The book is an excellent and practical breakdown of current knowledge in the area of astral projection, and the exercises, along with the author's accounts of his out-of-body experiences, make his account extremely readable and enjoyable. Suitable for all public libraries and for specialized collections dealing with New Age and perhaps even psychology materials.

—*Library Journal*

Magnus is passionate about his subject, knowledgeable in personal experience and adept at describing his topic with clarity.

—*Publishers Weekly*

ASTRAL PROJECTION

AND THE NATURE OF REALITY

Exploring the Out-of-Body State

JOHN MAGNUS

HAMPTON ROADS
PUBLISHING COMPANY, INC.
for the evolving human spirit

Cover design by Marjoram Productions
Cover digital imagery © PictureQuest/BrandXPictures. All rights reserved.

Hampton Roads Publishing Company, Inc.
1125 Stoney Ridge Road
Charlottesville, VA 22902

434-296-2772
fax: 434-296-5096
e-mail: hrpc@hrpub.com
www.hrpub.com

If you are unable to order this book from your local
bookseller, you may order directly from the publisher.
Call 1-800-766-8009, toll-free.

Library of Congress Cataloging-in-Publication Data

Magnus, John, 1977-
    Astral projection and the nature of reality : exploring the out-of-body
state / John Magnus.
        p. cm.
    Summary: "Provides a brief history of astral projection and then guides the reader
through a step-by-step course for reliable projection. Also explains how we create our
own astral world and offers techniques for taming both our mind and the nature of our
reality"—Provided by publisher.
    Includes bibliographical references.
    ISBN 1-57174-447-9 (5-1/2x8-1/2 : alk. paper)
    1. Astral projection. I. Title.
    BF1389.A7M33 2005
    133.9'5—dc22

2005019900
ISBN 1-57174-447-9
10 9 8 7 6 5 4 3 2
Printed on acid-free paper in Canada

To all the brave souls who project their minds

into beauty and bring it back.

And to my wife, Barb, for being.

Contents

Acknowledgments

I would like to give a big hug to everyone who has contributed to the making of this book.

As this book has progressed, I have come to realize that nonphysical people surround us. They visit me in my dreams and astral projections. A few of them have been fiercely interested in the contents of this book and so have unselfishly put ideas in my mind. A huge gratitude goes to these muses.

Another gratitude goes to the astral projectors—Andrew Charles James, Andrew Musch, Barb Lanier, John Floyd, and Julia Melges-Brenner—who have reviewed the contents of this book and provided invaluable feedback. I also thank them for the techniques they have shared.

I would also like to thank the good people at Hampton Roads: Frank DeMarco, Richard Leviton, Sarah Hilfer, Tania Seymour, Jane Hagaman, Anne Louque, Diane Lynch, Virginia Colburn, and everyone else who has pitched in.

And to my wife, Barb, whose soul (I have seen it) is as shining blue as the firmament: Thank you for opening my eyes when they were closed, and for our leaps of faith.

I also wish to send a thank you to all people around the world who make an effort for the benefit of someone else. You probably do not realize what a tremendously positive impact you have on people's lives.

Preface

The Rise of a Book

Journal Entry, July 11, 2002

I wake up after an afternoon nap. I have the whole outline of this book in my head. Strange, I never had any special passion for writing such a book, but now I can't wait to get started. I am motivated like never before. The top of my head is tingling like crazy, as if someone or something is feeding me information. Plus, I am irritated, possibly because my logical mind can't make sense of where I am getting the inspiration.

A few years back, seemingly for no particular reason, I became curious about what lies beyond the physical. Could there be something more? I sure hoped so, because if there were not, life would lapse back into the boredom and complexity of modern Western society. Imagine my surprise when, a week later, I stumbled upon accounts of near-death experiences on Kevin Williams's near-death site (www.near-death.com). It was as if I were guided to the information by a helpful energy, and I probably was. Previously, I had been ignorant of and uninterested in the concept of life after death. Because I am somewhat of a procrastinator, I had postponed thinking about death. I reasoned that death gets in the way of living. Literally, it does, but I now appreciate death because it makes life larger and more profound.

The near-death accounts I read about on the site were amazing. There was no doubt that there must be some sort of existence after the death of the physical body. The sheer number of witnesses—tens of thousands—should be proof enough to convince anyone but the most hardcore skeptic. In the face of the evidence, death now seemed quite a ride, and I could not wait to discover what was included in that ride. A desire began to grow in my mind. Would it not be awesome to see all these things in the beyond without actually having to die first?

Imagine my second surprise when I stumbled upon something called astral projection on the Internet. Now, this was a far-out subject. Apparently, there are people all over the world who engaged in the very thing I desired: seeing the world beyond the physical. I was surprised to discover that some people spontaneously experienced astral projection, and I was thrilled that others deliberately attempted to induce such experiences, armed with nothing but a meager amount of literature, their experience, and their wits. It seemed possible for me to go where I wanted to go without the hassle of dying after all.

After my discoveries, I practiced astral projection diligently for weeks. I tried out 20 techniques designed for leaving the body, all of which I found on the Web, free of charge. None of them worked as I had hoped. I concluded that there must be something I was not doing right, but what? Then one night, after two intense months of attempting to leave the body, that "something" revealed itself as if by accident. I fell asleep during a session. When I woke up, I had the surprise (and terror) of my life as I was sucked into another dimension of existence. I had finally accomplished my first astral projection. The missing ingredient had been the state of mind that can only be achieved when waking up after a period of sleep.

The realization brought about by my weird astral experience—that I was not the body, but something that could *leave* the body and *return* to it—radically changed my priorities. I started taking responsibility for my spiritual and emotional growth. I grew less interested in material pursuits. My academic labor suffered. It no longer made sense to me to acquire skills (in marketing) that had nothing to do with my spiritual growth. I confess that some of my education in marketing was blatantly contradictory to spiritual growth.

I abandoned the quest for financial security, something to which I previously had been prepared to dedicate my future. I realized that life is not a competition where the person who dies with the most money is declared winner. Life is precious, too precious to be viewed as a battle over money and security. It does not make sense to waste time on collecting resources that you have to leave behind at death anyway. Ultimately, it does not make sense to spend your life pretending to be someone that is not you, doing things that are not in your nature. What *makes* sense is to be yourself and to create something in life that you can take with you after that life has ended.

I realized that people in general, as I had, succumb to a sort of spiritual tunnel vision to such a degree that they remain oblivious to the immense value of their own lives, and I felt compelled to do something about it. Somewhere in these thoughts, the idea of a book was born, a book that would help people help themselves. A book that would help stressed-out modern men and women awaken to their own larger nature, in which they would take charge of their lives and make them better. It was an idea of a book, not just on astral projection, but also on the nature of reality.

I doubt readers of this book suffer from too much of the mentioned tunnel vision (or you would not be reading this), but at least I might advance your knowing of reality and inspire you to tell others about the awesome experiences that come with that knowing. From now on, with everything you say and do, you will inspire everyone around you to wake up from their state of tunnel vision and find a life truer to our form, as I did.

As a ripple upon water, the awakening will travel over the human species, which will then take a giant leap into nonphysical realms and accept them as we have accepted the physical realm for so long. With that sort of understanding of reality, there will be no limits to where we can go. Well, that is my romanticized idea of what will happen.

Originally, I practiced astral projection, aside from for the fun of it, to get personal proof that there was something more to existence than the physical. Specifically, I wanted to know whether death was the final curtain or if it was just a portal, as the near-death accounts had suggested. In time, my objectives expanded. Assuming that there is much more to existence than the physical, which certainly seemed evident, I had an urge to find out how the physical fit into this greater picture. I wanted to know how creation was structured—if it was structured.

This book is my report on what I have learned on this subject so far. Or, more correctly, this book reports my opinions and interpretations of what I have experienced. From what I have seen, creation seems to be a very subjective place. What I have perceived may or may not match what you have perceived or will perceive; therefore, I can't claim that what is revealed in this book is the absolute truth. I can only say that to the best of my ability I have drawn conclusions from my experience. In the end, we all have our own opinions, and this is something we should treasure. Take what knowledge you can use from this book and make it your own. Rip out the pages you do not agree with and make a nice warm fire with them.

I could write until my hands fall off about what I have experienced, yet nobody would benefit from it, simply because it is human nature (and a good nature it is) to remain unconvinced until personal experience says otherwise. There is no substitute for personal proof, which is why this book encourages you readers, with the help of some exercises, to find your own experience of the nonphysical realm. I want you to see what I have seen, but I want you to see it in your own unique way.

This book gives you the tools for exploring other worlds, physical and nonphysical. The tools consist of a technique for leaving your body and the knowledge to navigate once out of your body. If your motive for leaving your body is to have fun, then you are reading the right book. I can't think of anything more fun than astral projection. If your motive is a desire to understand reality, then you are also reading the right book. In this book, we will seriously consider what we are and what everything around us, physical and nonphysical, is. We will do this partly by making several deep dives into the astral and partly by reflecting and discussing the experiences.

To ease exploration, I have divided this book into sections I call Circles because I believe our lives are divided into circles of knowledge, each of which we must digest before we can take on the next Circle.

Each Circle contains a number of topics. Each topic is exemplified by journal entries and exercises. The journal entries represent a small portion of my personal experiences. Apart from the knowledge they communicate, I think you will find them fun to read.

Regarding the exercises—they are stepping-stones into the astral. Astral projection is not merely a matter of leaving the body and coming back to it. The exciting part is what happens between these two events. That experience depends on beliefs, moods, and other things going on in the mind. The exercises are meant to loosen up the mind, so it can fully benefit from the projection. Some exercises may seem to have little to do with astral projection, but they are a preparation for the experience. If all you want to do is see whether you can leave your body (which you can), then some of these exercises may be superfluous. But if you want to explore the astral projection experience to the fullest, I recommend that you carry out as many of the exercises as possible.

The first Circle, "Preparing for the Astral," gears you up for the astral. It discloses some groundbreaking opinions on the nature of reality. Although you do not need to know any of this in order to leave your body, it may help you understand what is happening. The second Circle, "Getting Out There," assists you in creating your first astral projection. Even if you have already had one or more projections, it is a good idea to at least look at the technique used. I use what I have found to be the easiest method available to get one into the astral from a starting point of waking consciousness. That means a lot, because I have tried many.

The third Circle, "'Mind' Your Step," assists you in getting to know how the astral works. Knowing how your mind works is key, because the astral is controlled by your mind. I would even go as far as saying that the astral *is* your mind. But then, of course, we would have to define the word "mind" to clear up misconceptions. This is something that has never properly been done, and perhaps it can't be properly done until we know more about what we really are. For that reason, I will not attempt to define mind here, either.

When you have finished the third Circle, you will have the tools you need to explore the nature of that which surrounds you. As mentioned, the tools consist of your skills in leaving your physical body at will and your knowledge of how to navigate the astral to get the best results for your explorations.

The fourth Circle, "The Nature of Reality," discusses the relationship between the physical and the astral, how we fit into the picture, and what may lie outside the borders of explored realms. There is so much to be discovered, a whole new world, so let us begin.

Preparing for the Astral

Get your mind and body in shape for the big exit.

If you ask a good quantum physicist what the true nature of
physical matter is, you will get the answer that it is nonphysical.

—Deepak Chopra, *Body, Mind, and Soul*[1]

In this Circle, we will discuss some preconceived notions of what
astral projection is and, frankly, shred them to bits. We will pave the
way for you to form your own opinion of the astral from your own astral
experiences (which will come in the next Circle), rather than from what
you have read in books.

What Is Astral Projection?

There are as many definitions of what astral projection is as there are astral projectors. I think it is a good idea to give my definition before we delve into the topic.

Projection, in this case, is the process by which you select a physical or nonphysical object and turn (or shift) your awareness (or attention) to it. It can also be viewed as the process of drawing an object, or the concept of an object, into your awareness, but those are just two different ways of looking at the same process. Every thought you have is a projection of awareness.

For example, one second you may be projecting your awareness to a memory of an article on strawberries that you read two weeks ago. The next second you are projecting your awareness to a memory of the sweet taste of a strawberry. As another example, if I have to sharpen a pencil, during the sharpening procedure I project my awareness to the pencil, then to the sharpener, and then back to my usual daydream. Projecting one's awareness to other realities takes a bit more effort, but it is the exact same procedure.

Awareness is the point of your mental focus. It is the clearest part

3

of your conscious mind. The functions of the mind can be divided into two major parts: the conscious and the subconscious. The subconscious controls the autonomic nervous system, beliefs, and memories. The two parts cooperate to implement complete mind functions. For example, if you decide to move your arm, you are consciously aware of the arm moving, but you have no idea how the subconscious manipulates the muscles. Likewise, you can consciously access memories but can't control how they are stored or fetched. You have no conscious control over your memories when the subconscious prevents you from remembering the names of people you meet.

Awareness allows access to the conscious parts of your mind, but not all at once. You can only turn your awareness to a small portion of the conscious mind at one time. For example, if you are listening to music and, out of the corner of your eye, see something moving, you turn your awareness to your eyesight to investigate whether the movement is a threat. For a few milliseconds, the hearing function slips out of your awareness and you can't hear the music.

Astral is trickier to define, and everyone seems to have his or her own idea of what it is. The *American College Dictionary* from 1967, for example, says the astral is "a supersensible substance supposed to pervade all space and form the substance of a second body belonging to each individual." That is a good definition (although not necessarily correct), but it still does not tell us what that supersensible substance is, how it relates to the physical, or how to reach it. Perhaps the confusion stems from attempts to define the astral with words that are commonly used to describe physical space. Or perhaps the confusion is caused by the fact that humanity has not even defined the *physical,* and we can't tell what the astral is without knowing what the physical is.

Some say the astral contains all the nonphysical realms. Others say that there is a continuum of energy frequencies reaching from the physical to the divine, and the astral is one of those frequencies, neatly tucked in between the physical and mental frequencies. Since there are too many unknowns, I will not attempt to specifically define the astral; I will only say that the astral is the realm where thoughts come to life. It is the dimension where dreams live, where we hang out when we are taking a break from physical reality. We are multidimensional beings.

Our consciousness exists in many dimensions, and the astral is one of them. Later in this book, we will get into the details of what the astral might be, and you will experience it for yourself.

Astral projection (sometimes referred to as AP) is the process by which you turn your awareness into the astral realm. The astral includes many different types of experiences, everything from dreams to the afterlife, and there is a plethora of ways to get there: dreaming, daydreaming, fantasizing, dying. We will be using the projection type that is known as out-of-body projection, which means that we interact with the astral as we do in waking physical reality: from a first-person view and with senses similar to the physical senses.

I am not too thrilled with the term out-of-body because it implies a physical part of you somehow escapes the physical body. In my opinion, out-of-body travel involves directing your attention to a nonphysical part of yourself that was never locked down by the body in the first place. It also implies that projections take place in the physical world, as the word "out" may be interpreted as a physical location relative to the physical body. Astral projection is *not* merely the process of leaving the physical body and floating around in physical reality, although it is quite possible to do so. The astral is a realm of its own which is very much larger (in nonphysical terms) than the physical. It contains millions of worlds that may or may not resemble our physical universe. We would miss out on too much if we were to limit our journeys to only our physical world.

Every being in the universe can practice astral projection. Whether you are young or old, short or tall, rich or poor, you can astral project. The ability to astral project is a consequence of how the physical body is constructed and how the nonphysical parts of your being connect to it. It is a natural skill. There is nothing supernatural about it. Astral projection is not a freak occurrence of nature; it is an expression of who we are. In fact, everyone astral projects all the time. If you could not project your awareness, you could never sharpen your pencil. If you could not project your mind to the astral, then you could never have dreams. What we will do in this book is not too far from dreaming, although I admit it is vastly more exciting.

The History of Astral Projection

Astral projection in one form or another appears throughout age-old literature. The earliest account I have found comes from Ramtha, a spirit channeled by JZ Knight. Ramtha describes how, around 33,000 B.C., he had an out-of-body experience (OBE).[2] If this channeled information is to be trusted, it hints that people have practiced astral projection since pre-historic times.

Between three thousand and five thousand years ago, Egyptian priests were so familiar with the ability to leave the body that they wrote the *Book of the Dead* to guide the departed awareness to the afterlife:

> Moreover, grant ye that the Ba-soul of the Osiris Ani, whose word is truth before the gods, may come forth with your navel cords in the eastern part of the sky, and that it may follow Ra to the place where he was yesterday, and may set in peace, in peace in Amentet. May it gaze upon its earthly body, may it take up its abode and its Spirit-body, may it neither perish nor be destroyed for ever and for ever.

Astral projection was also used in priesthood initiation rituals. The priest apprentice could, for example, be assigned to present himself partially or totally materialized in front of a group of people while in an out-of-body state. He would leave his *khat*, his physical form, and step into his *kha*, the astral double. The astral double was thought to be the personality appearing as a subtle copy of the physical form, attached but capable of roaming free.

At the dawn of Greek philosophy, astral projection spread from the religious into the intellectual realm. Plato proposed that what we see in this life is only a dim reflection of what the spirit could see if it were released from the physical. In *The Republic* (circa 360 B.C.), he illustrated the idea by saying that life was like sitting chained in a cave with our backs to a fire. We can only catch the shadows of the people passing between us and the fire. In time, we would come to assume that those shadows moving across the cave wall were the only reality. If we were released from the chains and turned around and saw the people passing by, we would not understand what we were seeing; we would continue to think the shadows more real than the people who cast them.

Plato also relayed the story of a warrior named Er, who died in battle but came back to share his experience of the afterlife:

> When Er and the spirits arrived, their duty was to go at once to Lachesis; but first of all there came a prophet who arranged them in order; then he took from the knees of Lachesis lots of samples of lives, and having mounted a high pulpit, spoke as follows: "Hear the word of Lachesis, the daughter of Necessity. Mortal souls, behold a new cycle of life and mortality. Your genius will not be allotted to you, but you choose your genius; and let him who draws the first lot have the first choice, and the life which he chooses shall be his destiny. Virtue is free, and as a man honors or dishonors her he will have more or less of her; the responsibility is with the chooser— God is justified."

Through the account of Er, Plato presents the soul's opportunity to choose the details of its lifetime and the amnesia placed upon the newly born. These are concepts confirmed by near-death and prelife hypnotic regression accounts more than two thousand years later.

In his essay, "On the Delays of the Divine Vengeance," bundled in Moralia, the Greek historian Plutarch shares the story of Thespesius, also known as Aridaeus, a man of ill-repute, who had a bad fall in A.D. 79. Thespesius ended up in a two-day coma, during which time he found himself outside of his body. Thespesius spent the time exploring another inhabited dimension. His body pulled him back just in time to prevent his burial. The experience prompted him to turn his life into one of ethics and values.

The Greeks contemplated a subtle body similar to the Egyptian *kha*. Plotinus suggested that all souls must be separable from their physical bodies. Aristotle taught that the spirit can leave the body and is capable of communicating with other spirits. Homer spoke of three components: the body (*soma*); the impersonal psyche; and the seat of intent, will, and feelings known as the *thumos*.

The ability to leave one's body influenced the Greek language. The English word *ecstasy* is derived from the Greek word *ekstasis*, which means "to stand outside oneself." This may very well carry the literal meaning of leaving one's body. The fact that it later came to mean an exalted state of mind attests to the fact that people leaving the body would find themselves in a euphoric state.

Astral projection accounts are also plentiful in the Bible. The prophets seem to receive visions in altered states of mind, often away from their bodies:

> Then the spirit lifted me up and I heard behind me the noise of the Lord rumbling as the glory of the Lord rose from its place. (Ezekiel 3:12)
>
> The Spirit which had lifted me up seized me, and I went off spiritually stirred, while the hand of the Lord rested heavily upon me. (Ezekiel 3:14)

The accounts carry on into the New Testament. After the crucifixion, the apostles set out to spread the new religion. In the midst of political turmoil, Paul gave a second sermon to the Corinthians. He relayed the following story about a heavenly trip to drive home a point:

> I know a certain Christian man who 14 years ago (whether
> in the body or out of the body I do not know, God knows) was
> snatched up to the highest heaven . . . and there he heard things
> which cannot be put into words, things that human lips may not
> speak. (2 Corinthians 12:2–4)

It is believed that Paul was referring to himself. This example hints
at the difficulty in formulating astral experiences into words. Telepathy
is widely used outside the physical, and the emotions and understandings that are transmitted between minds are not easily translated into
words.

The Apostle John's revelation took place in an altered state, in a
strange world, most likely outside his body. This can be considered an
astral projection of impressive length and content.

> I was in the Spirit on the Lord's day, and I heard behind me
> a loud voice like the sound of a trumpet, saying, "Write in a
> book what you see, and send it to the seven churches: to
> Ephesus and to Smyrna and to Pergamum and to Thyatira and
> to Sardis and to Philadelphia and to Laodicea." (Revelation
> 1:10–11)
> After this I looked, and, behold, a door was opened in
> heaven: and the first voice which I heard was as it were of a
> trumpet talking with me; which said, "Come up hither, and I will
> show thee things which must be hereafter." And immediately I
> was in the spirit: and, behold, a throne was set in heaven, and
> One sat on the throne. (Revelation 4:1–2)
> So he carried me away in the Spirit into the wilderness: and
> I saw a woman sit upon a scarlet colored beast, full of names of
> blasphemy, having seven heads and ten horns. (Revelation 17:3)
> And he carried me away in the Spirit to a great and high
> mountain, great city, the holy Jerusalem, descending out of
> heaven from God. (Revelation 21:10)

Bible accounts resemble both modern astral projection and alien
abduction experiences. It would be reasonable to assume that the prophets

made an interpretation of the experiences according to the beliefs and culture of their time. Ramtha spoke about becoming the wind, the Greeks about standing outside themselves, and John and Paul about rising to the heaven in the spirit. From the sparse wording, we can only speculate about what really happened.

In the seventh century A.D., Muhammad, the founder of Islam, enjoyed an equally impressive projection through what he terms the seven heavens. Sahih Bukhari, full name Abu Abdullah Muhammad bin Ismail bin Ibrahim bin al-Mughira al-Ja'fai, put the story in writing sometime during his lifetime (A.H. 194–256 or A.D. 809–869), roughly 200 years after the event occurred.

> While I was at the House in a state midway between sleep and wakefulness, [an angel recognized me] as the man lying between two men. A golden tray full of wisdom and belief was brought to me and my body was cut open from the throat to the lower part of the abdomen and then my abdomen was washed with Zam-zam water and [my heart was] filled with wisdom and belief. Al-Buraq, a white animal, smaller than a mule and bigger than a donkey, was brought to me and I set out with Gabriel. When I reached the nearest heaven, Gabriel said to the heaven gate-keeper, "Open the gate." The gatekeeper asked, "Who is it?" He said, "Gabriel." The gate-keeper, "Who is accompanying you?" Gabriel said, "Muhammad." The gate-keeper said, "Has he been called?" Gabriel said, "Yes." Then it was said, "He is welcomed. What a wonderful visit his is!" Then I met Adam and greeted him and he said, "You are welcomed O son and a Prophet." (*Hadith of the Night Journey and Ascension Al-Isra' wa Mi'raj,* volume 4, book 54, Number 429, as narrated by Malik bin Sasaa)

In each of the seven heavens he visited, Muhammad conversed with well-known personalities from the Bible. It is interesting to note that his experience took place in the border state between sleep and wakefulness. This is the state most beneficial for astral projection.

The Egyptians are not the only ones who have compiled a book to ease transition into death. *The Tibetan Book of the Dead* or *Bardo*

Thodol (meaning "liberation through hearing in the intermediate state between death and rebirth") was written by Padma Sambhava in the eighth century, 100 years after Bukhari's book. It is composed from teachings delivered orally for many generations. The *Bardo Thodol* is read to the dying to give them a preview of what is to come and to warn them of the danger of getting entangled in dream-like worlds of their own creation.

The idea of the subtle double from Egyptian and Greek beliefs resurfaces in Tibetan Buddhism as the bardo body, which is thought to be an invisible and ethereal copy of the physical body containing a psychic nervous system. The bardo body is capable of traveling anywhere instantly, simply by desiring to be at the destination.

The wealth of projection knowledge kept by Tibetan Buddhists was exported to America by Paul Twitchell, who became the first American ECK master in 1965. Twitchell promoted a movement known as Eckankar, which includes the knowledge of ECK (the God consciousness) and what he terms Soul Travel. Soul Travel is a skill that utilizes astral projection to reach the ECK realm in order to assist people such as astral projectors and the newly deceased.

During the second millennium A.D., astral projection left a smaller imprint in literature. In the west, Christianity had become the common lifestyle. People relied on priests to inform them about life and the thereafter; astral projection was never the topic of the sermon. Even though Paul, the apostle, had spoken openly about it, religious leaders were quick to frown upon anything paranormal. Such experiences were reserved for saints and prophets.

Yet astral projection was practiced by witches and shamans in lands recently converted to Christianity. According to pagan tradition, witches could experience mental flight by rubbing their bodies with herbal extracts of aconite, belladonna, and hemlock, each lethal if ingested. Mexican shamans used mind-altering plants such as peyote, and the Vikings used poisonous mushrooms to achieve the same effect. The cultural shock to these newly christened pagan populations would cause friction for many generations.

Christians in general were afraid to discuss their astral experiences, fearful of the reactions of their brethren. This fear was often justified.

First, there was the Inquisition, beginning in the thirteenth century and lasting until the nineteenth century. Witchcraft was condemned by the Christian church in the fourteenth century. From there it went from bad to worse: 300,000 people were executed for heresy during the sixteenth and seventeenth centuries. Common belief says that most victims of this persecution were not sincere practitioners of witchcraft; nevertheless, this hardly encouraged sharing of knowledge regarding astral experiences, an atmosphere that lasted for centuries.

Paranormal practices became the province of occult groups, such as the Rosicrucians, the Golden Dawn, and the Cabalists. Knowledge of astral projection was passed secretly from one generation to another, from master to apprentice. The secrecy was unfortunate, for there is much we could have learned from these groups. Millions of people had spontaneous out-of-body experiences, and most of them understandably became terrified of the event. It was inevitable that such events would occur since all that is required to achieve such experiences is one of many favorable states of mind, and the natural sleep process sometimes jumps into such states. Their terror stemmed not from the projection event itself, but from the fact that they did not know what was happening to them. They were confused and scared that they might be falling physically or mentally ill. But because of the secrecy, there was no information on such phenomena and therefore no help available to them.

In the eighteenth century, Count Saint Germain made fantastic claims. It is said that he discovered the Elixir of Life and the Philosopher's Stone, that he could enlarge diamonds and make gold from lead and silk from flax. He also told of events that could be attributed to the astral projection experience: "For quite a long time I rolled through space. I saw globes revolve around me and earths gravitate at my feet." Horace Walpole and Voltaire both wrote about the Count, but he was largely dismissed as an eccentric by his contemporaries.

In the eighteenth and nineteenth centuries, astral projection resurfaced as a legitimate topic thanks to sincere investigation on the part of people such as the Swedish philosopher Emanuel Swedenborg; the French novelist Honoré de Balzac, in his story "Louis Lambert"; and the Frenchman Allan Kardec, founder of Spiritism. Swedenborg, especially, produced a wealth of material that still draws crowds today.

Still, the distribution of material remained limited. Astral projection did not enter the mainstream forums. The Age of Reason had begun, and there was not much room for phenomena that could not be observed by physical means. Astral projectors found it necessary to reinvent the wheel: Without access to astral research, they had to come to an understanding of the astral projection experience armed with nothing but their wits and courage.

In 1875, Madame Helena Blavatsky founded the Theosophical Society. Again, the idea of a subtle body resurfaced. Blavatsky divided the person into seven bodies, each one more subtle than the one preceding it. Her contributions would become a large part of Western metaphysics.

In the early twentieth century, astral projection became a highly discussed topic in psychiatry as people sought help to deal with astral experiences. It was an intriguing feature of the psyche. Professor Carl Gustav Jung reported seeing events in his hospital room while his body was in a coma. In 1913, Dutch psychiatrist Frederik van Eeden first used the term lucid dreaming when referring to the type of dream in which the dreamer knows he is dreaming.

In the 1920s, Sylvan Muldoon, who had experienced spontaneous out-of-body travel beginning at age 12, teamed up with psychic investigator Dr. Hereward Carrington to shed light on the subject. This effort resulted in *The Projection of the Astral Body*, published in 1929. It represented the most practical and comprehensive guide to astral projection of its time. As the title suggests, it relies heavily on the existence of a subtle second body.

Muldoon and Carrington's later book, *The Phenomena of Astral Projection*, presented nearly a hundred cases of out-of-body experiences, categorized by whether they were produced by drugs or anesthetics; occurred at the time of an accident, illness, or death; or were set off by a suppressed desire. Published in 1951, it was at the time the largest collection of out-of-body accounts.

Robert Crookall produced an impressive repertoire of astral literature. Between 1964 and 1979, he authored at least 22 works on astral projection. Even though he did so with a good deal of repetition, he managed to cover many aspects of astral projection, such as techniques, cases, the afterlife, and the nature of the soul. He advocated the idea that each person has a super-conscious mind that is responsible for psychic phenomena such as telepathy, clairvoyance, and telekinesis.

Robert Monroe, a businessman who found himself floating near the ceiling one day, went through a remarkable transition from questioning his sanity to becoming a fearless participant in events unexplainable by logic. The author of *Journeys Out of the Body* and *Ultimate Journey,* he also founded The Monroe Institute of Applied Science to conduct research that would help him understand what was happening to him. As it turned out, The Monroe Institute helped a lot more people.

The Institute developed Hemi-Sync, a tool that uses binary sound frequencies to affect brain waves, thereby inducing anything from alertness to sleep. Most noticeable is its capability to put the body to rest while the mind is kept from lapsing into unconsciousness. Monroe designated the body-asleep/mind-awake state as Focus 10, and states of mind beyond that had higher Focus numbers.

Dr. Charles Tart is a parapsychologist with a sincere desire to prove the validity of astral projection and altered consciousness in general, thereby bridging the gap between spiritual and scientific communities. He conducted research into lucid dreaming, astral projection, ESP, and the psychedelic effects of LSD and marijuana.

In the late 1960s, Tart brought subjects into the laboratory who could leave their bodies at will. The electrical activity in the subject's body was monitored while her awareness attempted to see a target not visible from the bed. Tart's first subject, Miss Z, was tested in a laboratory where a five-digit number was placed on a shelf about five-and-a-half feet above her bed. After three unsuccessful attempts, Miss Z awoke to report that she had seen the number 25132. She was right on all five digits.

Tart's second subject was Robert Monroe. Although Monroe did not hit the target in an out-of-body state, he did observe a man in the monitoring room who later was confirmed to be the technician's husband.

As a result of material put forth in the twentieth century by the abovementioned authors and others—Sylvester A. West, Hugh G. Calloway, Karlis Osis, Ingo Swann, Susan Blackmore, Celia Green, Stuart Twemlow, Dean Shiels, Scott Rogo, William Buhlman, Robert

Bruce, Robert Peterson, Bruce Moen, and many more unmentioned—public interest in the astral projection phenomenon grew. Astral projection practitioners emerged from out of their hiding places to share in and partake of astral projection knowledge in the public domain. No more did you need a master from whom to learn astral projection. There was plenty of information widely available on how to do it, much thanks to the Internet. Currently, thousands of people are practicing astral projection all over the world in deliberate attempts to leave their bodies.

Once again we have the opportunity to make use of our skill to leave our bodies and visit worlds beyond the physical. If we choose to see through the fear surrounding the subject and its implications on our perception of reality, we can grow like we have never before. With the knowledge of astral projection comes an understanding of a greater reality, similar to stepping out of Plato's metaphorical cave.

In the near future, if we decide to embrace and investigate the astral projection phenomenon, the mechanics of the out-of-body experience will be largely understood, and astral projection will become a skill that will serve any person who wishes to use it. Astral projection techniques will be so highly developed that with just a couple of days of practice, anyone will be able to leave their body. We might even invent tools that will assist us with getting into the necessary state of mind. Astral projection could even be taught in public schools as part of the curriculum.

In a more distant future, we might use astral projection to transcend the limits we have allowed the physical to impose upon us. We will communicate with those who have passed on and with those who live far away, perhaps even in other galaxies. Never mind communicating with them—we will actually be *meeting* them, awareness to awareness. With astral projection as common knowledge, interstellar communication will be a natural thing. In time, we will use astral projection to gather information on who we are and where we come from.

Prepare for Adventure

Before you throw yourself into adventures in other worlds, there are a few things you will need:

1. Bed
2. Small pillows
3. Astral projection journal
4. Dream journal
5. Notepad and pen
6. Tape (or digital) recorder (optional)

Many exercises can be executed on the fly. They do not require any special equipment or preparation other than a slightly relaxed state of mind. You can do these wherever you are (except while driving), provided that you will be undisturbed for a couple of minutes. Going through preparations such as a series of relaxation techniques is just a waste of energy and will in time wear out your motivation for doing the exercises. Aim to do the exercises on the spot and do not put too much effort into them.

When we get deeper into the astral projection technique in Circle 2, most exercises must be carried out before, during, or directly after sleep (this is where the bed comes in handy). Because they must be performed at particular times, this may slow down your reading. I advise you not to read past an exercise until you have executed it. It is better to read slowly and do the exercises than to skip parts.

Except for the sleep exercises, you do not need to use any special techniques while going to sleep. You do not need to put the body to rest nor do you need to lie in any particular body position. Just do what you normally do when you go to sleep.

Sometimes I get a burning sensation where my body weighs against the bed, especially in my heels and elbows. If you experience the same, you might find relief by placing a several small pillows under your knees, wrists, and ankles. This should relieve the pressure.

You will need a journal. I keep two: one for astral experiences, and one for regular dreams (I am not implying that dreams are unimportant). I keep both as digital files on my computer. Additionally, I keep a notebook and a digital sound recorder by the bed, so that I can record an astral projection or dream immediately after waking up.

I confess that I have an exceptionally poor memory. But even if you have a strong memory, keeping a journal is of utmost importance; in this book, we will be accessing certain states of mind that we are not used to. Our long-term memory is not trained to function in those states, therefore we have a tendency to forget our astral experiences all too quickly. To remedy this, try to write everything down as soon as you can.

A dream journal is perhaps even more important than an astral projection journal, not for its contents, but for the beneficial effect it has on your subconscious. (The word "subconscious" here refers to all parts of your mind that are not accessible to your conscious awareness.) The act of documenting your dreams instructs your subconscious that you are interested in your dreams and want to improve your ability to remember them. The subconscious then does its best to make remembering easier for you. After as little as a week of documenting your dreams, you will notice a great improvement in dream recollection.

I encourage you to write even when you do not remember any dreams. Even the act of *trying* to write will improve your ability to remember. As your memory improves, you will also get better at remembering astral projections, because dreams go hand in hand with astral projections. They take place in similar realms.

Exercise: Dream Recollection

1. Before you go to bed, put a notepad or a recorder (digital recorders are great, but a simple cassette recorder will work fine, too) next to your bed.
2. Set your alarm clock to go off slightly earlier than you normally wake up.
3. When you wake up, do not move an inch. Turn inward and sense the feeling of the last dream you had. Get into that feeling. You will find that when you are tuned into the feeling of the dream, the memory of the dream is easy to access. The trick is to remember not to move when you wake up. Remain in this state until the details of the dream begin to surface. This could take up to two minutes.
4. Write down or record any dreams you remember. Draw what you saw. Dreams can vanish from memory in seconds, so be quick.
5. Get out of bed or go back to sleep if you have time.
6. Later in the day, read your notes or listen to your recording.
7. If the dreams were important to you, file the notes or recording in your journal. Otherwise, throw them away. Your experiences will mount up quickly, so it is important to keep a clean journal by saving only the important notes.
8. Repeat the exercise every night until you can easily remember your dreams. After that, continue the exercise, but skip setting the alarm clock.

Not only will your memory improve as you document your dreams, but your mind will also become more alert during sleep. This is a prerequisite for astral projection and lucid dreaming. Aside from the benefits of remembering, you will find it very satisfying to read about your progress in retrospect. There is no greater joy than reading and reliving all your previous astral projections.

Awareness

Awareness is, according to my definition, the point of you that has the highest concentration of consciousness. If you think of consciousness as the thing that *is*, then your awareness is where you *are* the most.

Awareness is very flexible. You can move it around your consciousness any way you want, inside and outside your body. For example, in one moment, you can be in one thought, and the next in another. Both thoughts exist in your consciousness, but you may elect to turn your awareness to only one of them at a time, since that is most comfortable. Or you may want to hold both thoughts in your awareness simultaneously. This is a bit trickier, but still doable.

The Center of Thought

The *center of thought* is the physical area (actually it is a nonphysical area, but it is easier to think in physical terms) from which you take the energy you need in order to think. Your awareness moves here automatically when you want to experience your thoughts. In philosophical terms, this is where the *thinker* resides.

By simply moving your center of thought, you get a new perception of the world because different body areas supply different types of energy—energy that we use to form thoughts. Generally, the head supplies analytical energy, the heart compassionate energy, the chest imaginative energy, and the belly courageous energy. Each type of energy affects our way of thinking in different ways.

Since we are beings of habit, we always use the same body area from which to get thought energy, unless we deliberately instruct the thinker to take energy from elsewhere. For example, I am a very analytical person, so my center of thought is, by habit, attracted to my head. But whenever I feel I analyze too much, I push the center down to my chest. This gives me a richer perception of the world. There I can perceive feelings and concepts untouchable by logic. I am not saying that being analytical is bad. It is neither good nor bad, it is just another way of being.

Exercise: Thought Center

1. Find your center of thought. Where in the physical body are you thinking right now? You may feel it as denseness or a slight aching.
2. Push the center of thought to the center of your chest.
3. As you push it, fill the old space with good energy, which you suck in from the universe.
4. Keep the center of thought in your chest as you go about your day, every day.

Observing Yourself

When you shift (project) your awareness away from your physical body, a small amount of consciousness remains with it. That consciousness may even be so strong as to make up a part of your awareness. In many of my astral projections, I have experienced a split awareness, where one part is in the astral and another part remains with the body. It feels like being in two places simultaneously and, when you think about it, it actually is.

Considering that there is always consciousness remaining in your body, the body will always be perfectly safe when you astral project. Also, the consciousness that remains with the body is capable of managing your body without the help of awareness. Your body will not suddenly forget to breathe. On the contrary, astral projection could actually be beneficial in this respect. For example, if like me you are an analytical person, your awareness can block the flow of energy from the higher self into the physical body. But when you shift your awareness away from your body, as you do in astral projection, the analyzing ceases and the energy flow resumes. The much-needed higher energy can then reach your body. The flow aligns your body with your higher self, allowing you to be more you (if that makes any sense). This is also a benefit of meditation: When you meditate, you are not looking for something, you are just stepping aside to allow your natural flow to resume.

I have named the obstacles of the flow the *mind veil*. It is what keeps you separated from your higher self. The veil is kept in place by certain beliefs, such as that you are separate from others and that life is a struggle for achievements rather than a flow back to you. If you loosen or reprogram those beliefs, in a conscious attempt to resume the flow, you may break through the veil and sense your higher self. This may also happen if you shift your awareness away from your body long enough.

Wednesday, March 27, 2002
From an Elevated Point of View

These last few days I have been standing on a high nonphysical mountain peak from which I see things from an awesome perspective. I see others' problems and the solutions are immediately obvious to me. This is my mind veil coming off. I can see in my mind without distractions. But still, I can't communicate the solution to the person in need for there is no way I can make them understand. There is no way I can show them what I feel. I can't even describe what I feel in words. This is ultimate wisdom. It is a knowing, not knowledge. But this wisdom can't be shared easily. Only wise hearts can understand wise concepts. Human languages are inadequate.

Shifting your awareness away from the body is easy: Just focus your awareness on a point outside your body.

Exercise: Awareness

1. Focus your awareness outside your physical body, one foot to the right of your right cheekbone. If you are having trouble with this, just think of it as turning your attention to that same place and listening for any sound or movement out there.

2. Keep your awareness there constantly. It will try to move back to its habitual center of thought. When it does, just move it back outside your physical body.

3. After a few hours, you will notice a slight feeling of being outside your body, observing yourself in action.

4. After a while, this role of observer will benefit your spiritual growth. By way of metaphor, it is easier to see the opportunities during a soccer game if you are watching it from the audience platform than if you are playing on the field.

You can focus your awareness outside your physical body because the physical brain is neither the origin nor the cause of your awareness. In fact, your awareness does not need your physical body in order to exist. In 1981, the *Nursing Mirror* published the article, "Is Your Brain Really Necessary?" It was based on an investigation conducted by neurology professor Dr. John Lorber of the University of Sheffield. Professor Lorber found several hundred people with irregularly small brains. Some had no detectable brain at all, and yet they functioned perfectly well in society. IQ tests given to some of these individuals made it evident that IQ is not dependent upon the size of the brain. Dr. Lorber's research shows that the mind is able to function perfectly with only a fraction of the brain.

For fun, try on the following idea in your mind for a minute: *Your awareness is actually never in your physical body.* It is in some nonphysical place, eavesdropping on the input from the physical senses (hearing, sight, smell, taste, and touch), which are in the physical body. You can view the physical brain as the link that connects the physical body with the awareness. I think of the brain as a giant antenna. It assembles input from the physical senses and presents the result as a chemical-electrical state. Your awareness then reads this state of the brain. In this scenario, the physical body is a vehicle the awareness uses in order to interact with the physical world, and that vehicle is remotely controlled.

This raises an interesting question: If the awareness is you, then what is your physical body? Quite possibly, the physical body is just a figment of your imagination. Perhaps the physical body is something your awareness has invented. Perhaps even the whole physical world is something your awareness has invented for you to play with. If we assume your imagination is a part of you, then this would mean that the physical world, including the physical body, *is you*. Experiencing the physical world would then be a perfect opportunity for you to learn about yourself. But of course, until we have explored more of our nature, the body-awareness relation will remain an area of speculation.

Friday, April 5, 2002
The Return of the Veil

I have come down from my amazing trip, in which I saw everything from a very high place. I am my old boring self again. I think the mind veil was removed during this last week or two. I was more "soul" than I have ever been. I felt in understanding, even union, with everything. I understood everything that happened. I understood it, but I could not explain it in words. A friend asked me for help. I could clearly feel the solution for his problem, but I could not express it in words. The few words I managed to stutter did not do it justice and were completely misinterpreted. How frustrating.

When the veil was lifted, I was no longer fearful or worried. I was free of the human condition! My state of knowing knocked all those things out of the way. Those emotions are unnecessary, but it is hard to get rid of them when one is in the "normal" human state. I felt immortal, invincible. If troubles would come my way, I knew without a doubt that I would survive. Even if the body failed, I would still be intact.

I saw the spirit world. It appeared to me as a giant sphere floating in a dark void. It was made out of smaller spheres of brown smoke. I felt the nature of the sphere: It always pulls a person in the right direction, so one is never done for if one makes mistakes. There is always a chance to get back on our feet, should we fall. You might think of it as a compass that is continuously available to us. The compass points out the right direction, no matter how lost we get. This is the nature of existence. But of course, we ignore the compass most of the time.

I have spent most of my life looking for reasons to do things. Without the veil, I did *things just because I felt like it, or because I knew they were right. There was no need for reasons. In fact, there was nothing called reasons. There were no logical concepts of cause and effect. I could see how everything interacted in the sphere, and it was far from logical.*

I have searched tirelessly for the purpose of this life. I felt like I was running around in circles, trying every path to see which way was best for me. When the veil was lifted, the purpose was obvious. It came to me as a feeling that I could not put into words. Not only that, but I knew the general purpose of all lives. This too was a feeling, or state of knowing. Now I am no longer in that state, so I can't access that feeling.

When in this state, I grew very headstrong. My will could move mountains. I was single-minded, locked on target. I was confident that I could do anything if I put my mind to it, which I did. Now that the veil is back in place, I get distracted by little things, this and that, and what I intended to do never gets done. Little doubts get in my way. From what I have seen in the spirit world, I know I am putting obstacles in my own way in order to stop myself! What a waste of life it is to doubt yourself.

I lost touch with my human emotions. I no longer felt guilt, remorse, or pity. I felt that everyone was capable of taking care of their own lives and changing them for the better, so I am sorry to say I was annoyed by complaints made by people around me. Everyone has the power to take action and make what is wrong for them right, but instead they choose to blame everything and everyone around them. They do this subconsciously. From my point of view, it feels like such a waste of time and energy. If people put as much effort into fixing themselves as they put into complaining, they would soon run out of things to complain about.

I no longer cared where my life would take me. I did not even care if I made mistakes, although, in my state of knowing—where I could see the truth behind everything—there was little risk of making mistakes. With my newfound power, I could get out of any situation, because I was no longer a slave to obligations, emotional debts, or even consideration. The truth is that each person has the power to manage any situation. You can hurt them, disappoint them, or even dump them on their wedding day. They will get back on their feet eventually. The power is within them. It is our nature to endure and overcome. It is a beautiful nature, and the only reason we feel like giving in sometime is that we temporarily forget that beauty.

The only thing that can truly hurt a person is that person allowing himself to be held down by strings to unhealthy life situations. Take a look at your own life. Is there anything you do not feel like doing? Then break free, go your own way, detach from your responsibilities. Everyone deserves freedom. You are a free being. You are unbounded and unrestricted. The only thing holding you back is you.

This may sound cold for a human, but when the mind veil is gone, the word "cold" does not even exist. In fact, all judgments are gone. Forgiveness is natural. There is no need to ask for forgiveness or go through any painful process to forgive someone. The soul has no need for judgments. In fact, judgments are unhealthy. Judgments create emotional attachments. Attachments hold you down. In a way, judging another person is sentencing yourself to a life emotionally attached to your judgment of that person. Treating another person negatively in thoughts or in acts is the same as changing the perfectly beautiful nucleus that is you.

Each person is complete in himself. We already have everything we need inside. We have no need to compete for anything. In spite of this, we cling to each other, trying to make the other provide what we think we are lacking. We try to bury the competition, so we can get what we want for ourselves. Where does this behavior originate?

I think that a long time ago, as we went from tribes to larger societies, we forgot our tribal pledge to help each other. Since then, we have come to view our fellow beings as competitors—predators fighting over the same prey. We act as if we are dead scared that what we are striving for will suddenly run out, not remembering that it can never run out because we already have it within. Little do we know that there is no way we can get what we want by taking it from whatever is around us. We have to change this behavior. We have to realize who we are.

Our ultimate desire is to be free. How do we go about achieving this? We search all around for something to provide us freedom. We hope that we will have good political leaders who will respect our free will, and we strive to build up some wealth to provide financial freedom. We fail to see that freedom is a state of mind, and there is no way on Earth a politician or money can set us free if our minds are enslaved. We have to free our minds before we can become free. What is more, we have to do it ourselves, because there is no other person who can do it for us.

One person does not need another to be complete, although we sometimes team up to help each other remember this wholeness. I confess when the veil started to come back and the feeling of connection to everything was fading, I was beginning to realize that I had a strong subconscious need to be loved. It dawned on me that I had been on a wild goose chase for someone to give me love without realizing that I was already loved more than I could ever ask for. All that heart-aching loneliness had been completely unnecessary. Most of my teenage years I had subconsciously been looking for a person who would give me love. And when I found it, I would feel trapped, like an addict trapped by his drug. In this case, the drug was love. At the same time, the other person would be trapped. Now I realize I loved myself. The whole universe loved me. Not because I was me, but because I was. My quest for love-providers is over. I am content and self-sufficient. I now love people unconditionally. It does not matter whether they are half a world away; they are still in my heart. It does not matter if they step all over me or try intentionally to hurt me. Love is unaffected. That is unconditional love—loving without wanting anything back.

Remember that love for oneself is one of the most fundamental and important workings in the universe. This seems to come automatically when the mind veil is lifted. When you love yourself, the need for others to supply affection disappears. And with that, jealousy and other negative emotions that the ego uses to manipulate you into securing affection disappear. As a result, love becomes your natural state. Not human love, but love on a much higher level. It is so natural, you do not even reflect on it. You no longer worry about whether other people love you back, for you know they do, even if they do not realize it themselves.

Love is always there, it is our natural state, but there is so much junk piled on top of it, most of the time we can't sense it. Achieving love can't be the goal of your life quest, but remembering that love *could* be. That is a worthy quest.

Between Ego and Soul

The Birth of the Ego

Compared to our spirit home world, physical life is relatively recent and unexplored. You and I, as spirits, incarnated into this physical life in order to find out what it is and to see if our physical vehicles (our bodies) can survive it. Physical life is a challenge, there is no denying that. Whether we are big or small, rich or poor, clever or slow, physical life is difficult. That is because we are exploring a newly created frontier. Until we figure out how to deal with the physical, we will continue to struggle.

During our initial exploration of the physical, we discovered that, compared to our nonphysical counterparts, our physical bodies are very frail and require a lot of attention. To help us with this, we developed egos to monitor the physical bodies and make sure they had all the food, water, and shelter they needed in order to survive, as well as the means to get food, water, and shelter in the future (something we in modern times call security). Had we not had our egos, our bodies would probably not have lived long enough for us to explore much of the physical.

We designed the ego specifically to compare what was beneficial and what detrimental to the physical body. Before that, it had been unnecessary for us to value one thing over another, but in the physical world we did not have that luxury. With the ability to compare came categorization. We started filing experiences according to whether we thought they were good or bad for the body. This became a habit and soon we were judging everything that came our way. We became incapable of appreciating experiences simply for occurring. If we attempted to remain nonjudgmental, the ego always interfered as it colored the experiences either good or bad. Our perception of the world around us turned black (bad) and white (good). Soon we found it difficult to think in any other terms. In our true nature, we would not have applied any color at all. The closest we could get with the ego was gray.

With categorization came judging other people. This is something we would never dream of doing anywhere else. But in the physical, the ego felt we had to know whether a person was a threat to the physical body. As if that were not enough, we started judging *ourselves*, sorting our own actions as to good or bad. At the risk of our actions ending up in the "bad bucket," we had to invent *reason* in order to estimate whether the consequences of an action were likely to turn out good or bad.

In order to make good estimations, reason had to be able tell cause from effect, concepts belonging to reason only. To achieve this, reason organized events in a timeline. With that, the concept of time was born. Reason had the amazing ability to not only tell whether an event had occurred in the past or will occur in the future, but also to tell whether we should worry about the event. And because reason is so dedicated, worry became a big part of our daily physical lives.

With our new tool called reason, we rationalized away all other modes of thinking. We found them to be unreasonable. In time, reason replaced our usual means of thinking: intuition and knowing. By shutting down intuition, we severed the link to our true nature. But it did not stop there. Reason weighs evidence and experience against possibilities in order to tell what is probable and what is not. In this manner, reason considered all previous experiences in the physical and, ignoring the fact that it had no experience outside the physical, concluded that it is reasonable to assume that there is nothing more to the world than the physical. With that, we had put the finishing touches on our new reality: We denied our true nature and the existence of our spirit home world.

The Reign of the Ego

The ego takes its job of ensuring physical survival very seriously; therefore it goes to extremes to secure food, water, and shelter. In modern society, we need money to trade for everything, including food, water, and shelter, so naturally the ego works very hard to collect money in abundance. It reasons that the more money we have, the larger our chance of future survival. Those egos already in possession of food, water, and shelter know the value of those possessions and so do their best to trade them for as much money as possible in order to secure their own futures.

This is the basis of the economy of Western society. Food, water, and shelter are the needs of our physical bodies, and the economic system of trade is what the ego invented to secure them for the future. This system, of course, only works for the egos that have something of value to trade for money or food, water, and shelter. The egos that lack these means of trade—that is, poor egos—are painfully aware of this fact. Ironically, when we invented money in order to increase our security, we invented poverty, the opposite of security.

As souls, we recognize that all beings are equal and that we depend upon each other to survive. The way of the soul would be to share and make sure nobody lacks the fundamental physical needs. But the ego chooses to go the opposite way. Fearful of actually becoming one of those poor egos, it invents ever more ways to stay wealthy. The ego's favorite weapon in this fight is greed, which seems, for some inexplicable reason, to grow as our wealth grows. When we give in to the fear of becoming poor, we allow the ego to increase its influence on our lives.

This subconscious process influences our physical lives to such a degree that in many cases the ego's need for wealth becomes the only motivating factor in our physical lives. Our original motivation, the exploration of the physical, has been pushed aside. On only a few occasions do we allow our desire for exploration to guide us, and that is when we go on vacation. And we only allow that to happen if that vacation does not undermine the ego's means of collecting wealth. In Western society, we call it a paid vacation.

Passions

The act of physical exploration is motivated by passions, subjects that highly interest us. Every person has a set of passions, which guide us to the physical situations we wish to explore. For example, if I, as a soul, have a passion for exploring the physical cosmos, I might want to incarnate into a physical family with ties to NASA. Or perhaps I would select a father or mother who is a pilot. My passion for cosmic exploration would then further assist me by motivating me to becoming an astronaut. As an astronaut, I would be in an optimal situation for exploring the physical cosmos.

These passions are extremely important to who we are and to our physical and mental well-being. If we allow the ego to suppress our passions, we lose touch with our initial intention to explore and find ourselves wondering what on Earth we are doing on Earth. When we come to a point where we forget why we are in the physical, the physical becomes a nightmare—we feel depressed and lost, like a leaf being cast about in the wind.

During childhood, we are well aware of our passions. We know what our specialties are. Our specialties—what we do well—are simply what we think is fun, anything we are passionate about. We want to contribute to society with these specialties; unfortunately, as we are schooled, we realize that Western society is a very harsh and competitive place in which to live. We learn that we have to be streamlined in order to survive in Western society. Little by little, we learn that our childhood passions can't help us acquire food, water, and shelter.

To survive, we have to suppress those passions, maybe brush them off as childhood fantasies and focus on attaining the means (education, practical experience) to secure food, water, and shelter. In the end, society never benefits from our specialties because we choose to abandon them. This is as troubling as it is unfortunate. Our transformation from individuals who are motivated by passions to individuals who are motivated by the need to physically survive is, of course, brought about by the ego.

With our passions comfortably buried in the cellar of our minds, our egos can get a firm grip on us. From now on, our lives will be a constant nonpassionate struggle for security: a job, money, a car, a spouse, a house, and a retirement. I caught myself the other day thinking, "I am so poor, how will I afford grave care when I die?" And I am only 25 years old! The ego never ceases insisting that we secure our future, so much so that we actually live more for the future than for the present.

Sometimes our passions rise up to the surface and grab our attention, but they are quickly denied as the ego kicks in and tells us that those passions do not have bearing in this society. During certain times of change, passions regularly pop up in order to wake us up from our ego-induced slumber. This results in a conflict between passion and the ego. This conflict frustrates and confuses us, so some of us take to alcohol or other drugs in order to escape the ego or forget the passions. In the midst of this, we ask ourselves: "Is this life?" Is it? No. Living without pursuing our passions is a waste of life. If we deny our passions, we deny the reason for which we came to Earth, which is to extend ourselves by exploration. It is a suspended existence, in which we are never satisfied. The ego can never be satisfied, because we can never guarantee that we will always have access to food, water, and shelter, and other things of value in the physical world. Absolute personal security is unobtainable. Satisfaction can only be won by fulfilling our passions.

Exercise: Reclaiming Passions

Imagine that suddenly, as if by some incredible quickening of compassion, all humans on Earth decide to work for each other, making sure everyone has food, water, shelter, and other things that make physical life comfortable. It is not so farfetched; we already have the technology to feed every person on this planet.

Imagine that all dull jobs are automated. All food and other resources are grown and harvested by machines, which are run by a never-ending supply of solar and ocean wave energy. In that scenario, you would never have to pay rent or buy food, but you would have everything you need anyway. Consequently, you would never have to take a job unless you really liked that job. What would you be doing in this moment? What would you dedicate your life to doing?

Anything you come up with is a passion. Write them down in your journal. Then ask yourself how human society would change because of this global decision to help each other. How would people interact? How would human society change in 20 years?

Needless to say, passions are the tools of the soul. With our passions, as souls we try to affect what we aspire to in life, thereby directing how our lives turn out and what life situations we get ourselves into. Fear, on the other hand, is the tool of the ego. The ego's job is to keep us physically safe, and there is no more effective way of staying safe than being afraid of everything. The downside is that the fear induced by the ego often becomes unreasonable. Often we feel more fear than what is healthy. We might go about our day feeling nauseated by fear, worrying that our past will catch up with us or that we will not be able to provide a future for ourselves and those we love.

The Beauty of Choice

Considering all the fear brought on by the ego, why don't we just remove or remake the ego? First, we want to learn from the mistakes we made in inventing it, and in order to do that, we have to wait and see how the ego turns out. Second, the ego has proved to be a great teacher in more ways than one. The ego forces us to face our fears so that we can understand ourselves. As we begin to understand ourselves, we realize that living in fear is not something that is forced upon us. We choose whether we want to be subjected to fear, just as we choose whether to follow our passions. The ego is our own invention and, as such, we can choose when we want to use it and when we want to give it a rest. But before we can control the ego to that extent, we have to get to know ourselves. We have to rediscover our nature.

The ego keeps manifesting difficult situations so that it can produce fear in us. That fear, in turn, keeps us under control and demonstrates to us the necessity of the ego. Hardship is a way for the ego to tell us: "See, you do need me in order to get out of this mess and stay clear of it in the future." At the same time, that fear reminds us to acknowledge our true nature. Fears are strong only until we embrace them. Hardship is hard only as long as we fear it. By embracing our fears as parts of ourselves (which they are), we can accept them so that we can let them go. At the end of the day, we keep only what propels us to explore further. We keep only the core of our nature: our passions and loves. A side effect of the ego's reign of control is that it gives us a chance to embrace it and discover our true nature, which lies beyond it. That is the ego's gift to us.

One day soon, human society will be shaken to its core. We, the Earthlings, will take the next step of evolution, which is the evolution of mind. We will realize that there is more to our world than what our egos allow us to see. We will no longer be content with the ego's idea of survival. We will want to do more than survive: We will want to live. We will discover that we, as human beings, have the power to change our lives and pursue our passions.

We will turn our hope away from the leaders we have elected to guide us, and instead direct it to within us, where real power lies dormant. We will once more find hope in a life of bliss. We will possess the kind of expectation that children have before harsh physical society eats them up and their fantasies and passions are stored in the attic along with their toys. We will wake up and take control of our lives because the human race is too good for anything less. A dormant life force will once again awaken in the heart of each of us, and it will pour over planet Earth. Humankind will bloom once more.

This evolution will not only give us insight into our true nature, but it will lead humankind out of its self-invented, three-dimensional cage. I look at the history of humankind, over hundreds of thousands of years, and I can sincerely say that we have seen nothing yet. We are not even using one percent of our capabilities as human beings, although we are very cocky because we have achieved that one percent when other animals have not—as if they would care. We are seriously underestimating our potential.

The waking of consciousness to this evolutionary step manifests in a cultural change. The egos that have much to lose (those egos owning riches and power) will resist this development. They will want to keep things as they are, keep the fear and the ego intact because they have no problem in providing a future in the physical for themselves. They will fear that knowledge of other-dimensional worlds and off-planet species will diminish the value of their possessions. In truth it will, but they will also gain something that no riches can buy: self-knowledge. This fear will delay the development, but in the end resistance is futile. Evolution can't be stopped. The change is coming and maybe it will begin with channeling, telepathy, telekinesis, and UFOs. In this book, it starts with astral projection.

The Ego and Astral Projection

What does this have to do with astral projection? Everything! Our quest to perfect the ability to leave and reenter our physical bodies at will is part of our exploration of the physical and part of the evolution of the human mind. Those of us who take up this quest—and we are many—do it because we have the passion to do it. Another way to put it is to say that we are inclined by our souls to investigate the boundaries of the physical. This quest is an effort to understand what the physical is and what we as physical beings are. We are on the brink of discovering those truths. In a few years, our view of life on Earth will have changed. It will be of greater impact than Copernicus's claim that the Earth revolves around the Sun.

However, astral projection is at odds with the ego's idea of physical survival. First, the ego thinks astral projection is a waste of time, since it does not do much to further our wealth or in any other way increase our physical security. Second, the job of the ego is limited to the physical realm, therefore it does not care about anything outside the physical, including the astral. Thus the ego will object whenever we attempt to shift our awareness away from the physical, as we do in astral projection. It will even try to trick us into shifting our awareness back to the physical.

Your first astral projection will probably go without a hitch, but it will allow the ego to see that astral projection is not in its best interest. Once it has drawn that conclusion, the ego will attempt to sabotage your subsequent attempts at astral projection. This includes diverting your attention as you attempt to astral project, scaring you when you successfully project, suppressing your memories of the projection after you return to your body, and advocating the theory that "it must have been just a dream."

Third, since physical survival is the ego's mission, it will freak out whenever it experiences something that resembles physical death, such as the exiting of the physical body that precedes an astral projection.

In order to prevent the ego from interfering with our astral adventures, we have to understand how the ego works and what its motivation is. We already know its primary motivation: physical survival. But how does it work? The ego is not an external entity, but an integral part of every human. As with most elements of the psyche, the ego has a conscious component and a subconscious component. We use the conscious component when we reason. This one is easy to manipulate—we do it every day. Per definition, we can't directly access the subconscious component of the ego, but we can feel its effects in the form of motivating emotions. You might say it works like a black box. We know what we put into it: situations, experiences, and memories. We feel the outcome in the form of greed and fear, but we can't see what happens inside the box.

The ego resembles a machine more than a living soul. As such, it does not have access to energies in the form of inspiration and creativity, like the soul has. This is to the advantage of the soul, which is our true nature. It does not take much creative thought to outsmart a machine like the ego. However, we want to do more than to circumvent the ego. We want to make it work *for* us—the soul—instead of against us. After all, that was the ego's original purpose, before its interaction with our thought processes became so complex, so how hard can it be?

Exercise: In the Absence of Fear

1. When you wake up tomorrow, tie a short thread around one of your fingers like a ring.
2. Tell yourself: "Each time I look at this ring, I will feel no fear or worry."
3. Go about your day.
4. Every time you see the ring, remember your pledge. Release any fear or worries you may have at the moment.
5. At the end of the day, evaluate whether the absence of fear and worry made your day easier or put you at greater risk of harm. (What you have been doing throughout the day is consciously interrupting a subconscious process: the ego's control mechanism by fear. In other words, you have nipped the ego's takeover in the bud).
6. Ask yourself: "Did this absence of fear and worry threaten my future security or endanger me in any way?" Most likely, you will find that the absence of fear gave you clarity of thought, which helped you see more opportunities around you. Seeing those opportunities increases your chances for future security. Now we see that the ego is defeating its own purpose by not allowing you to take advantage of the opportunities. With that realization, the ego automatically transforms to work for you instead of against you.

The Belief System

Loss of Information

All of us have a set of beliefs that assists our reasoning. Let us call this set of all beliefs *the belief system*. Without these beliefs, reason would not be able to estimate the outcome of an event. Consequently, we would make mistakes that would endanger our physical survival. The ego can't have that, and so it ferociously defends all of its beliefs.

In order to maximize our chances of physical survival, we invent beliefs to keep us focused on the physical. This limits the input from our surroundings, especially our nonphysical surroundings. It is imperative to our survival to perceive only objects that immediately affect us. Nonimmediate input is eliminated so it will not take attention away from potential threats in our immediate surroundings.

Let us look at an example. Many projectors report hearing voices and noises prior to the exit from the body. Such sounds surround us constantly and we would hear them all the time if we were not so intent on ignoring them. On one hand, the ego considers them a nuisance because they take attention away from potential physical threats in our immediate surroundings; on the other hand, we are afraid to hear them because is culturally unacceptable, to such a degree that we lock up people who claim to hear voices. We can only hear noises in sleep states and other trances, because then the ego is offline (asleep) and we no longer care how well we fit into the current culture. When the ego goes offline, so do the beliefs that make us ignore the noises.

This applies not only to noises, but also to most things unseen. For hundreds of years, psychics have been saying that spirit guides and other nonphysical beings surround us at all times. Why have we never seen them? Our beliefs do not allow us to see. If we wish to see them, we either have to seek out the beliefs that make us blind or establish new beliefs that make us see. Perhaps we should stop merely regarding spirit guides as possible and start believing in them as real. But we are reluctant to believe anything that we have not experienced. We do not want to be misled. We have a Catch-22 here: We can't see the spirits until we believe in them, and we can't believe in them until we see them.

Another example is the popular syndrome (I say "popular" because nearly everyone seems to have it) known as Attention Deficit Disorder, or ADD. Doctors can't understand why kids today can't concentrate (that is why they label the problem in such an obscure way). The child's attention goes in all directions. The cause lies in the belief system.

As mentioned, the belief system is arranged to maximize physical survival, which means that our beliefs maximize input from objects that potentially threaten us and minimizes input from objects that are likely to pose no threat. This works well in straightforward interactions with other beings and objects. But we live in the age of information—our lives are packed with information. Wherever we go, we are bombarded with information: billboards, commercials on TV and radio, warning labels, lists of ingredients, Internet pop-ups, and bulk e-mails. With Procter & Gamble's new printing technology even Pringles will have surface-printed text!

Look around the room you are in now. Can you find a single artificial item that does not have text on it? You can't even have a drink of juice without being informed of how many calories your body receives. Even worse, pictures and voices in commercial ads are especially designed to catch our attention and direct it into the TV, radio, or Internet. Marketing people want our undivided attention so they can encourage us to buy their products.

The time of straightforward interaction has passed and our belief systems can't keep up. Kids don't know where to focus their attention because their belief systems can no longer tell which objects pose physical threats and which do not; consequently they can't make out which input to eliminate and which to keep. They are drowning in input from their surroundings. These kids have difficulty paying attention in class because their belief systems incorrectly eliminate information coming from their teachers. Commercial ads, on the other hand, are not eliminated because they are designed to attract attention. Is there any wonder kids are confused?

There are two cures to ADD, and stuffing our kids with mindaltering drugs is not one of them. Either we remove all commercial ads (wouldn't that be nice?) and cut back on the amount of information given for every little unimportant thing, or we encourage the belief system to adapt to the higher information load (which will mean more personal limits and stricter habits).

Censored Information

The belief system not only filters sensory input, but also adjusts some input to fit the beliefs. This causes us to get a censored, even propagandized, view of our surroundings. Why is our perception twisted in this way? Because our reason can't cope with ideas and objects that do not conform to what we estimate reality to be. By filtering the input, the ego does not have to worry about landslides within the belief system, which would no doubt disturb our functioning upon the physical plane.

The belief system is formed by experience. In our younger years, each experience established a belief in our minds. For example, if as toddlers we put our hands on a hot stove top, we experienced pain and established the belief that stove tops are dangerous. Similarly, we established beliefs that gravity pulls us down, winter is cold, cemeteries are spooky, birds have the ability to drop nasty stuff from above, the Earth is round, space is vast, and so on. There is almost no end to how many beliefs we have established for ourselves.

Once a belief is established, it is reinforced when we experience events similar to the one that established the belief. Every time we reinforce a belief, it gets rooted more firmly in our belief system. Eventually, the belief becomes integral to how we interact with reality, at which point it starts filtering sensory input. Input that is contrary to a firm belief is plainly rejected so that it will not upset our perception of reality.

For example, a woman levitates without support. Three men witness the event. The first witness, who believes that humans can fly, has no problem in seeing the levitation and so accepts the event. He does not even consider the levitation anything out of the ordinary because it is our beliefs that dictate what is ordinary and what is not. The second witness believes that humans cannot fly. He is convinced that the levitation is a trick, a hoax, because it is the only reasonable explanation. As such, he does not even feel the need to investigate whether his assumption is correct. This is the ego's best defense against upsetting notions. (For example, how many people feel it is unnecessary to read UFO literature simply because, even though they have not investigated it for themselves, they are already sure that UFOs are unreal or elaborate hoaxes?)

The third witness has a deeply rooted belief that humans can't fly. The man does not see the levitator at all, even though he is staring right at her. The event is totally filtered out by his beliefs.

A major disadvantage to the difficulty of changing a belief system is that the world around us, however we perceive it, is changing rapidly. Everything is changing, and all the time. Even our own beings are changing more quickly than the ego, in its need for stability, would like to admit. But the beliefs that we have reinforced all our lives simply can't change that quickly. Our whole existence could be shaken to the core—and our beliefs simply wouldn't allow us to know it. What used to be our points of reference, our beliefs, have now become our mind veil.

Exercise: Affecting Beliefs

1. For one whole day, consciously decide what you believe in.

2. When you read something, or when somebody tells you something—whatever it may be—check your wristwatch.

3. If the time shows an odd-numbered hour, then decide that you don't believe whatever you are told. Tell yourself, "I don't believe that."

4. If the time shows an even-numbered hour, decide to believe in whatever you are told. Tell yourself, "That sounds reasonable. I believe that."

5. Consider how these statements affect your belief about the information over time.

6. At the end of the day, think about your beliefs. Are they different from what they were at the beginning of the day. Do you find yourself believing in things that up until today you were skeptical about? If so, then you know that the belief system is a machine that can be consciously programmed. In other words, given time, you can teach yourself to believe in anything you want.

How do our beliefs affect us in the astral world? Let us look at an example. An astral projector projects into an astral forest and finds it very beautiful and serene. The projector enjoys it tremendously. But why would there be a forest in the astral? For no particular reason, other than the projector believes that the astral looks like the physical and forests are very common in the physical. Our beliefs dictate our perception. What would the projector have seen in the astral if he had no preconceived belief about what the astral is? He would have, to the best of his ability, seen the true nature of the astral, which is a big part of our own nature as multidimensional beings. In other words, the projector had a chance to discover a piece of his own nature, but his beliefs interfered. I like forests at least as much as the next person, but isn't exploring the nature of our being grander than exploring a forest?

In the medical world, a placebo is a "fake" cure, often given as sugar pills or staged surgery. In Dr. Henry K. Beecher's 1955 paper "The

Powerful Placebo,"[3] the placebo effect was found to improve the health of between 21 and 58 percent of the trial patients. A placebo uses the patient's belief in the cure to promote healing. If the patient has a belief that says medicine is able to heal her particular ailment, she can be healed without the medicine as long as she believes she is taking it. The placebo is an example of how beliefs govern our reality.

So here is the big question: According to physics, the creature called the bee has wings too small to allow its large body to fly. Yet it spites us by buzzing around like an acrobat in the air. Now, imagine that same bee flying to college to study physics and aerodynamics because it wants to advance within the hive. After graduation, it looks upon its own body, measuring the wing–body ratio. Will the bee still be able to fly, or will its newly created beliefs in physics keep it on the ground?

Friday, December 6, 2002
Levitation Teaching

This experience takes place somewhere between the dream world and the astral. I dream I am sitting on a bench in the square of my hometown with what seems to be my family. I do not recognize these people, but they feel like family. A man who reminds me of Don Juan (from Carlos Castaneda's books) appears. Perhaps the feeling of this man being a teacher makes my mind draw the parallel to Don Juan, who is also a teacher. Intuitively, I know this man is dead, but I can see him anyway. He seems to be here only in spirit.

He is levitating, floating a few feet above the ground. He explains that he has come to teach us all the art of levitation. He encourages me to try. I try several times, but each time the thought that "it is impossible" pops into my mind. Consequently, it is impossible; you can't do something if you believe that something can't be done. The man encourages me over and over. A younger man next to me starts levitating. He seems to have no trouble learning, but I do. I finally decide that the best way to stop the limiting thought from popping into my mind is by stopping my internal dialogue. I think this is what Don Juan would have done.

The second I stop my inner dialogue there is a big blast! I suspect the blast is in the waking physical world. Apparently, I now know I am not awake. I can see pieces of a firecracker flying in front of my dreaming eyes. I suspect a firecracker has been set off right next to my left ear in the physical. Who would do such a thing? Whoever it is, he *would not hesitate to hurt me. I could be in great physical danger. I fight to wake up. I manage to wake up purely as an act of will. It takes me ten seconds to reach a fully awake state of mind.*

I look over to my left and see my wife Barb sitting peacefully at the kitchen table. I conclude the cat must have caused the noise, perhaps dropping his can of food off the counter onto the floor, but later when asked, Barb says there never was any racket. In fact, the whole morning has been unusually calm.

I believe that during the night, I spent a good amount of time at an astral learning center, where I took a class in how beliefs affect our reality. The people I perceived as my family were my fellow students. Perhaps they feel like family because we spend so much time together in the astral. We were all given a lesson in how beliefs govern our realities. In this case, the lesson could only be learned in a dream environment, where most of the beliefs of the physical world are intact. Therefore, the class moved into the dream dimension, at which time the dreaming me became aware of the teaching. The teacher showed us how the belief of gravity could prevent us from levitating. There was absolutely no reason why I could not levitate, since there is no gravity in the dream dimension, except that I believed it could not be done.

The blast signaled the end of the lesson. Apparently, the whole lesson was designed to lead me up to the realization that inner dialogue holds our beliefs in place. When we stop the inner dialogue we are free to see without the filter of our beliefs. When the lesson was learned, the teacher felt it unnecessary for me to stick around, so he tricked me into waking up with a big blast.

Mind Evolution

However much of our sensory input our beliefs filter out, there is often a small piece of indefinable (according to our belief systems) information that slips through the cracks in our beliefs and reaches our mind. When it flows into our consciousness we can't make sense of it because we have no prior experience or belief to which to relate it. This is the case during our first astral projection.

When we leave our bodies for the first time, naturally we run into new experiences, because we are in unexplored territories. We desperately try to make sense of what is happening. During my first astral projection, I tried to reason logically, but that did not meet with much success in the astral. In spite of our efforts to understand, if the belief system can't relate, the experience will remain an unknown until our subconscious has had time to digest it. What the belief system can't grasp, we can't grasp. After a while, we just have to give up trying to make sense of it; label it "Cool experience of the first degree," and store it in the back of our minds.

The reason we can't make sense of our astral experience is that the beliefs we hold about the nature of reality conflict with it. In time, we subconsciously find a need to modify our beliefs to incorporate the undeniable astral experience. This is a natural process in which the belief system learns and adapts to changing life conditions. The process is designed to optimize survival in the physical but might just as well be used to optimize nonphysical exploration. As the belief system is restructured to allow new rules for reality, we find ourselves in an uncomfortable situation, not knowing what reality is or what physical life is. In short, we don't know what we believe in anymore.

When the rearranging is finally complete, we find that we suddenly believe that leaving the body is as natural as day and night. A new belief, that a person can leave his physical body, has been established. At the same time, the belief that "I am a physical being" has been altered to include at least the possibility that the awareness of that being can be focused outside the physical, and the belief of death as the final *game over* is dangling by a thin thread (see figure 1).

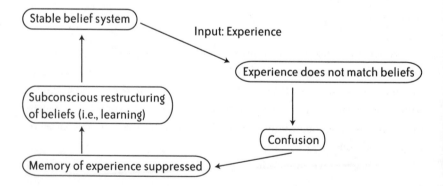

Figure 1. The belief system's learning process in response to an astral projection experience.

Sometimes it feels like we are standing still, as if we have stopped evolving. Remember then that most changes take place in the subconscious. We are not aware of them.

Changing Thought Patterns

> ## Exercise: Thought Reactions
> 1. Go into the bathroom.
> 2. While in the bathroom, bring to mind what you ate for breakfast. If you skipped breakfast, bring to mind your last meal.
> 3. Think of what food in that meal was high in sugar content; for example, cereal.
> 4. If you can't find anything in that meal that qualifies, think about everything you have eaten during the last couple of days until you find a food with a high sugar content.
> 5. Go do all that now, then return to this book. Do not read further until you have completed steps 1-4.
> 6. Why did you have to do all this, you ask. We shall see in a minute.

There is an air of familiarity to how your mind works. When you think a thought, another thought follows immediately, as if triggered by the first thought. Every thought has a *thought reaction*. This is a process you have done so many times it has become a routine—a limiting routine!

We are creatures who like the security and reassurance that habits offer, so we do not often welcome change. However, in order to change our picture of the world, we have to change the way we think. As it is said: Change your mind and your body will follow. We will now stretch our mind muscles outside of our familiar thought patterns and our bodies will follow.

Changing Thought Patterns

For one whole day, think outside the box.

1. When you hear a sound (for example, the sound of a motorcycle), do not think, "Yeah, that's a motorcycle," as you usually do. Instead think, "Yeah, that's an antelope." Your thoughts will get slightly confused and this will allow you to observe how your mind works.

2. Whenever a thought pops into your mind, and you know exactly what thought will follow as a reaction because you have already done it so many times, cut off that thought and replace it with a wild thought of your own invention. For example, when you pour your milk in the morning, instead of thinking ". . . and I will use my balancing skills so I won't spill . . . " think "This is a magical glass of milk, forged in the fires of Mount Doom. It holds the milk in place with special magical powers." Keep feeding your mind such *unexpected* thoughts.

3. Notice how the feeling of familiarity disappears from your mind. You are changing your thinking routine and, consequently, your thought patterns. This opens up your mind so that you will see more possibilities than you are used to.

Now, let us go back to the Thought Reactions exercise, in which you went into the bathroom. When you thought of sugar, did you look at your teeth in the mirror? If so, this is a live example of how thought reactions work. During the 1980s, I was bombarded by propaganda that said sugar ruins teeth. This formed a fear of sugar in me. If you were exposed to the same propaganda campaign, then you might have the same fear.

In the case of the exercise, when you thought of sugar, the fear kicked in and the reaction to that fear was a thought to check your teeth to make sure they had not been ruined by the sugar you ate. This is the automated subconscious process of thought reactions. Now that you have experienced the workings of thought reaction for yourself, you can learn to interrupt it and turn it into a conscious process.

Physical Realities

To reap the true power of the astral, you have to understand what the astral is and how you, as a conscious being, relate to it. But there are many traps along the path to that understanding. I write about this here and in the next chapter because the biggest mistake I made—the deepest trap I fell into—when I first started with astral projection was to assume that the astral is another version of the physical. It is not.

The truth is that, on a superficial level, the astral is whatever you make it into, so if you want to make it look like the physical, you can (imagine the confusion this causes in the astral). But this is not what we want to do. We want to push through to the true nature of the astral and not get caught in another physical reality.

It is very likely that any preconceived notion you have of what the astral is will limit your adventures. Even the smallest expectation will affect your astral experiences, as they did mine. It is therefore important that you have a completely open mind about how the astral works. You must untie all ideas you have about what the astral is. Open your mind to new possibilities. Do not accept *any* limits.

Forget all you know about vision, hearing, touch, taste, smell, and everything else associated with the physical. They are not the tools of the astral. If you want to find out what the astral is, first remove all limiting notions of what physical life and reality are. If you are having difficulty accepting that the astral is a part of reality, you must rewrite your definition of reality, perhaps even your definition of life. Start from scratch and let your astral experiences shape your understanding of the astral.

Wednesday, March 13, 2002
The Recursive Creation

In meditation, in my mind's eye, I go to Goldie, one of my current spirit guides. I ask him to help me remove the mind veil:

"I want to see everything around me," I tell Goldie. "I want to see the whole of creation."

"One cannot see it all," Goldie says, "because it is infinitely recursive. Just like a proton is part of an atom, which in turn is part of a molecule, so is the Creation structured. The universe is part of something bigger, which is part of something even bigger, and so on into eternity. The physical world is part of the spirit world. The spirit world is also infinitely recursive."

This is a groundbreaking insight for me. There is no end to anything. There is no final destination to our souls' progress, for nothing ends.

"Then I want to see a pretty big picture."

Another spirit comes up and gives me a thing that looks like a lamp. I stare into the lamp and it blinds me with yellow light. The light changes color. The back of my physical neck is tingling. The energy pattern in my neck is opening. I see, not in visions, but in feelings, how the spirit world is. It is built from feelings that have no names in human languages. They remind me of beauty, hope, self-realization, openness, adventure, and creativity.

In this chapter, I attempt to loosen your beliefs about what reality is. You do not necessarily have to agree with what I write. The important thing is that you accept the possibility that there may be more to reality and life than you have been taught. This point of view will help you make the best of your astral experiences. I will try to remove any limiting expectations of the astral from your belief system, to give you an easier time learning from your astral travels. However, because changing a belief system is one of the most difficult things a person can do you may want to read this chapter more than once.

Limiting Beliefs

Too many people view the physical as the only reality. They believe that anything real must be physical. To them, there are two alternatives: astral projection is a physical phenomenon, or it is a hallucination. It is inconceivable to most of us that a person can enter another dimension, which is not physical, and still view the journey as real. Starting from this narrow point of view, those who attempt to validate or invalidate the reality of astral projection (and I have attempted it) are actually using the physical to try to prove that astral projection is real. This is impossible to show, of course, since astral projection is not a physical phenomenon.

As a brainteaser, what would happen if someone managed to prove that an astral projection can manifest something, let's say a cool breeze of air, in the physical? Would only the physical manifestation be viewed as real? We can't prove that the rest of the astral projection is physical, so that must mean that that part is unreal, right? The cause becomes unreal and the effect becomes real.

That way of thinking is widespread in modern science. It is the limiting factor in medicine. For example, it is a little-known fact that all disease originates in the mind—a realm that is viewed as unreal—and that many of the symptoms appear in the physical. Blinded by our belief in the physical, we try to heal the disease by wiping out the physical symptoms. We pay no attention to their origin. As a result, the disease survives and appears in other symptoms, like a tree that has been cut grows alternate branches. What we must understand is that the origin of disease is the key to health and symptoms are created merely *to assist* us, alerting us of the presence of the disease, so that we may deal with its origin.

Scientists refuse to enter research areas that are considered improper: astral projection, intuition, precognition, clairvoyance, telepathy, telekinesis, remote viewing, UFOs, and dreams, to name a few. Those who do jeopardize their careers and risk ridicule from their peers. But who decides what is proper and improper? The ego. The soul does not have the limitations of proper and improper.

Science has become institutionalized and has thereby lost the flexibility needed to investigate a phenomenon like astral projection. There is no greater tragedy than this. Somehow, we have extinguished the flame that drives science—the desire to know truth—and in so doing we have prevented research that could lead us into a better world. We could all be communicating telepathically by now, had we given the phenomenon the proper scientific investigation it deserved a few years back. Somehow, the desire to know the truth has been replaced with the desire to defend what we previously accepted as truth, for no reason other than we invested pride in them as truths. But humankind can't evolve by clinging to yesterday's truths. The human mind is evolving.

We are enriching our reality to include dimensions outside the physical. With this, new truths will surface. That is unavoidable. That is how evolution works and has worked since the birth of whatever was the beginning, if there ever was one. Some new truths will make us question old truths (or, rather, what we thought were truths), but this is only healthy. What is unhealthy, on the other hand, is to cling to outdated truths, as if they were our lifeline.

There is nothing wrong with the scientific model. What is wrong is that the current set of truths—truths that supposedly were collected using the scientific model—is contaminated by false assumptions about what constitutes reality. Our careless assumptions about what reality is have led us to a dead end. Here are some examples of false assumptions: the physical dimension is external; anything not connected to the physical is an illusion; reality is constant and, therefore, a fluid world is less real than a slow-changing world; and anything we can't grasp with our logical minds is unreal. The scientific model has a mechanism for replacing invalidated truths, but that mechanism is blocked by the assumptions of thousands of scientists. These assumptions, in turn, are based on beliefs held by scientists. As much as one tries, it is difficult to be an objective scientist. When presented with the results of an experiment, it is human nature to fall back upon previously held beliefs when interpreting them. It is difficult to come up with theories that conflict with the core of what one has been taught.

Sunday, March 17, 2002
My Essence

I have long wondered if I am a soul, unbounded by my physical body, or if I am a little consciousness belonging to a body, which is in use of and manipulated by a soul unknown to me. It is clear now that I am a soul. If I were the body, I would not be able to have astral projections.

One might argue that the body-bounded consciousness could project (perhaps with the help of the soul), but what would be the purpose of such ability? It does not make sense that a body-bounded consciousness can project, because it dies with the body. If it did not die with the body, it would not be bounded by the body in the first place, and that makes it a soul.

It is more likely that it is the soul that projects, and since I am the one projecting, I am that soul. The projections prove that I, the soul, am able to survive without a body. Therefore, I will survive physical death. Phew, what a relief.

It is not too difficult to conceive that our five senses can't perceive all of creation. If you subscribe to the theory of evolution, then a physical sense is a tool that our ancestors created, possibly by coincidence, in order to improve their chances of survival. For example, animals that live underground have no use for physical eyes because it is too dark for them to see and, so, they do not develop eyes.

In order to communicate what they were sensing, our ancestors came up with the abstract idea of everything that could be sensed and labeled it *the physical*. If biological organisms do evolve, it is conceivable that there are plenty of things around us that we can't perceive, because we have not yet evolved senses capable of perceiving them. It would be a very limiting mistake to assume that our current set of senses is capable of perceiving everything around us. Therefore, it would be incorrect to assume that anything is unreal just because we can't sense it. You can bet there will be an upgraded version of the human next year—one with air-conditioning—and another the year after that, and so on and so forth. Little by little, we create senses for what we can't yet perceive.

Many people view *mind* as an object that travels through the physical and sees what is there. But what we experience as physical is *inside* the mind. Our senses feed the mind with information and the mind creates the *experience* of the physical from that information. The same goes for the astral. What inspires us to create the experience of the physical or the astral is something entirely different and nobody seems to have a good idea of what it is. Therefore, claiming that astral projection is an illusion (and therefore not real) because it only happens in the mind is absurd. Where else would it take place? Reality, physical or astral, is something we create within our minds, not something that is served to us by something external.

The Nature of the Physical

Too many people have viewed the physical as the only true reality. That opinion is changing now because of research in quantum physics. Quarks are well known as the particles that build the neutrons and protons that in turn make up the atom, which was long assumed to be the indivisible building block of physical matter. Physicists are now looking for the building blocks for quarks. These theoretical building blocks are named rishons or stratons by some. When and if they find these particles, chances are they will have to start looking for the particle that makes up rishons or stratons. When that is found, the hunt begins for something even smaller. There seems to be no end to how many times we can divide particles into smaller discrete components.

These tiny particles are separated by comparatively vast distances of empty space. The farther down we look into matter, the more space we find. An atom is not a solid particle but an empty space inhabited by neutrons, protons, and electrons. Neutrons and protons are empty spaces inhabited by quarks. Likewise, a quark is not a solid particle, but an empty space inhabited by rishons. Rishons are also mostly empty space, and so forth. Every time we discover a new particle, it turns out to be the effect of a smaller particle lurking in a vast space. In fact, there is no particle to be found, only more empty space with the promise of an even smaller particle. The nature of matter is an elusive riddle of infinite emptiness.

Where we originally thought there would be building blocks, there is nothing. How can this be? What is this thing we call matter? How can physical matter be built from nothingness? How can physical matter *be* something that *is not?*

An analogy that comes easily to me, perhaps because I am a software engineer, is virtual reality. In software, a virtual reality is represented by information *about* the world. The software does not contain the actual world itself; hence the word *virtual*. One way of looking at it is that there *is* no world in the software (or anywhere else), only a *description* of the world. The description is then used to give the *impression* of an actual world. Of course, how well this impression is received depends on the perceiver, the human computer user. Perhaps this is how the physical world works as well.

Maybe there *is* no physical world, only a *description* of it. Where this description of the physical world comes from, I do not know. Perhaps we, as individuals or groups, create it continuously as we interact with our impression of the world. Likewise, how well this description gives the impression of an actual world depends on the perceivers—us—or, rather, our beliefs and expectations. Perhaps in cases where our impression of the world is faltering, we subconsciously adjust our description of the world to make it more convincing. Could the physical universe be a *description,* an ever-changing blueprint, rather than an actual place?

Behind the scenes lies a nonphysical energy field we call the astral. This field has no form, taste, or sound. It does not conform to how we believe a proper world should act. It is simply neutral nonphysical energy. There is nothing in it, except the ability to create anything. We draw energy from this field into our perception. Once in our perception, we mold the energy into shapes that fit our description of the world. The reality behind our physical experience is a subjective energy form sculpted by our individual minds.

There are an inconceivable number of ways to mold astral energy. If you happen to meet other beings living in the universe, you might find that they look at their surroundings in radically different ways. They do not share our beliefs about how a world should look. They have their own beliefs and so mold nonphysical energy to fit those beliefs. The result of that mold is what they perceive as being their surroundings. For example, UFO occupants have been reported to walk through walls, blink in and out of view, and enter dreams. Their view of the world evidently does not contain walls and doors or even a distinction between waking consciousness and sleeping consciousness.

Matter proves to be only one of many ways of looking at or conceiving of nonphysical energy. The only thing that makes this perception of energy special is that we as physical beings (the term we use) have developed senses—eyes, ears, and so on—to assist it. As we have the means to perceive energy in the particular way of the physical, we have made that perception our reality. Had we developed senses to measure energy in some other way, then *that* way would be thought of as reality. Reality is in the eye of the beholder. Give the beholder an astral eye and he will accept the astral as a reality too. Wherever we go, high or low, thick or dense, we eventually develop senses that allow us to get used to our surroundings enough to call it reality. This is because we are nonphysical beings, and we can adapt to any form of reality we choose to create.

This time around, we have extended our senses in order to interact with energy in a physical way. We have chosen to make the physical our current reality. Physical space holds no real boundaries for us, except the ones we create for ourselves. If we believe matter is the only proper or real way to perceive energy, then we will not be able to sense energy in any other way.

It is our nature, however, to constantly create new experiences, and the best way to do that is to extend into unknown territories, including the physical and the astral. Your whole childhood was a long period of getting used to your extended physical senses. You are now extending your senses to experience energy in an astral way. It will require time and effort but will be well worth it. You will not stop with the astral, though. You will never cease to expand yourself in this manner. You will never stop exploring new horizons.

Mind over Matter

In 1927, Werner Heisenberg proved that, because of their nature, it is impossible to measure the momentum of subatomic particles. For example, if we want to measure the position of an electron, we have to apply light or we will not be able to see it. The light (photon) will energize the electron, increasing its velocity. In other words, we can't measure a quantum particle without disturbing it.

Luckily, in 1925, physicist Erwin Schrödinger devised a quantum wave function to calculate how an electron is spread out throughout a subatomic space. This wave function is applicable to all tiny particles that behave as waves, including quarks. In later experiments, Max Born confirmed that an electron stays in one piece rather than spreads out, rewriting the meaning of the wave function. To Schrödinger's dismay, the wave function came to represent the *probability* of finding a subatomic particle at a particular point in space, rather than its actual position. The wave function gives several positions in which the particle is likely to be. The particle is said to be super-positioned, meaning it could be in any of several positions. The notion of super-positioning has been challenged by many physicists, including Einstein, because, according to Newtonian physics, a particle can be in only one place at any time so its probability should have only one position. However, it is evident that conventional physics can't explain the behavior of quantum particles.

Niels Bohr reasoned that the nature of the quantum particle is probabilistic. Therefore, it does not exist in any position but is simply probable to exist in several. Applying Bohr's theory, now known as the Copenhagen interpretation of quantum mechanics, we could say that matter does not exist, but the probability of matter exists. And if matter does not exist, space and time do not exist, although the probability of them exists.

A problem arises when we measure the particle. It then ceases to be super-positioned and appears in only one of the probable positions. This transition is known in quantum physics as the collapse of the wave function. The wave function incorrectly gives several probable positions when we know the particle to be in only one. This raises the question that is at the heart of the quantum problem: How does the particle pick one position over other positions of equal probability?

The collapse from a probable to a measured state is theorized by some not to be deterministic, but rather a random transition governed by the laws of probability. This would mean that the Universe is random and its future can't be predicted by looking at its current state, unless you are content with a probabilistic prediction. The nondeterministic nature of the Universe has been very hard for physicists to digest because, according to classical physics, the Universe is a machine-like system that is playing out an extremely long energy transformation ending in a state that was destined the moment the Universe began.

To further complicate matters, experiments have hinted that a measured particle picks the position in agreement with the expectation or guess of the observer.[4] Either the nature of physical matter is subjective or we do not have the understanding required to conduct productive quantum physics research. To combat subjectivity, Hugh Everett put forth a so-called many-worlds theory, which holds that when we measure a particle, the universe is split into several parallel universes, each holding the particle in a different single position and containing one copy of the observer.[5] A similar theory has been presented involving consistent histories.[6]

I postulate that as the nature of matter is to be in several probable places simultaneously, this is not the nature of human consciousness. The human mind can't handle the concept of a probability-based reality. It needs a stable reality in order to function. The human mind therefore takes the particle and forces it into a single position. This would mean that in every instant, you decide the position of the particles around you.

Does this sound familiar? This is exactly how astral "matter" works. It moves to your thoughts and expectations. What is the difference between the physical and the astral? The line between the physical and the nonphysical is getting blurred because the physical and the nonphysical are built from the same stuff, a stuff that can be found everywhere throughout existence. One is not higher or better than the other. They are different aspects of the same thing, or different ways of looking at the same thing, or different ways to give different impressions of the same thing—however you want to look at it. This thing is what we call the astral energy field for lack of a better word.

An interesting parallel is that of digital clocks. Have you ever looked at your bedside clock to find it saying 2:22, 3:33, or 4:44? This happens to me almost every night. It may seem like a coincidence, but in light of the Copenhagen interpretation, it is not. As time and matter are related, time is also super-positioned. It ticks forth in equal seconds only if you measure the movement of the clock. Otherwise, for all you know, time could slow down or speed up. When you wake up during the night, the time could be anything between midnight and morning. By looking at the clock, your mind gets confused by finding that time has a whole range of possible simultaneous values. It quickly decides that time should be something simple, for example 2:22, because a symmetric number like 2:22 is easier to come up with than, say, 2:13 or 2:29. Time then becomes 2:22 in your current reality. As a result, your clock shows 2:22.

The strides of quantum physics are one way in which our view of the physical world is changing. We are beginning to view the physical as an extension of the Creation, rather than the core of Creation. How fortunate it is then that many people are skilled in astral projection, because projection allows us to traverse the physical so that we may explore other parts of the Creation and find out how the physical relates to them.

Beliefs Influencing the Physical
Wednesday, April 10, 2002
Time/Space Fluctuations

I am waiting at a bus stop. I am growing impatient. I remember Art Bell talking about time/space fluctuations on the Coast to Coast A.M. *radio show. I decide that when I put my backpack on, the bus will come. I put my backpack on and the bus shows up around the corner! This means that one can change the world (or create a parallel time/space continuum for oneself) just by deciding that the change will take place. Thoughts create. Who knows, perhaps in an alternate space/time continuum I am still standing there, waiting for the bus.*

The physical is only an *interpretation* of the Creation. We perceive small amounts of information from an energy field with our physical senses and interpret the information according to our beliefs of what reality is. The interpretation is constructed by the mind. Too often, we claim that what we are seeing is how things really are. We cling to the interpretation as if it were the ultimate truth. To make it worse, in addition to our limited perception our beliefs and habits make us see some aspects in detail and others not at all.

Here is an analogy: A shoe salesperson and a dentist meet for lunch. The first thing the shoe salesperson notices about the dentist is that she is wearing size seven brown leather shoes. The first thing the dentist notices about the shoe salesperson is that he has a gold filling in one of his teeth. Likewise, I make no claim that I somehow created a time/space fluctuation in the journal entry above, but since I believe in them, it is easy for me to interpret the situation that way. Others, who do not believe in such things, come to different understandings of what occurred, whatever fits in with their beliefs. Perhaps the bus showed up by coincidence.

The astral realm is another interpretation, or way of looking at the Creation. Just like the physical, the astral perception of Creation also is contaminated by our beliefs. When I venture into the astral, I see, hear, touch, and even smell things. How is this possible? I did not bring my eyes, ears, fingers, or nose. Why do I insist on using senses that are inappropriate for my current environment? My *beliefs* about what is proper interaction with my environment force me to use my habitual physical senses. I am blinded by my beliefs of what reality is.

In similar ways, what we believe becomes our reality. If I believed the physical provides no visual input, I would be blind. Fortunately, most of us do not have that belief. Why not? Well, I think that we subconsciously pick up beliefs from each other. When we are toddlers, we expect our parents to show us how this reality works. We look at their movements and actions and apply what we see to our own belief systems. It does not stop with our parents, though. Our belief systems pick up something from every encounter with another being. This explains why we all have more or less the same beliefs about how the physical works.

We seek to establish some useful beliefs, so that we can function in the physical, but in doing so we also *create* the physical. The physical is no more than an idea or thought-form, and we shape that idea according to what we believe is contained in that idea. Even the laws of nature are not laws at all, but ideas that we have reinforced so many times that they have become habits of nature (see *The Gathering* by William Gammill[7]). We cocreate physical reality according to our shared beliefs. Our beliefs create our individual physical realities and affect the way others' realities are created around the globe (and possibly even around the universe).

In spite of all this, there is hope. We can make our own interpretations of the Creation and thereby change the world simply through our willingness to see things differently. When we use our imagination, we create an alternative world for ourselves. This alternative world bleeds into our shared reality, encouraging it to become more like we imagine. Some call the alternative world a fantasy or an illusion; still it is hardly any different from our shared physical reality. Both are created from thought and both exist only in our minds.

Imagination is our best tool for creation. In fact, our imagination decides how the physical world plays out. Imagination is also a tool we can use in order to sense parts of the Creation that we can't perceive with our physical senses. We can reach our intuition, creativity, and passions. We can talk to spirit guides, friends who have passed on, and other parts of ourselves. But our self-invented beliefs make us look down on imagination as something unimportant, when in fact it may be the most important sense we can ever hope to develop. A man can lose his physical eyes and get by, but where would he be without imagination? He would be cut off from the nonphysical realms and be forced to wander utterly lost, without any passion to guide him to where he wants to go.

Astral Realities

Sunday, December 22, 2002
Attempt at a Close-to-Physical OBE

I feel a need to achieve an OBE close to the physical, that is, to interact on the physical plane outside my body, in order to understand how the physical relates to the astral. How are the two seemingly different realms connected? What natural phenomenon holds them together?

In the evening, I decide not to go for an OBE. I have some feelings of disappointment that there might not be much of a Christmas this year, and those feelings might make the OBE an unpleasant experience. I wake up at approximately 10 P.M. After a short bathroom visit, I go back to bed and—in spite of my decision—drift into a weird state of mind. I just relax my mind and sit my astral body up. My physical body resists and I am pulled back down as if I am attached by rubber bands. I sit up again and add a little twist/rotation to the movement. I exit and glide down to the right. I stabilize the projection by sitting down and meditating on the center of my chest for a few seconds. Then I get stressed out. I want to do as much as possible, and I never know how long I am able to stay out here.

I know Barb is still awake next to me in bed. I float over to what I suspect is her physical body. I grab her arms and shake her violently while I yell her name over and *over. I think this is a good experiment. If Barb notices any movement or sound, then that is evidence that I am affecting physical matter from a nonphysical origin. The astral Barb I see wants to be left alone. She groans "no . . . no . . . no." I leave her alone.*

There is an invisible presence behind me. At the time, I do not reflect on it. The presence feels natural, like it is supposed to be there. The presence says to me, "That's not how it's done [projecting to the physical]." I just know that is what the presence wants me to know.

He feels like a male mentor who is correcting a fumbling student (me) while shaking his head in disbelief of my clumsiness. I know he thinks projecting to the physical is common knowledge and, therefore, I should already know how to do it, but he does not mind instructing me. But when all this is happening, I still have not acknowledged his presence. I am too busy carrying out my experiments to notice him. I want to return to my body to see if Barb noticed my attempt to contact her. In a few seconds, I return slightly groggy. She is peacefully reading in bed. It is apparent that she has noticed nothing and she tells me so when I ask.

I slumber off and slip into the astral. My astral projection is plagued by nightmare-like beings and events and I repeatedly wake up with my heart beating too fast and my mind blurred with panicky fear. In the last short astral slumber, I clearly hear footsteps walking rapidly and determinedly on gravel. I snap back to waking reality. I am terrified. Is there someone approaching the house at this late hour? We live in the middle of a desert. People seldom come here, and nobody ever comes after dark. I don't hear anything. Was it a warning that someone will come in the near future?

Finally, I calm down. I remember other occasions of astral noises. Nothing happened then, so I should be safe now as well. Perhaps it was that presence wanting me to know he is coming closer? I realize there had been a presence. I am very disappointed. The presence could have taught me valuable information (as a response to my request?), exactly the information I had planned to obtain, if I had only noticed him. I ask the presence in my mind: "If that is not how it is done, then how is it done?" No reply.

You are a multidimensional being. What that means is that you are capable of shifting your awareness from one dimension of existence to another. But that is not all. You are also capable of existing in all those dimensions and, with some training, maintaining your awareness in all those dimensions simultaneously. Take, for example, daydreaming. In a daydream, you have awareness in both the waking physical reality and in a dream reality.

Being a multidimensional being also means that all dimensions live *within* you. Together they make you into you. At the same time, you are you in all those dimensions. You do not change from dimension to dimension. You are one indivisible package.

Dimensions

So what are those dimensions in which you can exist? The three most apparent dimensions are the physical, the dream, and the astral. Your thoughts and actions in one of those dimensions affect your actions in the others.

For example, if, consciously or not, you attend a learning center in the astral, this would influence any dream you might be having. In the dream dimension, a school—perhaps your old high school or college— would be created and incorporated into your current dream. When you wake up (i.e., shift your awareness to the physical dimension), you will sense that somehow you have gained knowledge, even if you can't define that particular knowledge. You gained the knowledge in the astral learning center, but that is not easy to remember when your attention was in the dream dimension during the education.

Here is another example, something that happens to me frequently: When you project your awareness to the astral, you can sense another, separate part of you engaged in dreaming. It feels as if the dream is going on below the surface of an abstract layer below you, like a swimming pool, and your projected awareness is the only point of you that has the head above its surface. It is then clear that the dream is of your own making. You also see that the dreaming part of you is unaware of the fact that it is entangled in its own dream world. You can also notice how your actions in the astral influence the dream, taking place in the dreaming you.

These three dimensions are governed by thought. To make things complicated, we could say that what happens in the realm of thought affects what happens in those other three dimensions.

Subconscious thoughts are very influential in the three dimensions. In the astral, the subconscious mind has a direct effect on the astral "matter." Whatever lurks in the subconscious is mirrored in the astral people we meet and the astral objects that surround us. It is possible to affect astral matter with conscious thoughts, but the subconscious in most cases has the upper hand, simply because we can't directly control what goes on inside it.

In the dream dimension, the subconscious has even more power. This has to do with the fact that the conscious mind is "offline" and therefore can't question the events in a dream. Whatever the subconscious comes up with is manifested in the dream dimension as dream situations, symbols, and emotions. Should we question the events of a dream, the subconscious would lose nearly all its power and the dream would turn lucid. We would then be able to *consciously* affect the dream matter.

When we shift our awareness to the physical dimension, as we do when we are awake, we can manifest incredible things with our conscious mind. It takes a little longer to build a bridge in the physical than in the dream dimension, but when it is done, it will remain there until thoughts of wear cause it to collapse. Compare this to the dream dimension, where a bridge would disappear the moment you stopped thinking of it. However, the subconscious mind also affects us in the physical. Hearing, sight, touch, smell, and taste all take place subconsciously. When we move our bodies around, each muscle is controlled by the subconscious. Even our perception of our physical surroundings is gathered and compiled subconsciously. If it were not, we would be very clumsy in our movements, but we would also be able to consciously decide how we would perceive the physical world.

Wednesday, January 1, 2003
Earth-Close OBE

I am drifting off to sleep. It takes me an unusually long time to enter the hypnagogic state. When I finally do, a conscious part of me is awake and able to reason clearly, while another part of me is half unconscious, rapidly falling asleep. I get the idea that I should go to the bathroom before I fall asleep, so I do not have to get up in the middle of the night. I try to roll out of bed, but instead I break free from the body! I am floating two feet above it. I can't see anything, but I can hear. I hear Barb's light snoring. I roll in the air to break free from any attachments to the body. As I roll, I distinctly hear the snoring move, too.

The snoring comes from a stationary source—Barb. When I rotate, I perceive the sound from other angles, just as if I were rotating my physical body. I conclude that I must be projecting in the physical, because the sound is of physical origin and I can perceive it relative to the movements of my awareness. Then the drowsing part of me wakes up and I am called back to the body.

Beliefs Create

The astral is a place where your environment is created by your mind. This is true also for the physical dimension, but it is easier to see in the astral, because the effects there are immediate. I speculate that the reason for the slow rate of change in the physical is the fact that it is inhabited by so many beings, each of which holds a set of beliefs of what reality should look like. Their minds automatically apply those beliefs to the physical, creating it in every instance.

If one of those minds decides to create something different, say a green sky, then that mind would be at odds with every other mind that believes the sky is blue. Eventually, the green sky will take form, because one mind provides the intent for it to exist (more on intent later in this book), but you can imagine the time it takes the intent to penetrate the con- flicting beliefs of the other minds. There might also be nonphysical beings surrounding us, fully engaged in sustaining the shape of the physical.

The astral, on the other hand, is a highly individualized reality. Although there are plenty of cocreated astral worlds, in most cases when we project, at least until we learn to navigate properly, we end up in our own little astral world. There is only one mind (the projector's) inhabiting that world, so there are no conflicting beliefs to slow down the act of creation. The downside of this is that when that mind leaves that astral world, it loses its creator. There will no longer be any beliefs to recreate that astral world in every instance to make it persist. The astral world therefore dissolves into nothingness. Yet a cocreated astral world, that is, an astral world inhabited by several astral beings, will change just as slowly as the physical world. This leads me to the idea that the physical is just another astral world.

Thoughts Create

Because of the fast rate of change in the astral, when you project into it, you have the freedom to create anything your heart desires, just by thinking of it. The downside is that there are parts of us that are beyond our direct control. We label them the subconscious. The subconscious also thinks up things, which, to our frustration, pop into our astral environments.

The contents of the subconscious—what is on its mind—are old experiences. It is constantly trying to digest the memories of old traumas and events outside its belief system. Most traumas need to be dealt with consciously though, so this digestion may lead nowhere. As a result, the subconscious may be constantly packed with old, outdated, and painful thoughts. These thoughts manifest automatically in the astral as we project into it.

Therefore, you gain more control over your astral environment as you learn to tame your subconscious. It is vital to process all traumas and addictions, or you will be a slave to your subconscious and thereby to your astral environment. Like attracts like in the astral. If your subconscious is troubled, your mind will create or attract trouble in the astral.

As you might imagine, the subconscious can create many challenges for you in the astral. To make it worse, sometimes in the astral, restraints such as morals are not functional. Perhaps the reason for this is that morals are traits of the ego, and the ego is designed to work only in the physical. This may cause your addictions, for example, to run unchecked. For example, if a projector is addicted to coffee, then he will subconsciously create an astral world of coffee. The projector has no defense against this onslaught by the subconscious. However harmless coffee addiction may be, it gets in the way of what that projector wants to do in the astral.

Later in this book, you will experience firsthand how easily you can affect your mind and how much this affects your environment. Each thought affects another thought, and all thoughts accumulate to a resulting astral environment. This is great as long as we have control over our thoughts. The problem is we can't directly control subconscious thoughts. We will address this in Circle 3.

As mentioned earlier, to learn the way of the astral, we have to put aside all our beliefs concerning the physical. It is a costly mistake to assume that the astral looks and feels like the physical. Unfortunately, our beliefs about the physical are rooted deeply in our subconscious, and we can't just step into the subconscious and rearrange anything we want. The beliefs of the subconscious are formed by experience and so by experience must be loosened.

Subconscious beliefs kick in automatically when we are conscious, in the physical or astral. Actually, they kick in when we are unconscious in dreams, too. Have you ever broken a physical law in a dream? You probably have. You have probably gone flying at one time or another in a dream and marveled at the experience. Why is that such a special event? It is special only because you expected *not* to be able to fly. Why did you expect not to be able to fly? You assumed that the dream world had gravity, so you did not think you could fly. Your subconscious created gravity for you, and that is exactly how the astral works (it is even how the physical works). You will be subjected only to the things you create. What will happen if you manage to overcome this automatic application of subconscious physical beliefs? You will be free of any physical limitations. You will be free to do anything. That is the potential of the astral—to be able to create anything. The only thing limiting you is you.

A Call for Astral Research

Our sciences are hopelessly chained to the physical dimension. The general opinion is that anything that is not physically measurable is not real. This dangerous assumption is a great limiting factor to the progress of the human mind. We can advance our physical technology all we want and still be novices compared to other civilizations, both ancient Earth civilizations and other-dimensional civilizations. That is, unless we start developing our nonphysical technologies. When we finally do, we can only hope that the beauty of this new nonphysical frontier will inspire us as a race to abandon our destructive behavior.

So far, the research on the astral has been based on physical reality. A typical experiment involves a subject projecting from one physical room through a locked physical door and into another room, where he reads an integer correctly. This does not even approach the true power of astral projection. Researchers are trying to prove whether or not astral projection is real when they do not have the first clue of what the word *real* means. They make a huge mistake in assuming that there are things that are not real, and they make another in assuming that all real things relate to the physical.

Experimentation with the nature of the astral should not take place in a physical environment. That would be like testing your driving skills by taking a math test. Astral experiments must investigate the nature of the astral, not the nature of the physical. We must remember that the astral is the realm of the mind; it does not follow physical laws unless the mind enforces physical laws upon itself. What possible benefit could we reap by forcing physical laws upon the mind during exploration of a realm unchained by those same laws? I suggest more research on partnered projection and shared astral environments.

A partnered projection experiment involves a projection with two or more astral projectors. Upon reaching a nonphysical state, the participants attempt to communicate according to a predefined protocol, for example, speech, writing, sign language, or mind-to-mind. The messages communicated are kept from the recipients until the astral communication. If the participants report the actual message after returning to the physical, the experiment is a success.

By no means does this prove anything definite, as such communication can be attributed to anything from subliminal suggestion to telepathy, but it does teach us valuable points about the projection mechanism, allowing us to design more effective astral projection techniques and more precise experiments. The obvious problem with this type of experiment is having to find two or more projectors who are sufficiently skilled to be able to project simultaneously in a controlled environment.

A shared astral environment experiment closely resembles the partnered projection experiment, with the exception that the participants do not have to astral project simultaneously. When they astral project, they attempt to enter a previously agreed-upon world. They proceed to make changes to that world. They may, for example, erect buildings or write on a wall. Over a period of changes, if the participants' perceptions of that world match, the experiment is a success.

Basic Fears

As you will discover during your astral projections, your environment is a reflection of your state of mind. When you leave your body, you end up in surroundings that match your thoughts, among people who think like you do. If your mind is light and positive, you will encounter helpful people. If, on the other hand, your mind is heavy and fearful, you will run into fearful people. Fearful people have the tendency to hurt others in order to preserve the self. Therefore, I can't underscore enough the importance of freeing your mind from fearful thoughts.

As I see it, the mind is all you have, your only real possession. It is your responsibility to keep it in shape by regularly analyzing any fear harbored within it. In order to do that, you need to understand how fear works, specifically how it manipulates you. This chapter provides some insight into the dynamics of fear.

The Wrong Kind of Fear

For any human short of Buddhahood, life is a constant battle against fear. We despise the nauseating feeling of fear, yet we appreciate it as it keeps us safe from physical danger. But what *is* that danger and where is it?

In modern society, how often must we struggle to escape physical threats? We are no longer running from saber-toothed tigers; we passed that stage a long time ago. Physical threats appear almost exclusively in traffic, accidents, crime, and war. Fear in such situations dramatically improves our chances of survival. The problem is that we experience fear in far more situations than these.

Society has been evolving toward the goal of physical comfort for such a long time that we seldom have to rely on our physical bodies to carry us away from danger. Unless we are in a war zone or crime-stricken area, there is little pressure on the body to ensure our survival. The majority of today's threats are of the mind, not of the body. For example, a debt is not a direct threat to our physical survival and so we can't use our body to escape it. It is an indirect threat that can only be avoided by a mental maneuver.

If your boss asks you to give a presentation on your current project, you may be thrilled at first. However, you may not get any sleep the night before the presentation because the body is already preparing for battle. In the morning, your digestive system prepares by clearing and shutting down. Your palms sweat excessively throughout the day and your mouth is dry. As you step up to the podium, your tongue is paralyzed and your mind goes blank. You are unable to remember your prepared speech. You are inhibited by nervousness, which is another face of fear. This nervousness causes your body to prepare for battle. Are you going to do battle with the audience? No. In this common modern situation, the fear is misguided. It helps neither you nor the audience. If the fear had instead prepared you for mental exertion, you would have given a brilliant presentation.

Even though today's threats are distinctly different from those of our ancestors, our emotional response remains the same. Our reaction to a stock market crash is fundamentally the same as that of our ancestor realizing he is about to become breakfast. Fear speeds up our pulse, empowers our muscles, and shortens our reaction time. It also blurs the mind, preventing it from thinking clearly, because the last thing you want to do during a fight is to ponder and theorize. This does not work well with the threats of the mind. Further, we need our mind to be sharp and clear, so that we can consider our options. Therefore, there should be two kinds of fear: one that prepares us for physical battle, and one that prepares us for mental exertion. Unfortunately, our emotional makeup has not yet evolved to provide the second kind of fear.

Any fear associated with astral projection is a fear of the mind. For example, if we get confused and disoriented in the astral, fear may kick in. We prepare for battle. The problem is that we did not bring our physical body, so we have nothing to carry into battle. Even if we did bring the physical body, any astral threat would most likely not take physical form, and so the physical body would have no power over it.

A fear of the mind would help us here. Such a fear would make our minds clearer, thereby helping us to understand our surroundings. Unfortunately, this does not happen. By habit, we react to astral threats by preparing for physical battle.

No Worries

Worry is a common type of fear. Living in modern society, you are probably familiar with worry. As modern people, we worry about everything: Do we have enough money to pay next month's bills? Are our children safe at school? What poisons are in our foods? How much sunlight can our skin take before it develops cancer? How long can we keep up paying the mortgage? The list is endless. We all know what happens to people who are unable to pay their bills. We see them outside the mall every day, forced to live in humiliation and starvation, even though the country they live in enjoys one of the highest standards of living in the world. Today's Western society displays a giant plaque saying: "Produce or Perish."

The cause of our chronic worry is that it is programmed into our genes as a survival insurance. As our forefathers roamed the woods, worrying about predators and long cold winters was the best way to survive them. Even today, tens of thousands of years later, the most effective way to stay alive is to worry. That is why, even though we have evolved into high-tech people, worry is a big part of our daily lives. We may not worry about predators, but we worry about money and housing, the lack of which, in our culture, can prove to be just as lethal as tiger's teeth. Still, it is remarkable that, during all that time, we never managed to control or even understand that worry.

Add to that the programming of our culture. We have come a long way from the hunter-gatherer tribal society where the village news was spread around the campfire. From birth, we are programmed to consider the dangers of our society. The mainstream media constantly remind us of how many killers are on the loose, where the terrorists may strike next, and how many trillions of dollars of debt the country owes. Commercials try to scare us into buying their products, telling us that only their pills will save us from a most gruesome death, only their deal can protect our families, and only with their exercise equipment can we overcome our physical fallibilities that will surely result in rejection, abandonment, and, ultimately, death in a solitary bed.

We are being conditioned to be wary in every aspect of our lives. This programming has increased exponentially during the last decades. Only 20 years ago, people very rarely locked their doors at night. Today we put bars on our windows. Are we unreasonably scared or has the human spirit really stooped to levels where the average man threatens to obliterate his neighbor?

Turn on the news and you will hear only the worst of the worst. Rarely do we get good news. Naturally, hearing the worst-case scenario for years will program us into believing and expecting it. In our thoughts, the fear has become justified, and once justified in our thoughts, it becomes justified in our actions. At the prospect of theft, injury, freezing, or starvation, of course we worry. This worry is poison to our spirits. It has been rooted so deeply that it is part of our every thought.

Emotional Responses

All thoughts ignite emotions to different degrees. In other words, emotions are merely the effects of our thoughts. When thinking a thought—any thought—an emotional response will immediately follow to emphasize the thought and to encourage us to action. If we think of ice cream, the emotion of craving fills us, motivating us to take a trip to the freezer. Additionally, as a consequence of our conditioning, worried thoughts accompany the first thought: "If I pay for this ice cream, will I still have money for the bills? Will I get fat if I decide to eat this ice cream? Will my arteries be clogged? Will I have a heart attack? How will I pay for the visit to the emergency room? Who will take care of me when I am released from the hospital? If I die from this ice cream, who will pay for the funeral?"

These thoughts pass through our minds so often that we do not even notice them. We are used to being afraid of the consequences of our actions. As a natural emotional response to the fearful thoughts, worry flares up. We feel it as a slight nausea in our guts. Most people are so used to the nausea that they do not question its validity.

If we manage to shake the nausea off long enough to think, "Nah, ice cream isn't that good anyway," the emotions of craving and worry will be replaced with well-being. We no longer think ice cream is tasty, so there is no need to feel a craving. Who would feel a craving for something distasteful? The worry will also be neutralized because we have opted to take an alternative route that does not involve the dangers of ice cream.

There is a better way to neutralize the emotion of worry: You can remove the worried thoughts from the initial thought (ice cream). Without the fearful thoughts, no nauseous emotion will be produced. When you think of ice cream, and you feel the nausea coming on, simply think of ice cream again, but this time, identify the thoughts of worry and decide not to think them. If you do this with your every thought, you will feel tremendously liberated. Your thoughts will no longer be held back by worry. You will be able to see incredible opportunities in your life, opportunities that previously were locked out by fear.

Fearful thoughts have the potential of creating havoc when we leave the body. When you awake after a nightmare and are considering leaving your body, but you are concerned that it may turn into a scary experience, apply the Removing Fearful Thoughts technique to eliminate the fear created by the nightmare. If you leave your body with fear, you will most likely have a nauseating trip, but if you remove the fear just before leaving, your odds for a wonderful experience increase.

Exercise: Removing Fearful Thoughts

1. For each thought you think, examine your emotional response.
2. Do you feel nauseated or bad in any way?
3. Look back at your thoughts to the reason you feel bad. What thought brought on the emotion?
4. Is the cause reasonable? Is the emotional response justified? Are you really as threatened as the thought would have you believe?
5. If the response is not justified, decide to remove it. Simply do not allow it to occur. Think only the original thought, free of the worried response.
6. If you continue to feel bad, search for other thoughts that may be responsible. Remove them in the same manner.

Fear of the Unknown

The fundamental reason we worry to such extremes is that we have a severe fear of the unknown. In my opinion, fear of the unknown is humankind's greatest obstacle and has been since we learned to think coherently. Any time we try to find new ways, our fear of the unknown is there to discourage us.

History is full of fears of the unknown. For example, in ancient days, every sailor knew you should not sail too close to the edge of the world because you might fall off. Looking back at that time, we find such fears amusing; but at the time, we viewed them as appropriate concerns. Surprisingly, in spite of the centuries that have passed, we still have not learned to understand the fear of the unknown. Our fear of sailing off the edge of the world is gone, but fear of the unknown still exists. It has evolved and grown alongside the progress of our culture, appearing wherever our culture lacks experience.

A modern example is that of financial security. Most people seem to believe that you have to work hard when you are young to gather wealth because you never know how life will treat you when you get older. In believing that, we are letting the fear of the unknown get in the way of living. We postpone life until we retire or even until the moment of death.

Most of us succumb to this fear without even realizing it. We are so entangled in fear that we can't tell what is up and what is down. But however we reason it, we can't escape the fact that this fear is based upon *uncertainty,* not on actual threats. As such, it has no reason to exist unless we give it a reason. The nature of uncertainty is twofold. On one hand, we fear what dangers might lie within it. On the other hand, we are intrigued by what potential discoveries await us. By following the second hand, we can view the fears as warning signs, rather than stop signs, on our path to discovery.

A good way to stop being afraid of an unknown is to turn the unknown into a known. By probing the object of the fear and studying it, the fear dissolves as we realize that the object presents no threat, and there was nothing to fear in the first place. For example, as you read this book, you may feel slightly worried about what awaits you in the astral, but as you read on you acquaint yourself with the subject and, before you know it, you will have turned the unknown of the astral into the known of the astral. The worry will dissolve.

Fear of Change

From fear of the unknown springs not only worry, but also a fear of change. We are all more or less afraid of change, because we know that beyond change lie many unknowns. How often do you tell yourself: "Well, it can't get any worse." Not very often, I hope, because it is not true, and we know it. It can always get worse. Consequently, we strive to achieve stability in our lives, avoiding change at every turn. But do you know what? Stability is boring!

Life is an adventure, and there is not much room for stability in an adventure. How much fun would Tolkien's tales be if the Hobbits sat at home instead of setting out on adventures in Middle Earth? Changes will come, perhaps not involving magical rings and hordes of Orcs, but they will come whether we like it or not. We may resist, but that leads nowhere. It takes more energy and effort to resist change than to prepare for and embrace change.

The astral is all around us, all the time. We can access it and all its potential anytime. Anyone of us could enter the astral right now if we wanted to, just by thinking of it. So why don't we? The truth is that, deep inside, we do not want to. We do not want to know that the physical is escapable, that there are better ways and places in which to live. We do not want to find out that our whole hardworking lives have been an illusion. We fear knowing that our world is completely different, more subjective and at our command, from what we have thought throughout our lives. Can we stand the thought that at anytime we could have left our lives of hardship behind? That we did not have to go through any of it? Would we rather cling to the belief that each difficulty was a building block in our lives, a life that will never change?

But beyond this fear of seeing life's true nature, we find sobering thoughts: Everything so far, every hardship, in this life has been in preparation for this moment. Every step forward allows a second step forward, which allows a third step forward, which in turn leads to the realization that none of the steps were necessary, although they were necessary in order for us to realize that they were unnecessary. There is always a next step, and the next step now is to take off, leave the mundane life, and enter the astral.

Nothing to Fear but Fear

Tuesday, March 19, 2002
Lucid Dream

I dream that I am in my parents' house. Some strange event occurs in the dream. I think, "This is impossible. I must be dreaming. This is a dream." I keep repeating that it is a dream and I become increasingly lucid. Suddenly, something grabs me from behind and starts spinning me! I am frightened. I can feel my chest bubbling with terror. I manage to overcome the fear. I know that in dreams, nothing can hurt me except fear.

I spin around in circles, spiraling upwards. I stare down at my parents' bed in the living room, where it was ten years ago. The spinning stops and I am floating at the ceiling above my parents' bed. I get more in touch with my physical body. I can hear my girlfriend snoring. I try to focus on the lucid dream, but the snoring is very difficult to ignore. I wake up in my bed. I guess the affirmations for lucid dreaming with brainwave sounds really work—only it takes a week for them to take effect.

We as conscious beings cocreate our realities. Specifically, you create what happens to you in every moment. You are like a victim and perpetrator rolled into one. If you are afraid, then you will believe that the fear calls for a defense. You create the defense by building walls around you. With the walls comes isolation. The isolation spawns uncertainty of what is outside. Uncertainty spawns fear. And around it goes.

Your ego always makes sure it is correct. The ego hates to be wrong. That is what being an ego is all about. After a while of waiting for the threat that is not there, it *invites* the threat in order to prove that being afraid of it was not a waste of time. And threats can't show up at your doorstep unless you invite them, because nothing happens to you unless you allow it. In a manner of speaking, you have manifested a threat out of thin air just because you were afraid of such a threat.

If you instead detach the ego, you will live by a loving attitude. With that attitude, you will be able to manifest anything with little effort, even cool trips to the astral. You will also see the benefit of creating fear for the purpose of overcoming it and growing from the emotions it produces, but do not feel you *have* to feel fear. You will know that there is nothing to fear but fear.

Love Conquers Fear

Friday, January 12, 2001
Love Conquers Fear

I am walking in the woods, something I enjoy tremendously. I come upon a cliff. In spite of my fear of heights, I decide to approach the ledge and look down. My legs turn into spaghetti as I crawl toward the rim, inch by inch. I look down. There is a 30-foot drop straight down. I watch my reactions very carefully, so as not to be overcome with dizziness and fall to my death.

I remember something I read: Fear can't exist where love exists. To test this theory, I bring to mind the thing I love the most. I think of it and, especially, I think of how much I love it. The fear dissipates. This is incredible! I stand up. My legs are perfectly normal, not the slightest shaky. I lean over the edge and look down. I can see the ground below the cliff and it does not frighten me at all. In fact, I think the cliff is a nice little feature of nature, compared to earlier, when I thought it was a deathtrap. I climb down the steep end of the cliff. In my previous fearful state, this would have been impossible, but now I quite enjoy it.

One of the universal laws is that fear can't exist where love exists. Love dispels fear. Love is our natural state of mind; therefore, we can always feel love, in spite of any pain in our life. If we manage to break through the emotions of fear, grief, pain, and anger, we can access love, and then love will automatically dispel any vestiges of those negative emotions.

Exercise: Dispelling Fear

1. Close your eyes.
2. Relax your mind. Let it sink.
3. Move your center of thought to the center of your chest.
4. Create a small pearl of love in the center of your chest.
5. Let love beam out from the pearl in all directions.
6. Let the love bathe everything around you.
7. How do you feel? Have any worries and fears subsided?
8. Repeat the exercise as often as possible so that it will be an automatic response to fear in the astral.

Astral Projection Fears

Each person is unique and therefore reacts differently to his first astral projection experience. Some find it tremendously joyous while others panic. It is a joyous occasion, but it is human nature to let fear get in the way of anything fun. My first projection scared me out of my shorts, and I have talked to many other projectors who have reacted in similar ways. It is the kind of fear that makes you want to turn and run as fast as your legs can carry you, while screaming at the top of your voice. This is completely natural.

Our subconscious has no clue as to what is happening when physical reality falls away from our senses, and that is enough to scare even the bravest soul. Even if we have read everything there is to know about astral projection, fear is a possibility, even a probability, until we get used to the actual experience.

Fear not only keeps people from attempting astral projection, but it also keeps them from practicing astral projecting after succeeding the first time. Such fear fills no purpose because there is nothing to fear during a projection. If you fear anything about the projection experience, do not fret. The fear will subside as you get more used to it. I promise you that the fear will dissipate if you maintain a loving and adventurous attitude toward astral projection, in spite of the fear. And once you get past the initial fear, you will love every moment of your time in the astral.

There are many fears to conquer when attempting to leave the body, so to prepare for the first astral projection, we will look at some of the most common.

Fear of Not Being Able to Return

Will you be able to turn your awareness back to your body once you have turned it into the astral? Yes. It is *your* body and you have been associated with it during your whole physical lifetime. You turn your awareness back to your body every time you wake up. For a 30-year-old, that is about 11,000 times, so you have had a lot of practice. You know the procedure like you know the back of your hand. You have made it into an automatic habit to such a degree that you no longer remember how to consciously do it.

If you ever want to get back to your body while in the astral, all you have to do is think the word *body* and the memory of your body will pop into your awareness. Your mind will associate the memory with your actual body and then your awareness will be turned to your body. You will probably find that the opposite—remaining projected away from the body—is a lot trickier, at least in the beginning.

However, if astral projection turns into a compulsion, there might be a physical danger. Everything you intensely desire will come true. If you desire to constantly be in the astral, then it shall be so. If you have to abandon the body to fulfill your wish, then that is the way it has to be. Be careful what you wish for, for you might get it. Let me rephrase that: Be careful what you wish for, for you *will* get it.

Life is a beautiful gift that we have bestowed upon ourselves, and it is difficult to desire anything better than being alive. But sometimes compulsion gets the best of us and creates desires so strong that we can't avoid allowing them to come true.

In *The Divine Blueprint*,[8] Robert Perala presents a disturbing case. Perala's friend Devon was a frequent astral projector. She reportedly departed from this life during an astral projection in 1992. Her body had a seizure and she failed to return to it. We know much too little about the mechanics of the soul-body connection to determine a more exact cause of her death.

Upon her death, Art, Perala's friend, went into trance to find out what happened. He contacted some spirits who had been around her at the time. Reportedly, she was in the habit of astral projecting so frequently and for such long durations that her connection (some call it the silver cord, but I think that term is misleading since it might make us think of a physical cord, whereas the connection is nonphysical or semi-physical) to her body wore out. In spite of persistent attempts, she could not get back into her body. Understandably, she freaked out and tried for hours to get the attention of the living. When she finally acknowledged the death of her body, she regretted having had such a strong desire to spend time with astral beings.

This is indeed a tragedy, but Devon did not die in vain, because she taught us something valuable about ourselves. We are here because we love the experience of physical life. In order to sustain that experience, we have to take good care of our bodies. The moment we stop appreciating it, perhaps by desiring to escape life more than desiring to stay, the body falters and our desire is fulfilled. Like Devon, many of us have a strong desire to explore the worlds beyond. We want to know what is behind the physical. We have to balance this desire with the desire to experience life, or astral projection will turn into a compulsion.

Perala tells me he still thinks astral projection is relatively safe, and I agree. As long as we leave our bodies with *moderate* frequency and duration, there is no danger involved. I think once per week is an optimal frequency. If you project more frequently than that, I recommend you check your motives: Does life still intrigue you or are you trying to escape it?

How often do people die during astral projections? For understandable reasons, there are no statistics. If the projector's body dies during an astral projection, his kin will assume the body died during sleep. Devon's case is the only one I have come across, but perhaps there are more. We should seek to learn from these.

Some say the silver cord is the projected awareness's connection to the body. The notion of a cord may spring from a three-dimensional way of looking at the astral-physical connection. Space does not apply in the astral, and so the idea of a cord that limits the distance you can travel from your body seems awkward. The astral-physical connection is non-physical or semiphysical. It can take any number of visual forms. Depending on the perceiver, it may look like a silver cord, a magnetic field, or a rubber band. It does not have to be visible at all. I have seen the silver cord on one occasion, but that may well be because I intentionally searched for it. The cord I saw could have been created by my wish to see it. Undeniably, there is an attraction between the projected awareness and the physical body, but to confine it to a silver cord would be to discount the diverse nature of the astral.

Many projectors worry that severing the astral-physical connection—for example, a silver cord—would cut off their return to the physical body, leaving the physical body to its demise. But how do you sever something nonphysical? How do you sever a color? How do you cut hope, beauty, or tranquillity? There is no possibility of severing the silver cord by a violent movement. It can't get entangled or wrapped around anything, just as you can't wrap a color around anything. It would be extremely difficult to sever the astral-physical connection in a tangible manner.

Like anything nonphysical, the astral-physical connection is under the control of the mind. We can't take a saw and cut the connection, but we can probably will the connection away. By intending to permanently drop the connection to the physical, the projector can kill his body. This is purely speculative of course, as I would not want to try it. In the Devon case, the connection broke because of her will to remain in the astral. In a way, she chose the astral over the physical. The demise of her physical body was an act of will and intent. In retrospect, she felt it was a misguided intent.

Wednesday, January 24, 2001
First Contact

First, I want to say that up to this point, I have never had an OBE. I found astral projection and the like only two months ago. I have been meditating irregularly since then. Two weeks ago, I started doing some energy exercises.

During the day, I do energy-raising exercises. In the evening as I go to bed, I decide to meditate before falling asleep. I start with relaxation exercises: As I breathe out, I sequentially relax every muscle from my feet to my head. After a few rounds, I feel resistance in my thighs, something I have never felt before. Upon inspection, I notice that the resistance stems from an energy flow from my belly to my feet, that is, the opposite way. I have never before felt such a strong energy flow. Obviously, my legs want to do the exercise in the opposite direction, so I switch.

I imagine—no, not imagine—there is a circle of energy, coming in from the air, entering my heart chakra, flowing down my legs, and exiting through my feet. I radiate love to my surroundings for a while, and then I can't help but fall asleep. When I awake a few hours later, I am still in the same meditative state of mind. That is fascinating. My exercises continue, uninterrupted by sleep. . . .

My body is overheated. The heat must have been caused by the strong energy flow. I exit my meditative state, throw off the blanket and let the air cool me down. I am still tired, so I decide to go back to sleep. I notice how delicate my senses are. My pillow feels incredibly soft, and I am very thankful for that. I do not thank my pillow very often, so this is a special occasion. I roll over on my right side and wait to fall asleep.

Three seconds later something heavy comes over me. Swoosh! It feels like I am being compressed and sucked through a tiny pipe. Then I am falling downwards and to my left, fast. No, falling is not the right word. There does not seem to be any acceleration involved, which makes me think I am not subject to gravity. It is more like floating downward at a constant speed of three meters per second. This sensation is real. I can't doubt that I am moving. After six meters, I stop floating. I feel like I am being compressed. It does not hurt, but I am confused and worried about what is happening.

The physical world is muffled. I can only vaguely hear my girlfriend's heavy breathing as she sleeps beside me. I can't see, though. My brain feels like cold steel, much like the sensation you get when it is low on blood or oxygen. Suddenly, I am extremely scared, somewhat by the unfamiliar situation, but mostly because I think my brain is out of air and I am losing brain cells fast. I am terrified to such a degree that— had I any connection to my physical rear—I would have soiled my pants.

I instinctively know what this is. I am having an out-of-body experience! To cope with my fear, I do what I have told myself to do in scary situations: I radiate love in all directions. Then I feel a lot better, but I am still afraid. I have told myself a thousand times not to be afraid if I got free of my physical body, but I guess fear is a very strong emotion that is difficult to control.

An astral environment forms in my awareness. I find myself sitting in a huge classroom. There must be a thousand other students sitting around me. Everyone's attention is turned to a professor who is giving a lecture, but the information flow from him is too fast for me to comprehend. I try to take notes, but my fingers are clumsy. They can hardly hold the pen. It is as if I am using my hand for the first time in years.

Then I decide to take the ultimate test: to open my eyes. For some reason, I expect to see my own physical body from a third-person perspective. Unfortunately, the eyes I open are my physical eyes. This instantly brings me back to my body.

Then I spontaneously float downward again and find myself back in the classroom. This time, I can partly feel my physical body. After a few seconds, I return to my body. When I attempt to float out again, nothing happens. Ironically, it only seems to work when I am not trying. I thank my guiding spirits for helping me have this experience. Balls of light move across the inside of my closed eyelids a long time after the experience has ended.

A few hours after the experience, I reach some conclusions:

• The reason that the physical world was muffled was that my awareness was turned away from the hearing function of my brain.

• The reason that my brain felt cold was that it was no longer in my awareness. I have felt the brain my entire life. I only miss it when it is not there.

• Energy exercises are essential for getting in touch with the spirit realm.

• I never intended to leave my body. I just wanted to get closer to the spirit realm. Unexpected things happen when energy is in motion.

• I have never before had a "paranormal" experience, nor am I gifted or sensitive. I am convinced that anyone can have this sort of experience.

Fear of Physical Harm

The biggest fears in physical life are the fears of getting injured, too cold, too hot, or too hungry. It is only natural to have the same concerns during astral projection, just as I experienced the fear of brain damage in the journal entry above. These dangers do not exist in the astral per se because they are physical concerns, but we may think that as we project away from the body, it might forget to breathe or have an accident like rolling off the bed. In any case, these fears are unfounded. I have had a large number of astral projections, and I can honestly say that I have never had a physical accident, except one time a dream catcher fell down and got tangled up in my ear.

Possessive Spirits

I want to make clear that I have never personally experienced a possessive spirit and therefore am not an expert in this area. I can't even say whether it is possible to possess the body of a human. However, there is such a large body of documented accounts, stretching as far back as to the New Testament, that the topic is difficult to ignore.

The frequency of possession seemed to climax in the late seventeenth and early eighteenth centuries, at which time Catholic exorcism was extensively used. But then the witch hunts with their accompanying paranoia were in full swing, so we can't tell how many of the alleged possession cases were actual possessions. No matter, there are plenty of cases of suspected possession in modern times and we can observe them in order to learn more. I have talked to several people who believe they have experienced possession firsthand.

What concerns us astral projectors is that there are plenty of accounts that tell of projectors finding different sorts of creatures upon their return to the body. The creatures seem to be trying to enter the projector's body, although I have never heard of a case in which they have been successful. I think that the degree to which a body can be possessed has more to do with the beliefs, attitudes, and emotions held by the person inhabiting the body than the availability of the body. Even if you leave your body unattended, it is still your body (even if it is a loan) and, therefore, a possessive spirit has to go through you before it can access the body. In other words, whether your body gets possessed or not depends on what goes on in your mind and has little to do with the fact that you temporarily left the body unguarded.

One projector, Brian, suspected that his younger brother was being possessed from time to time. The boy, to his parents' delight, showed brilliance far beyond his age, presumably from the spirit. How this situation resolved, I do not know, but this demonstrates to me that not all possessive spirits have malicious intents.

Even so, it seems possessive spirits have the potential to mess up your life more than anything else. They can even kill you (your physical body, that is), or worse: make your body kill people around you. There are a few accounts of ordinary men and women who have committed horrible crimes. They claim to have been possessed during their crimes. Could they be telling the truth? Could their tales be the tip of an iceberg full of instances of possessed perpetrators who are confused as to what happened? How many innocents are imprisoned because of crimes committed by possessive spirits?

However bad this may sound, it is clear that possessive spirits are not sent by the Devil to ruin your day. The concepts of a Devil and evil are human-made. No beings are evil; they are just struggling in the situation they are in and using whatever they know about the world in order to get to a better place. In fact, beings who are intentionally out to harm other beings are exceedingly rare. Most possessive spirits just want the same luxury we have: to experience physical life. Hardly any are out to make trouble.

To us, as beings inhabiting the physical, they may appear twisted in their minds, but we must remember that when they possess a physical body, they have no notion of morality. They are overcome by their own addictions, just like we are sometimes overcome by our addictions in the astral or in dreams (more on this in Circle 3). They do things they would not normally do. They are not intentionally evil; they just can't control themselves. To them, physical reality appears the way most people view dreams: a new place of existence so radically different from what they are used to that they can't accept it as either real or important. As it is not real to them, they can't take responsibility for the consequences of their actions. Their behavior is not very different from ours. How often do we as physical beings take responsibility for what we do in dreams?

If you get involved with possessive spirits, you need help from an experienced healer or exorcist. There are plenty of them if you know where to look. A search on the Internet should reveal some of them.

Fear of Bad Spirits

Many projectors report seeing nasty creatures in the astral or in the hypnopompic state (the groggy state we enter as we awaken from sleep or deep trance). Some look like trolls or monsters. Note, however, that just because we perceive a being as harmful does not necessarily mean that it *is* harmful. A well-meaning being may be perceived as harmful if fear gets in'the way of our perception. A slight change of attitude, from fear to love, will change the way we perceive a spirit.

Exercise: Anti-Fear

1. Close your eyes.
2. Imagine a monster running toward you with the intention of ripping you apart.
3. Imagine that it suddenly changes its mind and runs toward you instead with the intention of hugging you.
4. Evaluate the difference in how you perceived the monster in the two cases. Did the monster change appearance when you switched attitudes?

What you see in the astral is completely under the control of your mind. Therefore, by deciding that something is not there, it will disappear. In a way, you allow objects to be present, and no object can be present without your consent. If you find yourself in a terrifying astral situation, you can consciously change it.

Exercise: See It Not There

1. Close your eyes.
2. Imagine again a monster running toward you with the intention of ripping you apart.
3. Imagine that the monster is not there.

I have only rarely encountered harmful beings. I think my fortune has to do with my attitude. Each time I astral project, I expect—even *know*—that I will run into fun experiences. Thereby, I *create* enjoyable experiences. If I instead expected scary experiences, my subconscious might arrange that for me by attracting harmful spirits. I recommend that you review your expectations, even in physical life, because expectations form the starting point of your experience.

In the astral, beings can't harm you directly. They can't cause you any physical harm, simply because you did not bring your physical body. What they can do is harm you psychically by hanging around you for a prolonged time. Their mood affects yours. This works just as in the physical: If you hang around a bad crowd for a long time, eventually you will start to adopt some of their destructive behaviors.

Protection

Prevention is always the best defense. The following exercise describes what I do to protect myself from any bad experiences. Practice it repeatedly on dry land, so to speak, so you will know it by heart as you astral project.

Exercise: Protection

1. Close your eyes.
2. Move your awareness to the center of your chest.
3. Form a small bubble of foggy white light in your chest.
4. Let the bubble contain your love energy.
5. Expand the bubble until it surrounds you.
6. Reinforce the bubble with medieval knight shields, or bulletproof glass, or whatever strong material you prefer.
7. Put another shielded bubble around your whole environment.

Now that you know how to deal with harmful beings, there is no need to be afraid of them. I must again underline that there are many more benign beings than harmful ones. The next journal entry describes an experience that shows how nice they can be:

Monday, July 8, 2002
UFO Dream and a Natural Society

As I lie in bed in the evening, I get an eerie feeling. It feels like the space of the room is cut in half, as if an invisible metallic wall divides the room. I feel a presence.

The image of a gray alien comes to mind. For the first time in ages, I am afraid of the dark, but I get over it. Eventually, I fall asleep.

I dream I am in a coastal town. One night, people see lights in the sky. I look up and see crosses of white light all over the sky. There must be 50 of them. They slowly descend toward me. There is a kiosk nearby from which people maintain the beach. I run there and see a video camera. I ask if I can borrow it. A man is relaxing in an armchair, reading something. He says, "Sure." I look in the camera and ask them if they have any tape. A woman walks over to a videocassette recorder and ejects a tape. "You can tape over this," she says and hands me the tape.

I run outside and capture the crosses of light on tape. They appear to be alien craft. Suddenly, I am beamed up into one of them. I run film the whole time. I can't remember what happens in the craft. When I return to the surface, I am thrilled to have captured it all on tape. I rewind the tape and play it. To my amazement, the whole tape was somehow filmed on the ground. There is not a single frame from aboard the craft. Then it hits me: My lower self stayed in the dream (apparently I know I am dreaming) on the surface, while my higher self ventured on more important business in (or beyond) the alien craft. In other words, my awareness went with my higher self into the higher realms while my lower self stayed with the camera on the beach.

I think this is an interesting phenomenon. Perhaps this is the way alien abductions are performed, and that is why abductees have a hard time remembering what happens in the craft.

I drift toward the waking state. I make some notes on a notepad so I won't forget my conclusions when I wake up. I realize that the notepad is probably not physical, so the notes will not be there when I wake up. Nevertheless, I think it is a good reality check: If the notes are present when I wake up, then I am actually awake right now.

I don't want to wake up, so I fall back into a slumber. In the dream, it is now the following night. The same lights appear and I film them once more. The same events repeat. I almost wake up again, but then decide to fall back to sleep. For the third time, I enter the same dream. I conclude there must be something about the camera, because each time I look through it, my awareness projects to my higher self. I decide to try that theory. I stare through the camera, waiting for something to happen.

Suddenly, I find myself on the driveway of my parents' house. I sit down for a minute. I put my hands together like Buddhist monks do. I focus on my chest and meditate for a while, just like I do during OBEs to prolong the projection. The surroundings change. The driveway and the buildings around me are still the same, but they are shimmering with a magical transparent white energy. I am now in a place of ecstasy.

Strange, I am in the same place, and at the same time it is different. With a simple act of focusing in the chest, I turn an ordinary place into a paradise.

I stand up and walk down the street. It is winter (it is summer in waking reality). Snow covers everything. Some buildings there in waking reality are not there now. Instead, there is a valley covered in snow. The snow has that magical glow. It is incredibly beautiful! I smile so much I am sure my physical face is beaming, too. If someone were to see my physical face now, she would be puzzled as to what is going on inside me.

I walk down another street. It ends, but I walk straight into what appears to be a park. The season changes to fall the moment I step onto the lawn. There are dark green trees that glimmer with life force. There are beings here, but they are not humans. They are short and wide. They are very friendly and jolly. They seem to be enjoying life. Nobody is stressed. Nobody feels they have to do anything. Life here is one of leisure, just like I think life on Earth should and could be. These folks remind me of the hobbits in Tolkien's tales.

I spot some small houses. I intuitively understand that they are in energy symbiosis with the dark green trees. They do not stand out like human dwellings do. They look like an integrated and natural part of the park. Everything is in harmony with nature here. It is a relaxing sight. I enter one of the houses. Some of the little chubby men are baking something. Coincidentally, I have some pastry with me. I ask them if they would like to trade one of mine for one of theirs. They smile and tell me I may taste theirs and I can keep mine. They are giving me food without expecting anything in return. This is indeed a glorious society.

I pick a cookie from a baking sheet. It tastes incredible! My mouth is watering as I chew it. I think that my physical mouth must be chewing, too. I reflect on how incredibly real the taste is. I know I am not using my physical taste senses. Is my mind making this perfect taste up or is it under the influence of an actual nonphysical cookie? I take another pastry from another baking sheet. I take a bite. Yum . . . banana bread! Amazing! This is the best banana bread I have ever had. If only physical food could taste this good.

I walk out on the balcony and find that I am on the second floor. There are two tennis courts below me. I climb down to the tennis courts and enter the first floor. The moment I enter the door, I lose lucidity and move into a dream.

Spirit Guardians

Before you go into the astral, you might feel more reassured if you have a spirit friend who watches over you. There are spirits (they are called spirit guides or guardian spirits) who dedicate themselves to helping projectors. If you are unfamiliar with the psychic process of directly addressing spirits, prayer will suffice. Whether you pray to Jesus, Buddha, Mohammed, your ancestors, or another spirit acquaintance, prayer works well. A prayer is a clear thought sent through the astral, and a request to a spirit must be clear in order for it to be distinguished from the mumble of all your other thoughts. If you know a spirit guide, you may ask it to find a guard for you, or, if you, as I, talk to yourself, ask yourself to find a guard. Do not feel embarrassed or unworthy to ask for protection. It is never wrong to ask for help.

Exercise: Requesting a Spirit Guide

1. Close your eyes.
2. Relax your mind. Let it sink.
3. Imagine that all current thoughts get caught in soap bubbles and drift off in the wind.
4. Put your hands in front of your chest, the fingertips of the three middle fingers together at a 45-degree angle, forming an upside-down "V" with your fingers pointing up. Your inner senses are very focused using this hand position.
5. In your mind's eye, form the image of the spirit guide listening to your request.
6. Think clearly to the listening spirit: "I request a good spirit to protect my awareness when I astral project."
7. If you worry about your body, request another guard: "I request another good spirit to watch over my physical body while I am astral projecting."

If you run into trouble in spite of your spirit guide, remember the bubble of white light and love, and pretend the object is not there, as you practiced in the earlier exercises. Pretend you are in the astral and go through the steps in your mind, so that you are well prepared should you get into trouble.

Monday, December 18, 2000
Queue of Souls

I am very tired. I know I should not do any spirit exercises, because I am very likely to fall asleep. Still, my curiosity makes me attempt another astral journey.

I want to talk to my guardian angels. To initiate contact with a spirit, you must picture yourself in its presence. The problem is, I do not know their names nor what they look like. It is very hard to start pretending that a person appears when you don't have a memory of the person and you must pretend in order to initiate contact and get the communication rolling. I relax and picture myself in a meadow. Focusing on my chest, I call out, "Are there any spirits around?" I can't find the word "guardian." I try again: "Are there any . . . damn, what is it called?"

Then I hear giggles from the right and up from me. At least I pretend I hear it. Or am I? The giggle is not directed at me, but at the irony of the situation. I smile and think, "Good, at least one of them has a sense of humor." Then I notice two more guardian spirits around me. I ask their names but fail to hear their response.

I remember thinking I should not have journeyed when I was so tired. Shortly after, I fall asleep. I start to dream. Surprisingly, my guardian spirits are still there, along with a bunch of other spirits. Then a long line of troubled souls come to seek my advice. They are coming from my right-hand side. Each of them presents me with two or three choices that they can do, and I am to pick one of the choices for them. Each soul carries a yellow menu, much like a Windows application menu. When I select a choice from the menu, that choice turns gray. Then the soul moves along and the next one asks my advice. I can feel that every soul in the endless queue is very troubled, but as soon as I give them my advice, they are relieved and happy.

This worries me, because a few days earlier, I decided to cut down on the amount of advice I give. This is because I recently gave advice that lead to the breaking of another person's heart. People are very much capable of making their own decisions, so I decided to give encouragement rather than advice. Still, here I am, giving advice.

Some racket in the physical world wakes me up. I am awake, but my eyes are closed and I am still with the queue of souls and my guardian spirits. I am in the same state as just before the dream. This is strange, why did I not just wake up to the physical world as I always do after sleeping? I say goodbye to my guardian spirits and some other spirits around me. I then return to the physical world. The clock tells me I have been with the queue of souls for three hours. I fall back to sleep.

Wednesday, January 02, 2002
Comforting Lap

Last night at 5 A.M., as I was lying in bed, it felt like I was lying on someone's belly and that someone was comforting me. I felt completely safe and serene.

CIRCLE 2

Getting Out There

Achieving your first astral projection.

To boldly go where no one has gone before.
—Star Trek: The Next Generation

Each chapter in this Circle builds toward you achieving your first astral experience; therefore, the exercises are of particular importance. Astral projection is a skill that we learn by doing, not merely by reading, so feel free to do each exercise with all the enthusiasm you have. Good luck on your astral projection pursuit, and do not forget to have fun.

Sleep States

Sleep is a natural process that we need in order to stay healthy. To take full benefit of the sleep process, we should let it take its natural course without the interference of alarm clocks. Unfortunately, our hectic lifestyle seldom allows that.

There are numerous states of mind from which we can astral project. Many of them are natural sleep states with a touch of altered awareness, which is to say there is nothing artificial or unnatural about them. Ordinary states of mind, such as a waking physical state, keep the awareness focused in the physical senses and thoughts, but when we attain a state of mind beneficial for astral projection, the focus is unlocked and we are able to shift our awareness away from the physical. The natural sleep process sometimes jumps into one of those states and we find ourselves conscious in a dream world. Certain relaxing or psychedelic drugs can also be helpful to achieve those states, although they are not necessary.

Let us look at what happens when a person sleeps (see figure 2).

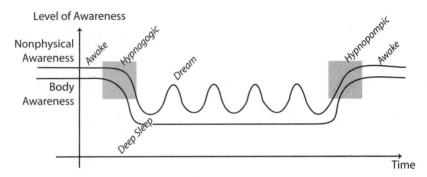

Figure 2. Sleep states.

Friday, July 19, 2002
The Astral Briefcase

Before going to sleep I think, "It is my birthday, so I am entitled to a cool experience." The next morning, Barb is outside the door fumbling with her keys. The noise wakes me up into a fuzzy state. I am half in the astral and half in waking reality. In the astral, I see a case resembling a briefcase or suitcase. Strangely, the case is also a red ball of energy. I recognize it immediately. I have never seen it before with conscious eyes, but I know it has been next to me for years. I think, "Aha! There you are! You are that thing that controls my sleep. Why have I not seen you before?"

The case is magical. It has something to do with the sleep process, though I am not sure exactly what function it has. Perhaps it is the thing that puts me to sleep at night? I float closer to the case. A buzzing feeling comes over me. My mind is buzzing and my physical body is tingling. I am trying to figure out what the case is and how it works. This could be the control panel to sleep. If I master the case, I will master all sleep states and, consequently, all projections. Unfortunately, I am becoming increasingly awake. The case disappears. I try to visualize it in order to attract it back, but that does not work.

Still in a fuzzy state, I make some notes: "The case is used for diversion, but it is also the goal. When you approach the case, you fall asleep." The purpose of the case seems perfectly comprehensible in my current state of mind. In retrospect though, I can't understand what the diversion or the goal is. I hope the knowledge will come back to me.

The Hypnagogic State

As we drift off to sleep, we enter the hypnagogic state (from the Greek words *hypnos,* meaning "sleep," and *agogos,* meaning "conduit"). This is experienced as the beginning of slumber. In this state, the awareness withdraws from the input of physical senses and opens up to the world away from the physical. We may hear voices or sounds in this state. They may even startle us. They sound very physical-like, although often lack the reverberation that follows a physical sound.

Tuesday, February 6, 2001
Shocking Sound

I raise energy as I lie in bed. I try to get my nonphysical energy in motion. My palms and soles, and sometimes my thighs, are tingling more than ever. After a few hours, I decide to go to sleep. I have a short daydream. I do not know what to call it. I am only half asleep, but I am dreaming. I dream I am a reporter or something similar and I have interviewed a group of marine biologists that is going on an undersea expedition. As they climb aboard a little boat, I consider coming along. Everyone knows that the boat could fail and we could all die. Should I take the safe way out and go home or should I risk my life on a wondrous adventure?

I jump onto the boat. The instant I land on its deck, I hear a very sharp sound in my head. It strikes as quick as lightning. It sounds as if an inch-thick steel cable is torn apart by an enormous power. I hope it is not my brain getting torn to pieces.

Once I get past the initial shock, I realize that the sound is only in my head. I am sure it is not coming in through my ears. It is kind of muffled and there is no reverb. Could the sound be related to my decision to choose adventure over safety? I have adopted the "no big deal" attitude in order to keep me calm, so I force myself not to analyze it too much. The next thing I know, I wake up in the morning.

Monday, February 19, 2001
Vibrations and Lucid Dream

After doing the dropping technique for some time (imagining myself falling through the mattress in small drops as I breathe out), the vibrations come. This is the first time I feel the vibrations. It feels like an electric current running through my chest. I approach the sleep state a few times. One time there are three powerful knocks: "Knock, knock, knock!" I think: "Who is knocking at my door in the middle of the night?" Then I realize the knocks are only in my head. They sound like the real thing, only they are muffled. I am frightened, but I fight it off by remembering love. I figure it could be someone knocking on my astral door. I try to visualize opening a door in my mind. There is no one on the doorstep.

A few minutes later, there is a tumbling noise from above me. At first, I think it is my upstairs neighbor dropping something on the floor. Then I realize again that the noise is in my head.

When I have done the dropping technique for a couple of hours, I decide to go with the flow and not fight the sleep. I move into a lucid dream. It is on a gangster theme. It involves two wild teenagers, one mafia don, and some gangsters. I am a hit man. My mission is to eliminate the don. I bluff my way into the complex and approach the don. Then I get the idea: "Hey, if this is a lucid dream, I can make the don float." I make the don float in his chair a couple of feet above the ground. Then I float myself. I can't fight sleep anymore, so the lucid dream ends.

Sunday, July 15, 2001
Spiritual Q&As

At night, I read in Bruce Moen's Voyages into the Unknown[9] that the four steps to contacting guidance are:

1. Get comfortable and relax.
2. Ask a question once.
3. Let go of it.
4. Expect an answer and be open to receiving it.

I try this a few times. Sometimes, I get imaginary pictures as replies. One time a woman's voice pops into my head and says with a bright but angry voice: "That's no way to behave!" It is kind of vague. I would categorize it as something between a thought and an audio input. I do not recognize the voice. I do not know where it comes from, but obviously, it is not of this world.

In any case, what I hear is not related to the question I asked. Sounds and voices like this one seem quite random, just like sitting on a railroad station bench, listening to the conversations of passing travelers; you can't control or anticipate what you will hear. Perhaps the sounds originate in beings living in other dimensions, and we can only hear them when we open up, as we do in the hypnagogic state.

Most people do not remember being in the hypnagogic state. This is because it is often brief and directly followed by unconsciousness. This is a shame, because the state provides the means to access hidden parts of us and nonordinary realities that live inside us. It is a gateway to our minds. In it, we can direct healing to our physical bodies, communicate with other parts of ourselves, and create our future through visualization.

In the hypnagogic state, we decide what we want to do during sleep and whether we want to astral project, dream, or gather otherworldly information. Our subconscious is very easily affected during the hypnagogic state. If we want to go projecting, we can program the time and destination into our subconscious, simply by picturing it in our minds.

As the hypnagogic state deepens, we lose consciousness little by little. The hypnagogic state climaxes with the release of the awareness.

Tuesday, February 13, 2001
The Border between Awake and Sleep States

I lie stretched out in my bed, feeling content and happy. I raise energy. I do not care whether I will have a successful session or not. I am content either way. After some time, I am drifting between awake and asleep states. I have a semidream. I am half dreaming and half pretending. I imagine I am walking around in my room. I know I am lying in my bed, so I know I am not having an OBE.

Suddenly, I walk into an invisible wall. I trip and fall through it. I instantly lose touch with my body. My brain, or what I think is my brain, has that weird out-of-air sensation again, just as it did during my first OBE. I try to find my balance, but the invisible wall surprises me to such a degree that I stumble and fall through the wall. I land on the street outside my house. I am embarrassed, because I know I am wearing nothing but my underwear. People are walking by and a man stops to help me to my feet. In waking reality, there are no people outside my house, because it is 4 A.M. The man is wearing late nineteenth-century Swedish clothing. Interestingly, the house was built in 1898. Unfortunately, I start thinking. I try to analyze and control the experience, and this ruins it. I feel increasingly in touch with my body and soon the sensation of being out of my body disappears. I fall asleep.

In retrospect, I think the invisible wall was the border between the awake and the sleep states. When the body fell asleep, I was released from it, as if I were released from an elastic rope to which I had previously been tied. I fell forward, which I interpreted as stumbling through a wall. My body fell asleep, but I was still conscious. This was a shock to my conscious mind, and I subconsciously translated the shock to the event of losing my balance. During the hypnagogic state, my awareness had been half turned away from the body. When I fell asleep, my awareness left my body completely, *which explains why I lost touch with my body. I am not sure whether my awareness actually fell out of the house or if it was a dream house.*

It seems I need to be in a contented state in order to have an experience. I must not care whether the session will be successful or not. The secret to success is to keep my consciousness alert but passive (i.e., not analyzing), while tricking the body to think that I am asleep. When the body thinks I am asleep, the awareness will be released from the body. The problem is that this is very difficult to accomplish without losing consciousness.

When the subconscious thinks we have lost consciousness, it unlocks the attachment to the physical body that is so strong during our waking hours. The physical body goes into a state of rest and the awareness, now set free, projects into the dream world. If we manage to stay conscious during this release, we will notice it as a signal from the physical body. The signal says, "Ping, you are ready to go!" Then we are free to project our awareness to any reality we wish by executing an astral projection exit technique. With some practice, we can gain the ability to remain conscious and sense this signal as we slumber off. It is an interesting experience, although not necessary for the astral projection technique we will be using.

Exercise: Probing the Hypnagogic State

1. Tonight, as you are falling asleep, close your eyes and tap your index finger on the mattress once per second.
2. If you drift off to sleep and wake up again, resume the finger-tapping.
3. How long can you keep tapping your finger before you lose consciousness?
4. Observe your mind very closely. What changes does your state of mind go through as you lose conscious control over your finger?
5. Practice this each night until you know the ins and outs of the hypnagogic state.

The hypnagogic state is excellent not only for astral projection, but for any other psychic activity: telepathy, channeling, clairvoyance, and more. We all have these abilities, but they are blocked by something close to reason. In the hypnagogic state, our critical mind and reason go to sleep. This removes the block and allows our psychic abilities to surface.

Saturday, August 16, 2003
Channeling Ramtha in the Hypnagogic State

I wake up in the morning. I might as well astral project, since I can feel I am about to fall back to sleep. But what do I want to do once I leave my body? Hmmm. "I want to speak with Ramtha!" Ramtha is a spirit channeled by JZ Knight. On page 16 of the book Ramtha,[10] edited by Steven Lee Weinberg, Ramtha describes how he, in a physical life around 33,000 B.C., had an out-of-body experience. He later ascended from the physical world and decided to contact JZ Knight to spread the knowledge of ascension. I affirm "I want to speak with Ramtha" mostly for my own sake, to ensure that I do not forget once I pop out, but, apparently, it is also a request to Ramtha.

Not a second later, my neck and back of head are tingling like mad. I am falling asleep now, but I do not realize that. The tingling must be Ramtha coming in. As he moves in, I phase out from my body. I am losing feeling of my body. I can take control of the body, but I sense that would mess up the session. I am a little worried that it might be some other malicious spirit, but I get over it. I am quite sure it is Ramtha, since I invited him. He is used to channeling, so the process is smooth. I did not have channeling in mind though; I wanted to project to him to have a talk.

My hand wants to move, so I assist it. One by one, other body parts want to move, too. I assist them. I think this is Ramtha's way to get used to my body. Then they do not need my help anymore. They move on their own accord, or Ramtha is moving them. My body moves off the bed and is dragged on its back across the floor. Cool. Into the next room we go.

This is a dream room with no resemblance to any room I know in waking reality. I mistakenly think I am still awake. In any case, the fact that the experience is a dream does not make it less real. There are about four people in the room, but none that I recognize. I am dragged here and there. I think Ramtha wants to give a speech, but nobody wants to listen. We return to the bedroom. Ramtha leaves my body and I wake up.

The reason we are discussing the hypnagogic state in such depth is that we will be using it to exit our bodies. We could just go into a trance from a waking starting point and exit the body there, but it might take hours to get into a good trance, causing strain on body and mind on the way. It is a lot easier to use the natural sleep process. Later in this book, we will leave the body in a hypnagogic state after waking up from a period of sleep. This is much more effective than attempting astral projection after a period of being awake, a *dry period*, as I call it.

The Release of Awareness

Prior to and during the hypnagogic state, massive amounts of the sleep hormone melatonin are released into the body, causing the body to fall asleep. The mind is used to following the body's impulses. For example, we think of food when the stomach growls and we think of going to the bathroom when nature calls. In the same manner, we think of falling asleep when the body needs rest. Thoughts of sleep cause the mind to lapse into unconsciousness. We have made this an automatic response to the body's desires, but it does not have to be that way. We can stay conscious while the body falls asleep by reprogramming the mind's response to the body's desires.

In order to reprogram our sleep pattern, we need to understand the body-mind relationship and the mechanics of the hypnagogic state. The hypnagogic state works like this:

1. The body is tired and releases the sleep hormone melatonin.
2. The hormone causes body organs to slow down.
3. The mind becomes groggy as a response to body changes. Dazed, we can't reason clearly, but our intuition is working.
4. The nervous system reduces its throughput, inhibiting sensory input.
5. The body cells produce more warmth for a while to compensate for lacking sensory input.
6. The body goes numb.
7. The mind withdraws from the bodily senses.
8. The mind lapses into unconsciousness. We can change this. It is unclear whether the mind needs rest, since it is a nonphysical object.
9. By now, the body is shut down, except for autonomic nervous system functions such as breathing, heart pulse, digestion, and cell waste disposal. The body is in a state of paralysis.

10. The mind withdraws from the body and turns its focus to the astral.

11. The body is healed. Healthy cells duplicate to replace damaged cells. Neurons increase or reduce their conductivity to adjacent neurons in order to optimize the body's response to orders from the mind. This also optimizes autonomic functions.

12. The mind creates astral worlds and plays out dreams in them. The mind is still subdued from the lapse into unconsciousness and so is unable to become aware of the fact that it is dreaming.

13. During dreams, the mind attempts to move the body as it usually does when it is projected into it. The brain receives the orders to move. Some brain activity is spawned as the brain triggers nerves to move muscles. Because of the paralysis, however, the nervous system does not carry the nerve signals. Only the eyes move as the mind accesses imagination in order to create imaginary worlds.

As you can see, if the mind manages to sustain its consciousness a few more seconds, it will remain aware when the body falls asleep and the mind enters the astral. This is quite an experience. To accomplish this, you only have to focus on something that keeps your mind riveted enough, a visualized object or sound, for example, to ignore the programming and stay awake.

The Planning Phase

Prior to the release from the body, most people just lose consciousness and experience (or rather, do not experience) their nocturnal time in the astral as deep sleep. But a hidden part of ourselves projects into the astral to meet nonphysical guides and friends. This part of us is normally inaccessible from our dreaming or unconscious minds. It meets up with guides to discuss the events of the past day and plan for tomorrow. It is as if waking reality is a game and we are secretly planning our moves as we sleep. The person inside the game, the reasoning, aware part of us, has no idea waking life is a setup and so takes the game seriously. To keep the game serious, we keep ourselves in the dark by secretly planning behind our own back.

Sunday, July 1, 2001
Astral Communication

I have a hard time falling asleep. My belly aches after too much chew and beer. I notice a sound in my brain, close to my right temple. It sounds like a mechanically repeating puff of wind. After two hours of sleep, I gain consciousness. I am in a state that I have not before experienced. At first, I think I am awake, but then I know I am not in my body. I can't tell whether I am having a lucid dream or an astral projection. It is probably something in between. My awareness is in a very subtle astral body. A less subtle body is dreaming. The dream affects me, but I am not participating in the dream. It is as if a second person is participating in the dream while I am observing it from a distance. It is an awesome feeling.

I am talking to a nonphysical being. How did I get here? I know intuitively that I have been talking to this person for a few hours. He is my teacher and guide. We have been going through the activities of the past day and have discussed what I could improve and how to encourage the physical me to make those changes. A hidden part of me must have had this discussion before I gained consciousness, because I do not remember any of it.

As far as I can figure, a hidden part of me talked to this person and, suddenly, the aware part of me woke up in the middle of the conversation. The part of me previously talking feels like an exact copy of me, only it lives in a place other than the physical. It has its own awareness but is still me. This is revealing and creepy at the same time.

The person I am talking to, a man with dark hair, is dumbfounded. He is completely taken off guard. He never expected this part of me to awaken while he was talking to another part of me. In a few seconds, he regains composure. I have so many questions I want to ask him, but I can read from his mind that he is uncertain whether enlightening me is in my best interest. I can feel pressure building up in his mind. He regrets having been discovered by the aware me, but he is also impressed by my interdimensional capabilities. His job is easiest when he is hidden. He quickly comes up with a plan to get out of here before I find out too much.

He introduces me to Sarah, a spirit helper. He says there are a vast number of beings like her. I look at her and see that she is a cricket. As I turn my attention to her, my guide disappears. She seems like a very jolly "person." I figure that while I am talking to her, I might as well present her with one of my problems and get some input. As I talk to her, I try very hard to speak with my physical mouth. Old habit, I guess. No matter how hard I try to speak clearly, only muffled sounds come out of my physical mouth. She seems to get the message from my thoughts anyway.

"I have a problem. When I am in a crowd, I always look at the bodies of women. I can't help it. Even when I am with my girlfriend, my head goes like a radar antenna. I love the aesthetics of the female body. But I don't want to do this anymore. Can you give me some advice?"

"You should stop doing it, because it will hurt you." (Actually, the answer was longer and more complex than that, but I do not remember it all.)

Not satisfied with the answer, I say, "There must be a better reason for not doing it, other than the fear of the consequences."

She gives me another reason, which I can't remember. I am not satisfied with that answer either.

My upstairs neighbor yells: "If you are asleep down there, then how come I can hear you talking?" (A strange thing for a person to say, but this is the astral, so anything can happen.) I am worried that the mumbling of my physical mouth will draw embarrassing attention from my girlfriend or a neighbor, and the yelling is probably a manifestation of that worry. My neighbor's voice comes in through the open balcony door. I could have sworn I closed the door before going to sleep, but apparently I must be mistaken. (The door is closed in the physical, but open in the astral.)

"Sarah, will you excuse me, I have to return to my body and go close the balcony door." Sarah nods.

I find myself back in bed, but not in my physical body. I roll out of bed and land on the floor. I am in a daze. My vision is blurred and distorted. It seems my eyes are glued to the ceiling. No matter how hard I try, I can't direct them away from it. I think: I will have to feel my way to the balcony door. This feeling of moving around is similar to my other astral projections, so I reason that I must be projecting. I float up in the air a few times on my way to the door, just for fun. Would it not be fun to float out the door? I check that I am not naked, to avoid embarrassing situations. I am wearing boxers and a small sheet. Hey, I wasn't wearing that sheet when I went to bed! Where did it come from? I throw the sheet to the floor. The boxers feel so real against my skin! I look out the balcony door. It is a sunny day. Small white clouds are sailing across the sky. I try to close the door, but fail. My hands can't work the handle.

I instantly pop back to my bed, but I am still outside my physical body. I continue to talk to Sarah. I can't get visual or audio contact, so we have to communicate with text. It is like Internet chatting. I can't remember what we talk about. The worry still bothers me, so I decide to try to go over and shut the balcony door again. I roll out of bed. My vision is distorted as before. Not being able to see anything but the ceiling, I crash into the armchair and a lamp on my way across the room. I try to close the door, but two plastic lawn chairs are in the way (they are not there in the physical).

Two young men are hanging around outside my balcony. They are sipping beer and talking like people talk when a party is over and things have calmed down. I recognize one of them. I close the door and float back toward the bed. I stop in the center of the room and lie on the floor. Perhaps I want to rest, or maybe I want to project. I get an impression that my girlfriend asks me, "Why are you lying on the floor?" Embarrassed, I get up, float over to the bed, and lie down.

As I lie on my bed, I think it would be cool to astral project. (Sometimes I mistakenly think I am in my physical body, which is confusing.) I visualize myself by the ceiling, looking down at the bed. In a second, I am floating by the ceiling. I am not sure if I am projecting into a higher astral body or if my current astral body is moving there. My girlfriend physically touches my body in her sleep. This causes me to pop back into the bed, but still outside my physical body (perhaps back into the astral body I projected from).

I visualize myself being in a beautiful park. I move there. My girlfriend touches me again and I pop back into the bed. I visualize myself being in a place where everybody is kind to each other. Nothing happens . . .

Then I pop out and fall into a void. A man, whom I can't see, repeatedly calls out my name, as if he is trying to find a missing child. I can tell from his voice that he has been yelling for quite a while, years even. I answer in thought: "I am over here!" My girlfriend touches my body a third time and I am back in bed.

I feel I have to write everything down, so I will not forget it. Suddenly, I have a pen and a notepad in my hands. I write as fast as I can. The sound of pen against paper sounds extremely real. Then I think: Hey, where did I get this pen and paper? I must be dreaming. Wake up! Wake up!

I have a false awakening. I get out of bed. My vision is still distorted, so I reason that I must still be asleep. I move around a few seconds in the room. Then I falsely awake again. When I realize I am still sleeping, I understand how difficult it is to know whether you are awake or asleep. What if I go to the bathroom when I am asleep, but think that I am awake? I slumber a bit. Then I wake up for real. I pinch my arm to see if I am still asleep. I seem to be physically awake.

This experience lasted almost an hour. It makes me realize that lucid dreaming and astral projection are very closely related. I am thankful for the opportunity to consciously communicate with what I think were astral beings. The man who repeatedly called out my name seems to be very eager to contact me. I wonder how long he has *been calling out for me, waiting for me to listen. This experience also raises intriguing questions to whether it is possible to project from a lower astral body into a higher astral body.*

Perhaps the hidden part of us that is engaged in astral activities is our truest being, residing in the place we call home, doing things it thinks are ordinary but are inconceivable to our reason. For some reason, we do not allow ourselves a glimpse into what it is doing. Because of this secrecy, sleep remains a mystery for most people, but not for long. We are finally developing tools to investigate it.

The Dream Phase

A buildup of the vitalizing hormone DHEA (dehydroepiandrosterone) arouses the mind enough to create dreams, but normally not enough to realize it is dreaming. True to its creative nature, the mind immediately creates worlds in which to immerse itself. Since thoughts create in the astral, there is no limit to how physical-like and convincing a dream can be.

A dream may occur directly after the hypnagogic state or after a period of deep sleep. A dream is often followed by deep sleep, then another dream, and so on until the body wakes up and calls the mind back.

We can tell whether a person is dreaming by looking at his body. Her eyes are often rolling (called Rapid Eye Movement, or REM) and other parts of her face are reacting to dream events. These signs may or may not be present, depending on how closely the dreaming mind and the body are connected at the time of dreaming. If a body is very deeply asleep, it may not be influenced at all by the dreaming mind.

Saturday, August 11, 2001
Astral Projection with Sight

I go to bed at 6 A.M. and awake at noon. I am wearing earplugs. I figure I can do an astral projection session, as I know it works best when one has just awoken. I ask my guides to help me become psychic. I ask myself to have the energy and will to train my psychic skills. I ask my guides to help me have an astral projection in ten minutes.

My body falls asleep remarkably fast. My mind remains awake. After 15 minutes, my body is completely detached from my awareness. I fall asleep for a short period. When I awake, I am ready to exit the physical body. I try rolling to my right, but there is too much resistance. I roll to my left and fall out of my body.

My vision is black. I float across the room. The room is full of furnishings I have never been aware of before. I place my astral hand on them and they feel extremely real. I float through the closed door and out into the corridor. The blackness disappears. I can see. My astral eyes are working for the first time! I am constantly afraid that I might try too hard to see and that I will start using my physical eyes instead, which would end the projection.

I have made it to the corridor without falling into some black void. Usually, when I pass through a door or wall, I end up in a totally different environment or in a black, empty space. I think, "All right, my first Earth-close projection!" I am convinced that my other projections have taken place in an astral replica of my room, which is the only illuminated thing in a vast void. I think this projection is taking place in a replica, too, but it is closer to the physical Earth.

I think I should visit my corridor neighbor. I have this perverted urge to snoop around in other people's rooms. I float to her door. I can't pass through it. Strange. Doors have never stopped me before. Perhaps my conscience is stopping me, because my intentions are not the best. I float down the corridor, thinking of what I want to do. I get the idea to go to my girlfriend instead. I have read that all you have to do to go to a person is think about that person. I think of her, but nothing happens.

I must be getting more involved with a dream now, because suddenly I am standing on the street outside my parents' house. For some reason, I am convinced that my corridor neighbor lives on the second floor of the house. I try to float through the window, but that does not work either. An old woman with a small dog walks past on the sidewalk. I have read about how animals react to projected people, so I float near the dog. At first, the dog is scared, but then it gets excited and happy.

I try to float up to the window again. I shoot up like a balloon, but I keep falling down like a rock, smashing my behind into the ground. It does not hurt, but it is an uncomfortable landing procedure. I practice levitation. I find a working method to keep me afloat: whenever I start falling down, I use the same method I use when I shoot off from the ground, only with less power.

My astral eyes are losing strength and I begin to awaken in my physical body. I am happy about my experience, but also exhausted, so I go back to sleep. When I awake, I am not sure if it was all a dream or an astral projection. I do not think a dream can

imitate the sensation of the exit, so I say it was an astral projection, but the last ten min-
utes were influenced by a dream production. The dream was about my parents' house.

There are many opinions of what dreams are. Those who have no experience in nonphysical realms say dreams are merely pictures spawned by discharging neural cells, created as the brain winds down after a day's thinking or created as the neurons rearrange their connections to each other in order to improve their functioning (i.e., learning). I am certain this is not the case. Dreams are not products of the brain, but rather of the mind, and the mind is not dependent upon the brain.

There are worlds upon worlds, and the physical universe and dream worlds are just some of them. Some worlds are created in an instant and blink out just as fast, while others have existed for billions of years. The thing that makes us question the reality of dream worlds is that they are short-lived and ever-changing compared to the physical world. But our nature matches that of dreams better than that of the physical. In our minds, we create and destroy worlds at the speed of thought. The slow-changing and mundane nature of the physical is so different from our nature that we get bored with it. How often do we not long for some action and adventure? It might be the reality of the physical that we should be questioning, rather than that of dream worlds.

The Hypnopompic State

En route to waking physical reality, we enter the hypnopompic state (from the Greek words *hypnos,* meaning "sleep," and *pompe,* meaning "a sending away"). We are then half awake. The awareness is split between the nonphysical realm and the input from the physical senses. This is, like the hypnagogic state, a very beneficial state for psychic activities. We have just returned from the nonphysical realm and can therefore recall what we did there, although it takes a lot of training to start the recollection process. In most cases, we are groggy and can't think clearly enough to start digging in memories. The good news is that we can linger in that state simply by telling ourselves to do so before we go to sleep. Having a hangover also seems to help.

Sunday, December 23, 2001
The Watch Mystery

I wake up and look at the bedside clock. It says 11:30 A.M. I look at my wristwatch and it says 11. I trust my wristwatch, so I conclude the bedside clock must be fast. Since the time is only 11, I go back to sleep. I wake up later and the bedside clock shows 1 P.M. Then I realize that I could never have checked my wristwatch, because it is not on my wrist nor within reach. And yet, I could not have dreamt the whole thing, because the bedside clock was accurate. It could have been a semi-dream, where the bedside clock was real and the wristwatch was part of the dream. It all seemed very real.

To make the most of the hypnopompic state, avoid using alarm clocks. You do not want to exit the hypnopompic state prematurely by waking up too abruptly.

Thursday, July 27, 2001
Morning Company

As I begin to awake, I suddenly become aware that a woman is lying next to me in bed. This is not a dream. My first reaction is that of familiarity, as if I think, "Ah, it is you." It feels like we have lived together for a very long time, but we have not seen each other for a while. She touches my face and it feels almost like a physical touch. I suck her finger and run my hand down along her belly. It feels very physical and exciting.

I am becoming more awake now and she is fading away because I need to stay in the hypnopompic state in order to sense her. I try hard to focus on her and she is there once more. We hug each other for half an hour or so. I suspect she is visiting me from a nonphysical world. I realize this does not happen very often, because I am physically incarnated and she is not. It is like we are very close friends. Then I become so awake that I lose contact with her. She disappears. I try to place the impression I got from her in order to identify her, but I fail. I can't remember having met this woman in this lifetime.

When the analytical mind is "offline," as it is in the hypnopompic state, the intuitive you is in charge of the experience. This part of you has exceptional power and knowing. Therefore, you may depend on whatever you experience in the hypnopompic state being the truth, however irrational and incomprehensive the experience is deemed by the analytical mind afterwards. It is not the truth as your rational mind would interpret it, but the raw, unspoiled truth understood by your subconscious.

The same can be accomplished with hallucinogenic drugs (though I think the word "hallucinogenic," implying that the drugs create hallucinations, is poorly chosen). Some drugs put the analytical mind at rest, so that we may experience truths that in normal circumstances would be deemed irrational and incomprehensible. Unfortunately, the effects of drugs are unpredictable. In order to use drugs you must know yourself thoroughly; the effects of such drugs depend on your state of mind and what goes on in your subconscious. It is difficult to maintain enough control to make use of the truths presented to you if your subconscious is in turmoil. Additionally, drugs can be detrimental to your body. But, of course, you do not have to take drugs to find truths. Just use the hypnopompic state.

Exercise: Exploring the Hypnopompic State

1. Before you fall asleep tonight, tell yourself to linger in the hypnopompic state before you awake completely in the morning.
2. When you wake up, do not open your eyes and do not move.
3. Do not initiate any thoughts. Just go with the flow of your mind.

Sleep Paralysis

During astral projection, just as during normal sleep, the body is paralyzed. The paralysis is little understood, but it is possible that it is caused by a lack of the hormone DHEA, which is manufactured in the adrenal gland. Researchers have not found a specific purpose for this hormone. It seems to have a more general function in that it promotes vitality and awareness by boosting the nervous system.

Melatonin is the hormone that regulates the sleep cycle. It is made in the pineal gland from serotonin. Melatonin production increases as the body gets worn out during the day. Melatonin inhibits DHEA production. As the DHEA concentration decreases, your nervous system slows down, you become increasingly tired, and your movements turn clumsy. Eventually, you lose control of your body and it falls asleep. During sleep, only enough DHEA is produced to maintain the autonomic nervous system functions.

The melatonin wears off while you sleep, allowing DHEA production to pick up. When the DHEA concentration has reached a sufficient level, your nervous system is active enough to allow you to wake up and take control over your body.

If you wake up before the melatonin has worn off and DHEA production has increased, your nervous system will be inhibited; therefore you will not be able to move your body. You are conscious, but your body is asleep. This is known as Awareness during Sleep Paralysis (Sylvan Muldoon attributed this physical state to a rigidity of the astral body he termed Astral Catalepsy).

Sleep paralysis is completely natural. If it were not for the sleep paralysis, we would all act out our dreams. Some people could then make a lucrative business out of returning sleepwalkers to their homes.

People often get scared when they wake up and find themselves paralyzed. This is understandable, since our bodies are defenseless in that state. If this happens to you, remember that it is only temporary. Then relax your mind and execute an exit technique, like *rolling out* (explained later). The sleep paralysis state is excellent for astral projection.

Tingling

Tingling is the physical body's way to call back the awareness. When you are going out into the astral, on many occasions you will also feel a tingling in your awareness. I suspect that the tingling kicks in because the body does not want the awareness to leave. The body tries to get your attention. But, since we are bold adventurers, we will not let that prevent us from projecting away from the physical plane and the body that helps us there.

When you project and there is no tingling, you can be sure that the body is fast asleep and does not need the awareness at the moment. This makes the projection more stable. On the other hand, if you feel tingling, you will know that the projection is unstable. You should then do some techniques to prolong the projection. These are discussed in the next Circle.

The tingling is very strong in the hypnopompic state because the body is waking up and is calling back the awareness. When the awareness answers the call by returning to the body, you wake up. It is interesting to speculate about what would happen if the awareness chose not to return to the body. Would a large enough part of the consciousness animate the body so that it may, unaware, perhaps by automatism, go about its day, or would the body just sleep until the awareness returns?

The hypnopompic tingling goes unnoticed if you follow the default sleep process (i.e., you are asleep and perhaps dreaming), but the tingling is noticeable if you are conscious, as you are during astral projection or lucid dreaming, at the time the body goes into the hypnopompic state.

Friday, August 16, 2002
Longest Lucid Dream

Naptime. I dream I am performing with a band in a tall wooden shack. I am hitting my head and bumping into things all the time. I am angry because I don't want to be there and when I try to do anything, I get hurt. Suddenly, I give up and throw myself on the floor. We get word that a forest fire is approaching, so the band starts packing. There is a forest fire near Vancouver, where I am in waking physical reality, so my dream must be affected by my thoughts about that. A friendly fellow notices me lying there, defeated, and drags me to the car. He and his companions drive me to a place safe from the fire. Then I realize that the guitars I have borrowed for the gig are still in the shack, too close to the fire. I feel responsible for them, so I set out to rescue them.

I start walking toward that place. There is an air show, just like there is one in waking life in Portland. The sky is dark and the planes, hundreds of them, are making maneuvers with lights so that they look like a huge flower. They can do amazing things with those planes. There are lots of people in the streets. There are so many people that I can't get anywhere. Everywhere I turn, I bump into people. I throw myself to the ground and give up again.

A little girl comes up and tells me I can't lie there. I get up and walk across a parking lot. I hear a voice in the loudspeaker system say, "If you are here and not in one of our cars, you must be watching the air show," or something similar. It made sense at the time. Then I hear the roar of a car from a tent. Probably a recording, but it frightens me. A dark blue car without a driver runs into the tent. It is on automatic pilot. "Good idea," I think, "but very dangerous. And noisy."

Somehow, I get into a small house. J (a former girlfriend) is there and we talk. I think, "I like it when J comes over. It doesn't happen very often, since we live so far apart." Then a man moves in and starts cuddling with J. I think it is good that she has found a new love, but I don't like him. At a glance, my intuition tells me he is narrow-minded and therefore, in some sense, dangerous. Then I see flames outside the window! A man who is supposedly a fireman is throwing teacups of water at the fire in a futile act to prevent its spreading. I tell J we have to get out of here because there is a fire outside. She does not move. I don't think she believes me. I start collecting my things.

Then it hits me. How can J be here? She was half a world away yesterday and now she is suddenly here. I know I am dreaming. I know what is going to happen next. I will announce that I am dreaming and then I will get a tingling sensation in my belly and become lucid. I walk over to J and say, "This is a dream." She shakes her head. She does not understand. I tell her over and over. What is worse, there is no tingling sensation. I am in complete control of my environment, but I don't have any of the bubbling feelings I usually have during lucid dreams and astral projections. I think this is odd. Maybe I am awake after all?

In retrospect, it is a good sign that the sensations are missing. I think the physical body causes the bubbling feelings. That is its mechanism to stop the awareness from leaving the body for too long a period. Tingling is the physical body's way to call back the awareness. It does the tingling when it is waking up. In this view, it is good that the tingling is absent. It means I am far from waking up. That, in turn, means the projection is stable.

"This is a dream." Does my physical mouth speak these words? I don't know, but I better be careful. I don't want Barb to think I am having a bad dream, because then she might try to save me by waking me up. I walk around and enjoy the freedom. I make myself float and then I make J float. I want to turn this into an astral projection but I don't know exactly how to do that. I try something that I can't remember. It has no effect. Then I try something new. I say, "Show me the most important aspect about Barb." A window appears in the air in front of me. Barb, in a white sports car, speeds by from right to left. She is wearing a white knit sweater, a scarf, and sunglasses. Interesting. I wonder what all the white colors mean and what the sports car means.

I say, "Show me the most important aspect of J." I can't remember what happens *next. I think I get sidetracked. I have plenty of time, so I do lots of things, but for some reason I am unable to remember any of them. Forty minutes pass. Then the tingling sets in. I am awakening. One second I am walking around in my own lucid dream and the next I am staring at the ceiling from the bed. The shift is instant. I try to get back into the lucidity, but fail.*

Affirmations

Positive Reinforcement

There are basically two kinds of beliefs: those that tell you what you *can* do, and those that tell you what you *can't* do. The first kind of belief can be programmed with positive reinforcement, also known as affirmation. This is the process in which you (or someone else) tell yourself that you can do things you used to view as difficult. The result is an increase in confidence and motivation. The second kind of belief can be programmed with negative reinforcement, also known as nagging. This is where you (or someone else, often your parents) tell (or hint to) yourself that you are incapable of succeeding.

Every time you think a thought like, "I don't think I can," you send a message to the belief system. The belief system does not have the ability to criticize, so it accepts the thought as a truth without question. It depends upon you to be critical. If you reinforce a thought by thinking it repeatedly, the belief system eventually turns that thought into an established belief. The set of all beliefs in your belief system shapes your view of how the world works. If you constantly doubt your abilities, your view of the world will be shaped accordingly, making you believe that the world is difficult to deal with.

116

Affirmations are messages sent to your belief system. They are positive thoughts that affect you in a positive way. It is a good way for you to accept the possibility that astral projection is possible. By telling yourself repeatedly that you can astral project, eventually you will believe that you can; then you will prove yourself right, because it is in our interest to prove to ourselves (and sometimes to others) that our beliefs are correct.

You may wonder if it is a good idea to establish a belief that astral projection is possible when you have no evidence to back it up. Do not worry about that. It actually works the other way, too: The evidence first appears after you believe in it. You change your environment by changing your beliefs. Your reality is a result of your beliefs. Everything is doable in this world. If you can envision something, then you can do it. Only limiting beliefs can prevent you from doing something. Besides, if you want to land on the moon, you have to shoot for the stars. Use extreme affirmations. Tell yourself you are able to do things you never thought possible. The higher you aim, the higher you will land.

Exercise: Affirmations

Affirmations can keep you motivated. The simple affirmation, "Astral projection is fun," will keep you practicing even when other obligations compete for your time.

1. Record the following affirmations on tape or on a computer:

"You are unlimited."

"You can do anything you put your mind to."

"You deserve an infinite number of astral experiences."

"You observe everything that happens in your mind during sleep."

"Tonight you will astral project."

"You are connected to everything."

"Everything is connected to you."

"The mind veil is removed."

"The time to doubt yourself has passed."

"The universe takes good care of you, whether you are with or without your physical body."

"Face the direction of the universe and follow its flow. Trust that the universe is going in the right direction."

2. Add a few affirmations of your own design. Make sure they are in the second person: use "you" instead of "I," since you will be listening to them, not speaking them. For some reason, perhaps low self-esteem, subconsciously we find it easier to believe what others tell us than what we ourselves say.

3. Actively listen to the recording until you know the words by heart. After that, play the recording, in your computer headphones or Walkman, in the background while you go about your business. Do not listen to it actively. Your subconscious knows what the message contains.

Visualization

The Art of Visualization

Exercise: Imagination

1. Close your eyes. Take a few deep breaths. Relax your mind.
2. Think of the word *horse*.
3. The word will trigger whatever memories you associate with it, probably a horse you have met.
4. The vision of a horse from a memory will be displayed onto your mind's screen. You do not see it with your physical eyes.
5. Reach out and touch the horse with imaginary hands.
6. Feel the texture of the fur. It feels remarkably real, doesn't it?
7. Lean forward and smell the horse with your imaginary nose. The horse needs a bath, doesn't it?

That is how simple visualization is. You pretend to walk around just like you do in the physical—seeing, touching, smelling, and hearing things from a first-person perspective. You turn your awareness away from physical waking reality and into your imagination. The longer you visualize something in your mind, the farther you will detach from physical reality. Also, the more often you practice visualization, the easier it will be to detach from physical reality and engage in the imaginary world that you are creating.

Would it surprise you if I told you that you have just taken a trip through the astral? You have just used your astral senses. What you have seen, touched, and smelled actually exists in the astral. You created it. By turning into your imagination, you projected your awareness to the astral dimension and created a horse. Visualization is the easiest way to enter the astral. Easy and yet very powerful. When you combine visualization with an altered state of mind—for example, a natural sleep state—you are able to fully project your awareness into the astral. No longer will it be as if you are imagining things in your mind's eye, but you will actually be there, among the objects you create. This is an awesome power and you will have a taste of it later in this Circle.

Visualization can have any depth you give it. You may play with objects in your mind's eye, or you may be among them. You can easily control this level of visualization by adjusting its intensity. The intensity is a measurement of how dominant the impression of your visualization becomes, compared to the impression of your physical senses. You can easily increase the intensity by tapping into your imagination and creativity. To allow your creativity free rein, I deliberately provide a minimal amount of detail in the visualization exercises. Exact instruction from me would only limit your creativity and, consequently, hamper your visualization's intensity.

Contrary to its name, visualization can be applied to senses other than vision. For most people, tactile (touch) visualization is best for engrossing the mind. For these people, a good way to increase the intensity of a visualization is to focus on imaginary touch more than any other imaginary sense. Since this varies by individual, I encourage you to find out which sense is most engrossing to your mind.

Exercise: Blind Visualization

1. Close your eyes. Relax your mind.
2. Visualize yourself walking around in your room.
3. Close your imaginary eyes. Your vision goes black.
4. Focus only on your imaginary hands. Touch the wall. Feel the texture. Really feel it. Touch the carpet. Touch your furniture.
5. Now focus on your imaginary nose. Smell the air. Take your time. Smell the scent of any paint or furniture oil.
6. Now focus on your imaginary ears. What sounds can you hear?
7. Open your imaginary eyes.
8. Touch the wall again.

In the exercise above, did the fact that you closed your imaginary eyes intensify your other senses? Which of your imaginary senses had the most powerful capacity to engross your mind?

Tuesday, February 12, 2002
Shaking the Soul

I fall asleep with my clothes on at 2 A.M. I wake up two hours later and decide to read some astral projection accounts in order to increase my chances for paranormal experiences when I go back to sleep. I stumble upon Robert Peterson's first book, Out-of-Body Experiences: How to Have Them and What to Expect,[11] *and do his exercise 22:*

> **Buzzing**—This exercise is similar to the musical imagination exercise. Relax completely, then try to get to that passive, quiescent frame of mind. As vividly as you can, imagine there is a coarse buzzing sound in your head. Pretend the buzzing is just a little bit too quiet to hear, but getting louder. Simultaneously listen intently for the buzzing to become loud enough to hear. As the buzzing becomes louder, imagine the sound is causing your soul to vibrate. Increase the volume of the imaginary sound until you feel like your soul is being rattled and shaken to the core. Maintain the imaginary buzzing and vibrating for several minutes. Repeat the procedure several times if necessary.

I fall asleep again with the feeling of being close to my soul. I am soon awakened by the disturbing sounds from chainsaws and tractors as the park maintenance people cut down trees outside my window. The noise keeps me from falling asleep. I remain in the state between awake and asleep for six hours. During that time, I am very close to my soul, which makes me happy. I have little control over what is happening, though. I get a lot of communication from my guides. Suddenly, four of them shout at me: "Shake!" This jolts me into an awake state. Simultaneously, the whole house trembles as a tree crashes to the ground outside.

Why Visualization Works

What we experience as the physical reality is not outside of us. The reality is within us, because the reality is our interpretation of the input from our physical senses (hearing, sight, touch, smell, and taste). You might say that reality is an image in your mind, representing the world outside, a world that we can only probe slightly due to the limitations of our physical senses. We can't grasp what the world outside is like because we can only sense bits and pieces of it. This makes you wonder what the world outside is, doesn't it? If the image is the reality we experience, then what is this field of energy that our senses read? Perhaps it does not even exist and the image is all there is. Or perhaps the world outside is of our own creation.

The subconscious fills in the blanks in the mind image when information is lacking. For example, I can see in front of me, but not behind me, so the subconscious creates the image this way: 1. The front part of the image of my surroundings is constructed from physical sensory input, mainly from my eyes. 2. The back part of the image is created from memories and experience. This part of the image is merely a best guess at how the surroundings behind me look.

This image becomes my perception of the external reality, if there is such a thing. Since the image always contains an element of our best guess, we can never be certain that our perception of the world is accurate.

Visualization is a way to replace our image of the world with another image of our own design. In visualization, we use our imagination to affect or replace our current image of our surroundings. The more intensely we visualize, the less dominant the input from physical senses becomes. Sometimes when you visualize, you will find that you forget the physical world, as if it never existed, and the visualization becomes your entire reality. Then you will have projected your mind away from the physical reality and into a new reality of your own creation. This is not difficult to accomplish and it is a lot of fun. The more you visualize, the more intense the visualized reality becomes.

Your subconscious is incapable of distinguishing whether sensory input is coming from a physical sense or from your imagination, therefore, it never pays any attention to where the physical body is. It only cares about where your awareness is. If you are visualizing walking through the corridors in the pyramids of Egypt, your subconscious will assume that you really are. It cannot distinguish between imagination and reality. Only the rational you can know the difference between the two. In fact, only the rational mind feels the difference is important.

Exercise: Elements Visualization

1. Close your eyes. Relax your mind. Take a few deep breaths.
2. Focus on the center of your chest.
3. Visualize yourself in your room.
4. Imagine stepping outside to find a tree.
5. Touch the bark of the tree with your imaginary hands. Examine the texture for a long time. Remember the sensation.
6. Pick up a handful of dirt and feel its texture.
7. Visualize the wind getting stronger.
8. Raise your hands in the air. Feel the wind rush through them. Remember the sensation.
9. Light an imaginary match and feel the fire.
10. Find a pool of water.
11. Touch the water with your imaginary hands. Sense the texture. Remember the sensation.

In order to properly navigate your physical body, the subconscious needs to make sense of its environment. It needs to have a coherent image of the surroundings. If such a coherent image is lacking in your visualization, your subconscious will force a completion of the image. It will force objects (that you are not deliberately visualizing) to pop up in your field of view. This is a very cool experience. Suddenly, you bump into objects you did not expect to find in your visualization. It is like walking through a new world. Actually, it *is* walking through a new world.

The world really exists in the astral, because you make it exist. The subconscious will most likely create an environment that resembles a physical environment because that is where it has the most experience, but it can also get inspiration from energies that are not of physical origin.

As your conscious mind becomes increasingly engrossed in visualization, the projection mechanism is set up in the background. Projection is a natural process that kicks in each night, but only if your conscious mind does not interfere. The conscious mind wants to be conscious of all processes. In other words, it wants control over everything. It is a bit of a control freak. The only problem is that it does not know how to manage some processes, such as intuition and astral projection.

If you have experienced intuition, you may have noticed that it is at its sharpest when you are absentminded. Without even trying to have them, intuitive thoughts pop into your conscious mind; and when you start trying to have them, they stop coming. This is because the conscious mind interferes with the intuitive process. The same is true for astral projection. To avoid this problem, we will use visualization as a decoy for the conscious mind. When the conscious mind is busy walking around in our visualized environment, the subconscious mind is free to arrange the projection.

Visualization and the Center of Thought

You can intensify your visualization by moving your center of thought. As explained in the chapter on awareness, the head provides energy that boosts the analytical part of your mind. The head has many subareas from which we can get different types of proanalytical energy.

The area between the eyes and the space in the air in front of that area (also known as the mind screen or the third-eye area) provide energy for accessing memory. These areas are particularly beneficial for visualization because they provide access to memories from which we can borrow descriptions for the objects we are visualizing. When focusing in these areas, the visualized objects generally appear more like physical objects.

Exercise: Memory Visualization

1. Close your eyes. Relax your mind.
2. Spend a minute in blackness. Imagine you are in a black void out in space somewhere.
3. Turn your eyes slightly upward. Move your attention to the space between your eyes, where the brow begins.
4. Visualize a horse, as you did in a previous exercise.
5. Are the sight, touch, and smell of the horse more detailed?

   By focusing on the third-eye area, memories become more easily accessible. With more memories from which to get visualization information, the horse should be more detailed.

Focusing on the mind screen is also a good method for storing things in your memory. When we focus on the mind screen, the visualization may be playing out too slowly. It may even turn dull, and since dullness is something we want to avoid—there is no point in visualizing unless the visualization is fun—we will have to focus on an area that provides more creativity and entertainment. I like the center of the chest because it holds plenty of creative energy. When we focus on the chest, we do not feel a need for the visualized objects to have detail or to resemble physical objects. Just like an abstract painter, we care more about the feeling and meaning of the painting than its semblance to real objects.

Exercise: Creative Visualization

1. Close your eyes. Relax your mind.
2. Spend a minute in blackness. Imagine you are in a black void out in space somewhere.
3. Move your center of thought down to the center of your chest.
4. Visualize a horse, as you did in the previous exercise.
5. Do the sight, touch, and smell of the horse contain details that surprise you, things you did not intentionally put there?

By focusing on the center of your chest, you are stimulating your creativity. The creativity fills out the mind image of the horse on its own.

Exercise: Personalized Areas of Focus

Repeat the exercise above, but concentrate on other places inside or outside your body that benefit your visualization. Each person has a different nonphysical energy configuration, so it is up to you to find what body parts benefit your visualization.

Whatever particular astral projection technique we use, it does not require that the visualization be precise. The visualization does not even have to resemble any other environment. The important thing is that it have an intensity that keeps the conscious mind riveted. Anything goes, as long as it is captivating and fun. Each person, of course, has particular tastes so I can't recommend one environment to visualize over another. One person may find pleasure in visualizing abstract concepts, while another may find it more enjoyable to visualize physical-like objects.

Practice, Practice, Practice!

Each time you practice, your visualization skill improves. You will also find it easier to detach from the input of your physical senses and to tune into your astral senses. Each time you practice, your visualized objects will look clearer, have greater detail, feel more intense to the touch, and smell better.

Use fun visualizations to stay motivated. I like pretending that I am invisible. Then I visualize sneaking into the neighbor's house or the girls' locker room. You have to keep the astral projection sessions fun. The ego, which wants to keep your awareness focused in the material realm, will try to prevent you from astral projecting by making you feel it is boring and a lot of work (which it is not, of course). So keep it fun.

Exercise: Practice Visualization

Each evening in bed, before you fall asleep, close your eyes and visualize yourself in one of the places that occupy your mind the most during your day. These are the places that are important to you. By connecting to them, you can use the energy you have bound to them for your visualization purposes. In my case, the places that occupy my mind the most are my childhood home and the school I used to go to 15 years ago. I do not know why. Perhaps it was those places that shaped my view of the world. Or perhaps I feel I have something unfinished there. Don't worry if you can't stay awake. If you fall asleep in the middle of visualization, the visualization will affect your sleep, giving you extraordinary dreams, sometimes even lucid dreams. Do this exercise every night for a week.

Visualizations Beneficial for Astral Projection

You can use any visualization to have an astral projection or a lucid dream. You can, as described earlier, visualize walking around in your bedroom, touching the carpet and furniture. However, some types of visualization are more beneficial for astral projection than others. I have sorted these into three types. Visualization type A moves you emotionally. Type B moves your location. Type C puts you in situations that you are not used to in every day life. Read the journal entry and then try out the different types of visualizations in the exercises below. See how they affect your dreams.

Friday, May 31, 2002
Native American

As I fall asleep, I visualize myself as a Native American sitting in a small green meadow. Suddenly the visualization turns intense. I feel like I am there. I have long black hair. I am hunting. My bow is ready, should any deer cross the meadow. In the distance, I can see a large dark mountain. I sweep my hand over the tall grass. I think, "Life is good." My entire being is content. I get the feeling that some of the images are memories from a past life as a Native American.

Visualizations in which you engage emotions are beneficial for astral projection because the emotions they invoke make them more intriguing and this will keep your awareness focused in the visualization, even after falling asleep.

Exercise: Happy Place Visualization

1. Go to bed.
2. Close your eyes.
3. Visualize being in a place that makes you totally content and happy. Perhaps it is a sunny meadow, perhaps it is with a special person. Only you know what makes you happy. The important thing is that you invoke happy, bubbly emotions.
4. Explore your surroundings. Remember to focus extra on imaginary touch.
5. Continue to visualize this as you fall asleep.

Visualizations that involve movement of yourself or of your surroundings are beneficial for astral projection because they put your mind in motion. The motion will conflict with the motion initiated by your dreams. The conflict may throw you into a gap (of motion) between your visualized world and the dream world. You can use this gap as a gateway to the astral.

Wednesday, January 23, 2002
Motion and Astral Projection

As I fall asleep, I use a visualization technique someone suggested on an online astral projection discussion forum. I visualize falling down a bottomless hole in the ground.

A while later I am dreaming that I am in a large unfamiliar city, in a subway station. I have lost sight of my friends and am bored, so I decide to go home. I have no idea which station I should go to. I get on the first escalator going up. I read a sign on the way up. I am not sure where I am supposed to go, but I am sure this escalator is going in the wrong direction.

I struggle to get off the escalator. I notice a constant motion going on in the background, initiated by falling through that endless hole in my visualization. The escalator represents another motion. I feel the two motions are in conflict. This struggle makes me unsynchronized with the movement of the escalator. The dream loses its synchronization and breaks up into shards and falls away into a void.

I fall into a dark space and keep falling. My vision is not working. I recognize the feeling: I am astral projecting! I am very glad because it has been a long time since I last astral projected. I am falling downward. I analyze too much, which breaks my state of mind, and I lose the astral projection state. I think I am awake, but it is probably a conscious sleep state. I relax my mind and get back into the astral projection state.

I am still falling through a dark space. It is fun! I am very happy. I expect the material of the worlds I am passing through to hit my body as I go through them. Suddenly it does, as if I have ordered it (which I have by expecting it). It feels like gusts of wind, but intuitively I know these are entire astral worlds. It feels like I am falling from a great height, at a great speed, and the wind is pressing against my body and face. This must be what parachuting is like. It is extremely joyous. I know I will never hit the ground, because there is none—none that can hurt my astral body, anyway. I try out some postures I have seen skydivers do. This is more fun than I have had in years.

I wake up, or so I think. I make some quick notes, so I will not forget what happened. When I wake up in the morning, I can't find the notes. Apparently, I had not been in waking physical reality when I made them.

Tropical Native Dream

Some time later, I am dreaming, with a bit of that magical astral projection or lucid state of mind. I am a young native on a small tropical island. I am sitting on a beautiful sandy beach. There are sparkles in the ocean waves. The dream is extremely detailed *and colorful. I lean down and drink from a small stream. This is perfect. Life is simple and I am perfectly happy.*

I walk toward the jungle. I look down and see a beautiful red ant. A ray of sun glitters on its back. Then I hear, or feel rather, the jungle getting worried. I turn around and see three large sailing ships approaching the island. One of the ships is close enough to land any second. I look at flags. They are black. Pirates! I have to warn the village. I run as fast as I can, but somehow I know it is too late. The way I identify with the young native makes me think this is a memory from a past life.

Do one of the following two exercises. Do the one that you feel is easiest. If you like trees, do the first one. If you like relaxing on the porch, do the second.

Exercise: Swaying Trees Visualization

1. Go to bed.
2. Close your eyes.
3. Visualize standing in a small meadow in a forest.
4. Feel the clear energy from the trees around you. The presence of trees opens you to receive energy from nature.
5. Visualize the trees swaying in the wind.
6. Sway with them, as if you were one of the trees.
7. Continue as you fall asleep.

Exercise: Angie's Hammock Visualization

1. Go to bed.
2. Close your eyes.
3. Visualize lying in a hammock on a porch.
4. Swing the hammock back and forth, as you fall asleep.
5. Continue visualizing this as you fall asleep.

Visualizations of falling or flying are good for astral projection because the mind is not used to doing those things, at least not in a waking physical state. The mind's expectations and your world initiated by visualization will be unsynchronized. This will again create a gap between the visualized world and the dream world.

Exercise: Endless Hole Visualization

1. Go to bed.
2. Close your eyes.
3. Just before you fall asleep, visualize standing next to a wide hole in the ground. You look down the hole and can't see the bottom, because there is none. It is an endless hole.
4. Throw yourself into the hole.
5. Feel yourself falling. Feel the sucking sensation in your belly. If the sensation is not there, create it.
6. Continue visualizing this as you fall asleep.

The next visualization takes advantage of the fact that we are conditioned to see ourselves from a first-person perspective relative to our bodies. The idea of being outside of our bodies is far from mundane, which is why it works well for astral projection.

Exercise: Barb's Zoom-Out Visualization

1. Go to bed.
2. Close your eyes.
3. Visualize looking at yourself from the ceiling.
4. Then, at your own speed, zoom out until your body is just a tiny speck.
5. Zoom back in until you are facing your body.
6. Then zoom out again.
7. Continue zooming in and out, as you fall asleep.

Visualization and Sleep States

As you may have noticed in these exercises, when you fall asleep during visualization your sleep is highly affected by it. Sometimes you end up in a weird state of mind. They are not really weird, because they are part of the natural sleep process, but they seem weird because we rarely consciously experience them. Visualization helps us become conscious in such sleep states so that we may use these experiences in different ways from how the subconscious can. One of the uses of such a sleep state is the astral projection experience.

To induce an astral projection experience, we will apply a technique I describe only briefly here, but I will delve into fully later in this Circle. First, you have to visualize in the hypnagogic state and fall asleep during the visualization. The visualization keeps the conscious mind somewhat alert, even after the physical body falls asleep. You can train yourself to remain conscious in visualization, long after you normally would become unconscious in deep sleep. Sometimes, I visualize for hours after my physical body has fallen asleep. However, this is not necessary for the astral projection technique we will use. We will let the subconscious (rather than the conscious) mind guide us into the astral realm. This approach requires less effort on the part of our conscious mind.

If you fall asleep while visualizing, the visualization will continue without your conscious interaction. The visualization heightens the dreaming you, causing an intensified dream. (By the word *intense*, I mean a heightened alertness of the mind. I am not referring to the contents of the dream.) You may be aware of this influence or you may not notice it at all. It does not matter (see figure 3).

If you wake up and then visualize again as you fall back to sleep,

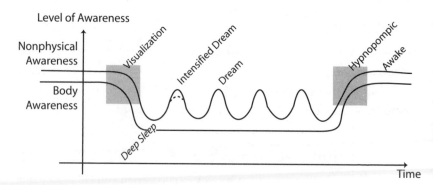

Figure 3. Hypnagogic visualization leads to intensified dreams.

the subconscious will take the visualization to be another dream. Thinking that you are sleeping, it will release the awareness from the body, just like it does when you fall asleep naturally. To avoid lapsing into unconsciousness, you may have to induce a preemptive release of awareness by applying an exit technique (such as the roll-out, discussed later) (see figure 4).

Alternatively, if you feel your body and mind are not unsynchronized enough to roll out, you may allow yourself to fall asleep during yet another visualization. You may repeat this visualization-sleep cycle any number of times until you wake up in an unsynchronized state fit for rolling out of your body. This is the core of our astral projection technique and will be explained in a later chapter.

As a side note, an intensified dream following visualization may be so heightened that you can muster enough awareness to turn it lucid, meaning your conscious mind will be alert and coherent enough to take control over the dream. This is a nice experience, although it is not our objective in this book. You may also spawn an astral projection from within the lucid dream.

How does all this happen during a night of sleep? Well, it is not so strange. It seems we have all been conditioned to stay unconscious when we sleep. Visualization tricks the part of ourselves that manages the sleep process, which, in turn, somehow circumvents the slip into unconsciousness, so that we can access more of our nonphysical functions.

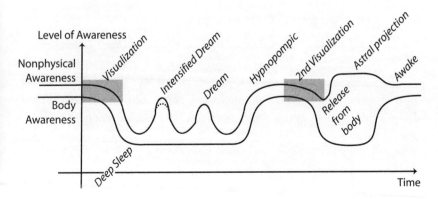

Figure 4. Repeated hypnagogic visualization leads to astral projection.

Since it is so easy to trick the sleep process with visualization, it is a wonder everyone does not consciously astral project all the time.

Exercise: Repeated Hypnagogic Visualization

1. Set your alarm clock to awaken you in the middle of the night.
2. Go to bed.
3. Close your eyes.
4. As you fall asleep, visualize whatever you like (something fun) with you as a first-person participant.
5. Fall asleep in the middle of the visualization.
6. When the alarm clock goes off, turn it off.
7. Get out of bed. Go to the bathroom. Avoid engaging in too many thoughts. Maintain your dazed state of mind. Avoid looking at yourself in the mirror as this will invoke your analytical mind and will wake you up.
8. Go back to bed.
9. Close your eyes.
10. As you fall back to sleep, visualize the same thing you visualized in step 4.
11. The next time you wake up, observe your state of mind, but do not analyze it. Remember how that state feels.
12. Repeat this exercise each night, but skip the alarm clock after the first time. If you wake up naturally during the night, do the visualization as you fall back to sleep. Otherwise, you can visualize and sleep a little extra in the morning after you awake.

Any time you wake up in a heightened state, you might find your mind buzzing or vibrating (although such sensations are not necessary). Do not be alarmed. You will not damage your brain or come to any other harm.

Attitude

There are a few attitudes that we can use to improve our chances for astral projection. As an analogy, in order to be as fast as he can, a sprinter may think of himself as a gazelle. The body of the sprinter does not look like a gazelle, but his mind does. In the same manner, we can play little tricks on our own minds, such as pretending to be a quiet observer.

Observer

The mind has little to do with the brain. There is no direct mapping between brain functions and mind functions. The mind is a nonphysical concept and the brain is a physical organ. The mind can exist without the brain and the brain can exist without the mind. There is no dependency between them other than the exchange of emotions, sensory input, and muscle manipulation information.

Understanding how your mind (not your brain) works is the key to whatever you want to do, including astral projection. And in order to understand anything, you have to first observe it. Therefore, always observe your mind, especially your subconscious, from an *external* point of view. By consciously taking the role of an external observer, you gain a sort of remote control of your mind processes. Distancing yourself in this manner provides some clarity of thought, which allows you to clearly observe your thoughts.

Exercise: Observing Yourself

1. Move your awareness (or attention) outside your physical body, slightly up to the right of your forehead.
2. Observe each thought that runs through your mind. Understand what caused it.
3. Observe what other thoughts the initial thoughts lead to.
4. Observe what emotions are invoked and what thoughts invoked them.
5. Go about your day with the same observant state of mind.

Motivation

The second you set out on the quest of leaving your physical body, your will splits in two. On one hand, you want to break free of physical limits and explore other worlds. On the other, you want to pay attention to material things, so that your physical body may prosper in your physical existence. The two are not easily reconciled and one always suffers at the expense of the other.

The conflicting interests (astral projection versus material survival) often result in mind fatigue in which you lose motivation to do one of the two. This is your mind's way of forcing you to choose one over the other in order to avoid a mental collapse. Most likely, the material side of you will be victorious. This is good, because it allows you to focus on money and physical health and other necessities of life. Your interest in astral projection will be put on ice for a while, but do not fret—it will be awakened again in the future. A passion always comes back to inspire you.

One thing you can do to bridge the gap between astral projection and material interests is to maintain a high motivation in both areas. In order to do anything, you must have the will to do it and you must nurture that will so that it will last until you have completed what you intended to do. Astral projection requires a particularly strong will, not because it is difficult, but because there are often limiting beliefs doing their best to quell the will.

Let's face it: Everything we have been taught about reality so far is obsolete, but our stubborn ego refuses to acknowledge that. The last thing the ego wants is to have its beliefs proved incorrect because it knows this would mean that all the time and effort spent on building the beliefs concerning the nature of reality are wasted, and all the wealth the ego has accumulated might become worthless.

Astral projection will disprove our obsolete beliefs about reality in seconds. The ego, therefore, tries to prevent us from astral projecting by manipulating our memories in order to spawn emotions that will weaken our will. It sounds like something Darth Vader might have thought up, but it is a natural process.

You have to maintain your will in order to keep it strong. Keep motivation high by focusing on the fun and adventurous sides of astral projection, rather than on the effort and time it requires.

As previously stated, you need will in order to do anything. Trying to accomplish something without having the will to do it can be harmful and may burn you out. Do not continue practicing your astral projection skills if you do not have the will. Instead, focus on building up your will for a couple of days. Astral projection really is fun, but do not practice it at the expense of your health.

Exercise: Motivational Reading

Look in books and Internet forums for accounts of astral projection. Read one of the accounts every day. This will keep your motivation for astral projection high.

Exercise: Motivational Affirmations

1. Record these lines on a tape recorder or a computer:
   "Astral projection is fun."
   "Visualization is fun."
   "Life is an adventure."

> "You are an explorer."
>
> "Jumping from one reality to another is fun."
>
> 2. Listen to the recording whenever you feel that astral projection is uninteresting.

Flow

If you have not achieved full control of your psychic abilities yet, your conscious mind will get in the way whenever you attempt to use them. If instead you concentrate on something different, such as daydreaming, your analytical mind will not get in the way as your psychic senses move into their natural state through which psychic energy flows unhindered. For example, sometimes I sit at my desk for hours, trying to solve a problem. When I go to the bathroom, my mind relaxes and the complete solution pops into my head, seemingly on its own volition. This happens to me all the time.

To take advantage of this phenomenon, first tell yourself what you want to do. For example, if you want the answer to a question, state the question clearly in your mind. Then occupy your mind with something unrelated. The answer will come when the flow is established.

Anything is easier if you find the flow. The *flow* is a state of balance that athletes always look for before a contest. It makes their bodies seem like they move on air. It gives you luck, joy, and intuitive information. In order to find the flow, you have to stop trying to do whatever it is you want to do and instead just allow it to happen to you. Also, you can't take your efforts too seriously. Taking things seriously puts pressure on your mind, which blocks the flow.

Exercise: Flow Affirmations

1. Add these lines to your affirmation tape or computer sound file:

   "You astral project because it is fun."

   "You do not really care whether you successfully astral project or not. The sheer fun of exploring it makes it worthwhile."

   "Astral projection is as natural as dreaming."

2. Listen to the recording every day.

While brightening up the atmosphere, you have to stay motivated. This requires a delicate balance: An increase in motivation should not spawn an increase in seriousness. Remember to have fun and you will accelerate your learning.

As an analogy, the secret of becoming a good communicator is to focus on *what* you want to say and *to whom* you want to say it, not on *how* you say it. Do not attempt to control your mouth as you speak—your subconscious already does this for you. Just think of the message you want to communicate and the mouth will do the rest. Astral projection works the same way. Do not think of how to astral project, just keep the will to astral project alive in your mind. Sit back and let the hidden side of you take you where you want to go.

Knowing

The greater part of creation can't be grasped with our analytical mind. In fact, analytical thinking is not natural to the nonphysical spirits that we are. It is a product of years of training in schools and academies. During our attempts to find out what this thing around us called existence is, we have been blinded by the belief that logic is the only trustworthy tool by which to understand it. Religions have gone astray and millions of people have been misled because some people, although with good intentions, have attempted to explain an uncomplicated truth with their heads rather than with their hearts. Repeatedly, we fail to understand who we are and what human consciousness is because we insist on thinking with our heads.

So how are we supposed to understand anything without thinking? It is not necessary to understand. Things do not have to make sense. Many realities outside the physical do not apply to thinking. Things just *are* and when we attempt to understand why they just are, we change them from just *being* into something that we created by thinking, something that they are not. This concept appears complicated, but only because we try to grasp it by thinking. In this light, René Descartes' philosophical axiom, "I think, therefore I am," seems misguided. It is quite possible to exist without thinking. It is actually easier to tell whether you exist when you are not thinking.

A Native American medicine woman once told me: "You are a very analytical person. You think up here (pointing to my head). But you have to remember that this (pointing to my chest) is where we all *live.*" Is it possible that logic has nothing to do with who we are, where we *live?* Could it be that logic is an artificial instrument and, therefore, is poorly equipped to investigate certain sets of problems? I think so. What we must do, in order to find answers to what we are and what existence is, is to sense with our hearts. Not the muscle, but the universal energy gateway that lives in it. Some people think with their heads. Some even think with their fists. But all people live in the center of the chest.

Our strongest tool for understanding is feeling, but only when feeling is not littered by thoughts. Feeling and emotion are not the same thing. Emotions often cloud feelings. For example, anger will surely prevent you from feeling a spirit presence around you. In order to use this feeling, you have to be well acquainted with your female energies, your *yin.*

Saturday, January 26, 2002
Firing Rationality

What I feel and what I think have been conflicting lately, leaving me confused and frustrated. I hereby decide not to use the rational part of me that analyzes and categorizes everything. From now on, I will let only my feelings guide me.

The worst thing you can do in the astral is to attempt to analyze what is happening. The astral changes at your command; if you invoke analytical thoughts, your astral reality will mirror them, undoubtedly preventing you from sensing what you came there to explore.

When I first astral projected, I knew I should not attempt to analyze the experience. But I did, even though I did my best not to. It is a habit analytical minds have. We choose to understand rather than to experience. If we want to stop analyzing in the astral, we have to quit the habit (or maybe I should use the word *addiction?*) of analyzing everything that happens to us, both in the physical and in the astral.

Consciously analyzing the astral projection experience often leads to false conclusions because our analytical minds can't grasp the whole experience. Plus, reason has a tendency to explain new experiences by drawing parallels to old experiences. Since astral projection is a totally new experience to most of us and so unlike anything previously experienced, comparing it to what we already know only limits it and thereby limits us.

There is a better way to understand the astral. What you experience in the astral, or anywhere for that matter, is sucked up by your subconscious. It is much more capable of handling things like the astral than your rational, analytical mind. Your subconscious does not forget. It will go over the experience until there is nothing more to go over. Slowly and invisibly, the knowledge will crawl up from the subconscious into your conscious mind.

Exercise: Turning to Feeling

1. Close your eyes. Relax your mind.
2. Move your center of thought to just below the center of your chest. This is a good place to sense intuition.
3. Put your palms together in front of your chest with your fingers up.
4. Look for a bubbling sensation in your chest.
5. Note that because you focus on the chest, thoughts seem less eager to pop into your mind. Your analytical mind will have to process fewer thoughts than you are used to.
6. Continue your day with the center of thought focused in your chest, with the analytical mind at rest and your intuition active.
7. Be observant of any feeling of spirits moving around you.
8. Practice keeping the center of thought in your chest every day, so that you do it out of habit in the astral.

Patience

One of the radical things I have noticed about astral projection is that each time I project, an experience has already been prepared for me. It is as if I (or possibly someone else interested in my mind evolution) have set up the conditions for the projection, including the environment and interaction. It seems as if our lives are under meticulous monitoring, but by a hidden part of ourselves. Each projection represents a lesson, designed to further my understanding of myself. Each lesson should be digested before the next projection can take place. Sometimes weeks pass without a single projection. Then I finally realize the impact of the previous projection. The next day, I am projecting again.

It seems nothing will come until we are ready, and in order to be ready, we have to reflect on and learn from previous experiences. Each experience builds on top of a previous lesson, and having an experience is meaningless unless we learned the lesson upon which the experience builds. Reflection can't take place in an impatient mind, so we have to calm our minds and give ourselves time to grow from our experiences. Ironically, slowing down is the fastest way to accelerate the frequency of experiences.

Love

I can't underline enough the importance of being in a good mood when projecting. When you enter the astral, you do not pick up a new set of emotions; you take with you whatever you are feeling. As Deepak Chopra might say, "Thoughts are things." Whatever emotions you have stir up thoughts, which turn into tangible things in the astral. Understandably, your astral projection could get ugly if you harbor negative emotions. It is no fun feeling scared during a projection, as I have on several occasions.

What is worse, emotions are often suppressed in the physical realm, but there is no such control in the astral. Whatever suppressed emotions you bring into the astral will be unleashed. You must therefore create the starting point of a good mood before attempting to enter the astral.

As mentioned in the previous Circle, love is the best antidote to fear and other negative emotions. You can, at any time, create a feeling of love simply by relaxing your mind, focusing on your chest, and letting the love radiate from there. The love will dispel any negative emotions. It only takes a few seconds to accomplish but will allow for hours of fun in the astral. Use this technique before any astral projection.

The Energy of Intent

Monday, November 11, 2002
One Type of Energy

The cat wakes me up in the middle of the night. He is running around like mad, staring out each window in turn. Barb is worried that there might be someone or something outside the cabin. I feel I have been taught something during sleep, perhaps in an astral learning center. One part of me was educated while another part of me dreamed about going to a university. Perhaps the dream was a consequence of the fact that I was in an astral learning center; one part of me affects another part of me.

What I was taught was a lesson in energy. I wake up and know that there is only one type of energy in the universe. It is everywhere and I can sense it. We all can. It feels like pockets of energy, spread about in the air and in matter. The higher concentration of pockets in a place, the more energetic that place is. I look at Barb and sense she consists of pockets of energy. Everything does. My subtle parts are in charge. My rational mind has yet to awaken, or I choose not to use it. Is that one type of energy love? No . . . it feels more like the energy of intent. In any case, I choose not to analyze it, because I know that my subconscious already knows exactly what the energy is and my analytical mind would therefore only get in the way.

I suspect from the commotion that there may be aliens about, so I get out of the *bed, which is made out of pockets of energy, and peer out the window. I am scared of the idea that aliens, or even worse—humans—could barge in here and take us away to perform painful experiments. I am afraid of the potential pain, nothing more. The prospect of cultural exchange excites me. The darkness and the wobbling light from the fire-stove put me in a spooked mood. Then I realize that if aliens come around, with their interdimensional communication devices, there would surely be a disturbance in the pockets of energy outside, and I would feel this like ripples upon a pond. Reassured, the fear dissipates.*

The next morning, Barb tells me she had a hypnagogic image of a tall, steel-gray alien looking at us through the windows as we slept. Perhaps he was gazing at us from another dimension and could only be seen in the hypnagogic state, when reason is asleep.

Everything you see, think, hear, feel, emote, and smell is created from the same energy. There is only one type of energy in the universe. From all my astral exploration, the closest I can come to describing that energy is that it is the energy of *intent*. Nothing in the universe would exist unless there were the intent for it to be. All matter, feelings, and thoughts exist because someone intended to experience them. This also means that if you experience them, you intended to experience them. The intent of having them attracts intent energy from the universe, which has energy in abundance, and forms the energy into the intended manifestation. There are two points to remember when it comes to this energy: 1. There is an almost never-ending supply of energy. The supply is as large as our intention to exist. 2. By simply intending something, whether physical or nonphysical, you can create it from raw intent energy.

The energy of intent can be tuned to vibrate at certain frequencies. How do you make that happen? By intending it of course! Your mind consists of several dimensions, as you are a multidimensional being. Each dimension of your mind has an energy mold. A mold is a mind function that manipulates energy according to your intentions. Each mold is tuned according to what energy frequencies that mold works with. The physical energy mold is tuned to process a low-frequency energy that we call physical matter. This mold sucks in raw intent energy from the universe and adjusts its frequency so that it can be shaped and held in place as subatomic particles. These are not solid particles at all, of course; they are just energy of intent vibrating at certain frequencies. There is no such thing as a solid particle. The physical energy mold intends for energy to interact in a certain way for it to form molecules. The molecules are in turn intended to form cells in your body. These molecules and cells are not solid particles at all, of course; they are just energy of intent vibrating at certain frequencies.

Everything is the same energy (see figure 5). Since Einstein published *On a Heuristic Viewpoint concerning the Production and Transformation of Light* in 1905, science has known that light can be described as both a particle and a waveform. In 1924, Louis de Broglie discovered that matter also behaves as both a particle and a waveform.[12] Apparently, we are living in the middle of a big wave. Perhaps emotions and thoughts will also be found to have wave properties.

The emotional and mental energy molds work in the same way as the physical energy mold, except they are tuned to process energies with frequencies representing emotions and thoughts, respectively. There are many more energy molds in our minds, but for the sake of simplicity, we will stick to only these three.

The three energy molds affect each other. For example, if the mental mold manifests (from your intent) a thought of inadequacy, the emotional mold will manifest, perhaps with a few days' delay, the anxiety of

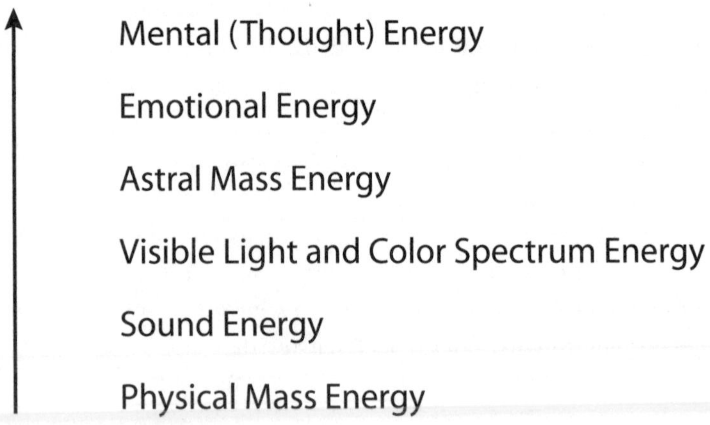

Mental (Thought) Energy

Emotional Energy

Astral Mass Energy

Visible Light and Color Spectrum Energy

Sound Energy

Physical Mass Energy

Figure 5. Energy frequency.

inadequacy. The physical mold will then deliberately fumble in its manifestation of fresh cells, thereby forming the conditions for disease to enter, creating the physical meaning of inadequacy. Likewise, the energy molds also affect each other in positive ways. A simple positive thought can turn the tide on an extended depression or disease.

The molds themselves are servants to your intent. Anything you intend to happen, the molds will manifest, given some time. See, you can have anything you want simply by intending to have it. The problem is that we as human beings almost always have doubts (born from beliefs) that tell us some things are unattainable or that we are not worthy of experiencing them. This is all wrong, because everything is attainable and we are worthy of everything. However, as long as we have those beliefs and doubts, our intent will be sabotaged and we will fail to manifest the things we desire.

Now, remember the answers to these questions: Is it possible for you to leave your physical body? Yes, because anything is possible. Are you worthy of an out-of-body experience? Yes, you are worthy of everything.

Exercise: No Doubts

Make these statements your mottos whenever you make a decision:
"Anything is possible."
"I am worthy of everything."

Manifesting through Intent

1. Tonight as you lie in bed, with your eyes closed, create your future astral projection by visualizing exiting your body and floating around. This is a direct instruction to your energy molds to adjust the way they process energy in order to make the projection happen.

2. Visualize other things you want in your life. Anything you visualize with sufficient intensity and perseverance *will* happen.

3. Visualize how your next day will be. For each thing you have to do tomorrow, visualize the best outcome for you.

Energy Exercises

When the energy throughput in the energy molds described earlier is consciously adjusted, odd and unexpected things may occur. If you intentionally increase the flow of energy through, for example, one of your legs, then the mundane energy patterns in that leg will be upset and you will get physical-like sensations that seem to belong to another dimension—which they do.

Tuesday, January 2, 2001
Astral Touch

I wake up at 4 A.M. and decide to have an OBE. I relax my body and clear my mind. Thoughts keep coming, so I decide to try to listen for a sound. I convince myself that my computer will soon produce a beep. When and if I hear the beep, I am to get out of bed immediately. Therefore, it is very important that I react to the sound as quickly as possible. This is silly, because my computer is not even turned on. Anyway, it works. My mind silences all thoughts in order to be able to hear the beep.

For a while, I feel a current run from the top of my head down to my chest. It feels just like the times I have touched electrical fences, only it does not hurt. I do not know where to go from here. I call out for help. Two spirits, both male, come to my assistance

148

(this could be pretending). I ask them what to do to get out of my body. One of them (the tall one) says, "You should go pee." I need to do that, but I think it would require too much effort to get back to my current state and I tell them so. He repeats: "You should go pee." I say, "Ok, I will be back in five. Will you be waiting?" They reply, "Yes." I regain control of my body and go to the bathroom.

I get back into bed, clear my mind by listening for the beep, and soon I am near them again. I try to talk to them, but they are in some kind of trance. They are sitting with their legs crossed, as some people do when meditating. I call out for them again. This time they respond. I ask them why they were in trance just now. They reply that they were trying to connect to me. Then I realize that these guys are alive and engaged in meditation, just like I am.

I ask them again how to get out of my body. They say I should "relax and go with the flow." I notice that my forehead is not relaxed enough; it was strained when I listened for the beep. I relax it and follow the flow. I just passively float along anything that comes into my mind. I drift closer to sleep. A vision comes along: I am sitting at the kitchen table. I stroke the side of the table with my right hand, and it feels real! I can feel the wood against my fingers. I am alerted by this sensation, and it keeps me from falling asleep. Similar things happen two more times in the bed. I drift closer to sleep and feel my right foot kick, like a spasm. I feel it move and I feel it hit the sheets. However, I am sure that my physical foot does not move an inch.

Some time later, I drift closer to sleep again and feel my right hand caress the sheets for 15 seconds, but my physical hand does not move. Additionally, I feel those sensations in spite of the fact that my body is relaxed to the extreme that I can't feel it. Then I have to go to the bathroom again. I feel a cool breeze on my right cheek as I get up. The two following attempts fail; I fall asleep in my third attempt and nothing happens in my fourth.

I believe that the zone between extreme relaxation and sleep is the key to having an OBE. I need to explore that zone.

The sensations tell you that your leg can be so much more than what you have, by habit, viewed your leg to be. They tell you that this is a multidimensional leg, used for walking not only in the physical but also in the whole of creation, in all dimensions.

When energy is set in motion, nonphysical energy channels in the leg are energized. These energy channels compare to *nadis,* energy channels long known in Hinduism. When energy flows through certain energy channels, you can feel it as a sensation similar to a medium-strength electrical current running through your leg. Those energy channels are not physical channels, thus the sensation is not physical. Astral projectors know this sensation as *vibrations*. Note that you do not need to achieve this sensation in order to astral project. You do not even have to do energy exercises, but they may help.

Nonphysical energy channels mostly take on patterns of habit. They find one way to channel energy into your being that works and they stick to that. In order to explore new ways of being—astral projection for example—we need to upset those habitual energy patterns. Energy exercises are one way we can do that.

Energy channels that we do not use during our waking time tend to slumber. Just like a muscle that is never used, they grow weak and inefficient. To upset their slumber, all we have to do is consciously increase the energy flow through them.

Exercise: Circle of Energy

1. In bed at night, close your eyes and imagine a whole universe of energy.
2. Suck in the energy through your chest.
3. From there, it will travel all the way down to your feet.
4. The energy will exit your body through the soles of your feet and then make an arc up through the air to your chest, where it will join the energy from the universe as it enters your chest.
5. Keep this circle of energy flowing for about 20 minutes. Be careful not to overheat yourself.
6. Repeat this exercise every evening.

After 20 minutes of directing the energy flowing through your body, you might feel tingly, buzzing, light, and maybe even a little high. These are symptoms of inactive energy channels suddenly turned active. You have changed the nonphysical energy patterns in your body, so naturally you experience new sensations. This change in the energy patterns, even if it only lasts for a few hours, allows you to *think* in new patterns. It allows for a more dynamic, fluid, and open way of managing your thoughts.

Why do people climb mountains? It is dangerous, cold, and a lot of work. They do it because the act of climbing and conquering is outside of their habits of life. In terms of energy, mountain climbing provides a way to upset their energy patterns, both physical and nonphysical, allowing energy to flow in unused channels. The new flow of energy makes mountain climbers feel more alive. Now, we do not have to risk our lives climbing mountains in order to experience such a new energy flow. All we have to do is direct the energy flow with our mind to achieve a similar excited state of being.

When people climb mountains, their physical and mental energy flows change out of necessity. They must change in order to keep from falling off the mountain wall. In the case of astral projection, it is not necessary for the flows to change. We simply must put more effort into visualizing nonphysical energy flowing through our body.

Exercise: Creating through Energy

1. Close your eyes.
2. Intend your body to be more fluid, dynamic, open, and conducive.
3. Suck in energy from the universe through any point of your body.
4. Visualize the energy washing over your intent of fluidity, making your intent become reality.

If you want, you can use tools to help you direct energy. Crystals are especially useful. Any type of quartz crystal is good for sucking in energy of intent. If you have a couple of crystals, that is great, but you do not have to buy any new crystals if you do not have any. You can use an ordinary rock, a plant, or even dirt. Remember, the power to direct energy of intent lies within your mind, not in a physical object. The mind, however, often believes more in external physical objects than in its own abilities. It might, therefore, be helpful to pretend that the objects channel the energy, rather than the mind itself.

To optimize the energy flow, you have to find points on your body that are especially open to energy input. These points may coincide with chakras, as these have high concentrations of nonphysical energy channels. *Chakra* is a Sanskrit word that means "wheel." A chakra is thought to be an energy node channeling vitality into the physical body. The seven main chakras are aligned along the spine.

Exercise: Finding Energy Points

1. Close your eyes.
2. Say out loud: "I."
3. Scan your body for areas that light up, tingle, or feel especially alive when uttering "I." These areas have strong energy flows.
4. Make a note of where those areas are.

Once you have a couple of energy objects (rocks will suffice) and know your body's strong energy spots, you can optimize the energy flow through your body. Do the following exercise once after waking up, once in the afternoon, and once before going to sleep, for three days. This should get your energy flowing.

Exercise: Individualized Energy Flow

1. Lie down.
2. Place one energy object (crystal, rock, plant, etc.) on one of your areas of strong energy flow.
3. Place another energy object on another area of your body that has strong energy flow, preferably not too close to the first area.
4. Close your eyes.
5. As you inhale, visualize energy flowing from the first energy object, through your body, and out into the second energy object.
6. Rest during your exhale.
7. Continue steps 4 through 6 for ten minutes. You do not have to concentrate. Let your thoughts wander. The energy flow will take care of itself.
8. When done, just for fun, hold your palms an inch apart. Do you feel a warm, slightly tingling, presence of energy?
9. Also, put your right palm half an inch behind your head. Do you feel a cool breeze?

Exit Techniques

Most astral projections are preceded by the exit from the physical body. This is not an actual exit, as much as a shift of attention from your physical body to one of your nonphysical bodies. The fact that older astral projection literature refers to the shift of attention as an *exit* is caused by the human traditional belief that the physical is our natural state of being (which it is not). When researchers tried to explain the astral projection phenomenon in the old days, they naturally assumed that some part of us exited what they thought was the center of our being, our bodies.

What if there are parts of us that are never actually *in* our bodies, but flying free in nonphysical realms? For example, do you consider your dreaming self to be inside your body? That part of you never concerns your physical body. You never bring your physical body into a dream (which is not to say that this is an impossible feat). Therefore, dreams do not take place in the physical realm, which is the same as saying that dreams are nonphysical. There is no need for your dreaming self to ever dip into the physical. It would make sense that your dreaming self is purely nonphysical, which is to say that it never exits your physical body. The same applies to your astral self.

When you astral project, you shift your awareness from the physical body to a part of yourself already residing in the astral realm. The shift would be so quick that you would interpret it as an actual physical movement. After all, your awareness is currently tuned into the physical. A second later, you would find yourself in the astral. The impression of physical movement and the resulting new environment may trick you into believing you exited your body, when in fact it was a simple shift of awareness from one part of your being to another.

The exit is a difficult subject made even more complicated by a physical-centered language, but still, it is worth spending some time thinking about. Knowing the mechanics of awareness is fundamental to finding our true nature: Are we physical beings able to temporarily escape the limits of that physical body, or are we nonphysical beings able to tune into a physical body?

Sunday, June 10, 2001
Roll-Out

I am very tired in the afternoon, so I go to bed at 5 P.M. I do not plan to astral project. I open my mind to psychic communication. I slip in and out of Focus 10 (Robert Monroe's name for the "body asleep/mind awake" state) and slumber off a few times. After an hour and 40 minutes, I impulsively think, "Enough of this, let's get out!" I try to sit up, but there is massive resistance in my chest. I only manage to sit up at a 45-degree angle from my still-lying body. I think that it might be better to roll out. I have never used rolling as a technique to get out before, so something beyond must be inspiring me. I roll inside my physical body.

At first, I think my physical body is moving along in the roll, but then my astral body breaks free. I fall through the bed, through the floor, and out into a dark space. This is a disappointment, because I want to project inside my room. Far off in the distance, I see a planet or some kind of blurry light, and I figure that going there is the only fun thing to do. My awareness is becoming a bit stiff and attached to my physical body (although I am nowhere near it), so I roll a few more times and am free once again. I raise my right arm like Superman and swoosh off at an amazing speed toward the planet. I am overwhelmed by massive tingling and vibrations!

Halfway to the planet, I get bored. I still want to project inside my room. I know that visual input from my physical eyes will take me back to the physical realm. I open my physical eyes a bit and close them. I find myself back in my room. I roll out onto the *floor and float around for a few seconds. Then the experience ends and I am not able to create another astral projection.*

An *exit technique* is a sequence of actions that prepares and executes the shift of your awareness from the physical body to the part of you residing in the astral. Most exit techniques are designed to move, as if by accident, a semiphysical (some call it ethereal) part of you. When that part of you is set in motion, it calls upon your awareness for your conscious assistance. You will notice this as a distinct but abstract signal that tells you that you are ready to leave your body.

You will then gain more control over that semiphysical part as you move it further. You move it simply by intending to move it. Another way to move it is by attempting to move your physical body, which will by then be asleep. Because the body is asleep, your attempt to move instead moves the semiphysical part.

When we intentionally or accidentally move that semiphysical part of us, our awareness is shifted into it. In most cases, the awareness does not stop there but continues into fully nonphysical parts of us—the astral, for example.

However, in order to be able to move that semiphysical part to begin with, the physical body has to be deeply asleep or we will end up moving it instead. We find the "body deep asleep" state in all sleep states, but for us to be aware enough to control the exit, we have to limit our exits to the hypnagogic (falling asleep) and hypnopompic (waking up) states. In my experience, the hypnagogic state, after a period of sleep, is the most beneficial state for exits. Perhaps the reason for that is that the body is used to relinquishing awareness to the sleep mechanism during that phase. We are exploiting the natural process of falling asleep for our astral projection purposes. This means that we first have to fall asleep, wake up, and then almost fall asleep again before we can apply an exit technique. Do not worry, it is easier than it sounds.

Whenever the body falls asleep, the awareness is automatically released into the dream world. With the aid of an exit technique, we can perform a preemptive release of awareness. The only difference between the two kinds of release is that in a preemptive release, we remain conscious as the awareness is released from the body and shifted into a nonphysical part of us. This is called a conscious exit. There is another, less reliable, type of exit called unconscious exit.

To achieve an unconscious exit, you first have to prepare for exit right before you fall asleep. You can do this by visualizing or affirming something, such as: "When I see my hands in a dream, I will know that I am dreaming," or, "Tonight I will have a lucid dream," or, "Tonight I will realize I am dreaming," or, "My mission tonight is to investigate my Akashic records while I am asleep."

Then fall sleep. The part of you in charge while you sleep takes such commands without question, because the rational mind is not there to tell it what is important and what is not. It will do its best to carry them out. Later, in the midst of dreaming, you will suddenly realize that you are not in the physical reality, but in a dream reality. You will then choose between letting the dream play out or becoming conscious enough to take control of your environment. This can be a difficult choice, since reason will be too deeply asleep to help you figure out which one is more important to you.

Traditionally speaking, you will have a lucid dream, although it is common that the dream environment dissipates when you become conscious, making the experience seem more like an astral projection than a lucid dream. The difference between lucid dreaming and astral projection seems indistinct at times. However you define astral projection and lucid dreaming, they are surely related.

In this book, we only concern ourselves with conscious exits, which we will apply in the next chapter. For now, we will practice some exit techniques on dry land, that is, in a waking physical state. When we get into that dazed hypnagogic state, we will know the exit technique so well, even falling asleep will not make us lose the thread.

Exercise: The Roll-Out

1. Place pillows next to the bed, to cushion your fall in case you roll off the bed.
2. Lie on the bed.
3. Close your eyes.
4. Relax your body and mind with a few deep breaths.

5. Twist your shoulder forward as if you were to roll out of bed. Do not use the lower half of your body. Use only your shoulders and back to propel the rolling movement.

6. Continue the roll without using your legs until you almost fall off the bed.

7. Repeat the roll a few times until you know approximately which muscles you are using.

8. Pretend that you are disconnected from the physical body.

9. Visualize rolling *inside* the body without falling out. Use the same movement as in the roll above.

If you do the last step in the exercise above while you are almost falling asleep, your awareness will break free from the physical body and you will have an astral projection, and a smashing good time. Additionally, once you have exited the body, you may use the roll to repel any attraction from the body.

Roll-out is the easiest exit technique for me, but each astral projector has his own preference. Some might prefer to kick up a leg (that would be a semiphysical leg, then) or simply sit up. You might even meet success just visualizing being outside the body. The list of exit techniques is endless, but we will look at only one more. It uses the power of the mind and is, therefore, quite different from techniques in which you attempt to move your body.

Exercise: AP Now!

1. Lie on your bed.

2. Close your eyes.

3. Relax your body and mind.

4. Turn your attention to the base of your throat.

5. Gather all your power of thought in that spot.

6. Hush all thoughts as you wait expectantly for something important that will be declared by you in a few seconds.

7. Command: "AP Now!" (AP, of course, is short for astral projection.)

Since this exercise was done in waking consciousness, most likely nothing happened. However, in a hypnagogic state, that is, when you are almost asleep, your command will have immediate effect. The sleep states are controlled in the realm of the mind, so anything you mindfully command in such a state will have effect. The waking physical reality is also governed by the mind. Similar commands would have same effect there if it were not for beliefs telling us what we can and can't do with our minds.

Putting It All Together

Tonight you will set out on an extraordinary journey of exploration. You have prepared for this a long time (at least for several chapters). You have all the knowledge and techniques you need. Some of it you picked up in this and other books, but your astral self acquired most of the knowledge while you slept. For many of you, this is your first conscious astral projection and, therefore, it is an exciting and joyous occasion. Let us keep it joyous, so set aside all fears. They fulfill no purpose, for there is nothing to be afraid of. Please read the instructions below carefully and memorize them, so that you will have no problem executing them tonight.

Exercise: Astral Projection
Setting Up the Intent

1. Tell your family not to wake you in the morning. If they are open-minded, tell them that you will be leaving your body and must not be disturbed. If you suspect they might not understand this, instead tell them you will be meditating.

2. Be sure to turn off any alarm clock—you do not want to wake up too abruptly.

3. Before going to bed, write down all the things you have to do tomorrow. Put the list down and forget about everything you wrote. The list will be there tomorrow, so it is unnecessary to keep all those things in your mind.

4. In your mind's eye, imagine there is a deep well before you. Throw all your worldly worries and problems into the well. They can wait until tomorrow, too. You do not need them right now. Also, throw all expectations and fears about the future into the well, as well as all painful memories of the past. Right now, there is only the present. The present is the only thing you need right now. The past and the future can wait until tomorrow.

5. Tell yourself: "I have worked hard for this. I *deserve* an astral projection."

6. Then state: "I will lie down tonight and I will not get up until I have projected." No, no, no! Say it like you *mean* it.

7. Lie down in your bed as you usually do, in any position, preferably not sharing the bed with anyone. You do not want anyone touching your body while you are projected away from it, as this might call you back. Do not ruin your marriage over it, though.

8. Close your eyes.

9. Relax your mind. Let it sink.

10. Think clearly: "I intend to temporarily leave my body." Then visualize standing in an open field. Let the visualized person spread his arms and yell at the top of his voice: "I intend to temporarily leave my body!" Intent decides what happens in nonphysical realms. By declaring your intent, you instruct your nonphysical parts. Also, words may not mean much in human society, but in most nonphysical realities, including your visualization, they are binding verbal contracts. Anything you say in these nonphysical realms will come to pass.

Getting into a Good Mood

11. Take a few deep breaths to relax your body and mind. Think to yourself repeatedly: "With every breath I take, I get more relaxed."

12. Move your center of thought to just below the center of your chest. This will help the flow of imagination while at the same time prevent thought energy from flowing to your head, the body part associated

with reasoning and analytical thought. You will not need logic or reason during this first astral trip, and you will definitely not need to analyze what is happening to you. Invoking the analytical mind might bring you back to your body, since it will get dreadfully confused. The reasoning mind is quick to assume, and incorrectly so, that you are in danger of being physically harmed when you are released from your body. This fear, or panic rather, will cut short your projection. So, you can see the importance of not analyzing. It is not necessary to understand what is happening until you get back to your body. Until then, just go with the flow.

13. From a point in your chest, feel love for the Earth and all its inhabitants. Bring to mind something that you love immensely. For example, think of how wonderful it is to sit by a trickling creek and breathe the spring air. Take the feeling of love this generates in your chest and radiate that love in all directions. A feeling of love will guarantee a positive experience in everything you do, including astral projection.

Visualization and Affirmation

14. Visualize that you are standing in an open meadow in a forest. Visualize as intensely as you can. All sensory input from that meadow should be at least as intense as sensory input from the physical body.

15. Visualize the sun's rays hitting your feet. The warmth relaxes them.

16. Affirm to yourself repeatedly: "Tonight I will AP." It is the person standing on the meadow that affirms this, not the person lying in bed. Continue the affirmation throughout the whole visualization (that is, until you fall asleep).

17. The warmth from the sun spreads from your feet up through your whole body, relaxing the muscles as it spreads.

18. The wind gains speed over the meadow. A warm breeze of air caresses your face. Feel the breeze.

19. You see the green grass waving in the breeze.

20. You smell the distinct scent of the pine trees surrounding the meadow.

21. Visualize walking around in that meadow. Touch the grass, the bark of the trees, and everything else you come upon.

22. Continue visualizing walking around in that meadow as you fall asleep.

23. You may wake up many times during the night. Each time you wake

up, continue visualizing walking around in that meadow as you fall back to sleep. Also repeatedly affirm: "Tonight I will AP."

The Exit

24. Close to dawn, you will wake up in a fuzzy, floating state of mind. It may feel as if your mind is unsynchronized with the body, as if the mind can't gain command over the body. You may also experience several simultaneous buzzing sensations throughout your mind, each vibrating at a different frequency. You will have difficulty merging them into the single vibration required for coherent thinking.

25. Continue to visualize and allow yourself to drop a little closer—but not all the way—to sleep. The floating sensation increases.

26. You will receive a distinct signal from the body that says it is ready to release you.

27. Apply an exit technique. For example, push your right shoulder forward to get momentum to roll out of your body. Since the physical body is already asleep, your semiphysical shoulder will move instead. Your awareness will roll inside the body for a second and then eject from the body on the left side. If that does not work, push your left shoulder forward instead and roll out to the right side.

28. Have a nice time in the astral.

If at First You Don't Succeed . . .

If you did not succeed in leaving your physical body in the previous exercise, do not despair. Do not doubt your ability to astral project, because every being in the physical universe can do it, including you. Sometimes you just have to work on it, and astral projection is well worth some effort. Do not give up. We will have you out of your body in no time.

The first thing I want you to do is to estimate how intensely you visualized in the previous exercise. The key to astral projection using this technique is the intensity of the visualization. (With the word *intensity*, in this case, I mean the richness and detail of the visualized sensory input. I am not referring to the speed at which events played out in the visualization.)

In an optimal visualization, you should lose all notion of the physical body lying in bed. Your whole attention should be focused on the imaginary meadow in which you are walking. The way to do this is to intensify the sensory input from that meadow, so that everything you see, touch, and smell on that meadow is overwhelming. It even feels more detailed and intense than would similar input from the physical world. Now, you do not have to remove all attention from the physical body in order to project, but it helps.

Exercise: Second Try

1. Tonight in bed, with closed eyes, repeat the visualization of the sunny meadow from the previous exercise, but this time with extreme intensity (i.e., richness of vision, hearing, taste, smell, and touch).

2. Walk around in that meadow for a few minutes, touching this and that.

3. Repeatedly affirm: "Tonight I will AP."

4. Visualize a huge hole in the ground in the center of the meadow. Its diameter is large enough to fit ten cars.

5. Walk to the edge of the hole and look down. The hole is so deep that you can't see the bottom. It goes on for thousands of miles.

6. Yell "Geronimo!" and jump into the hole.

7. The hole is so wide that you never have to worry about hitting its walls.

8. Feel the resistance of the air as you accelerate in the fall. The air flaps in your face and whole body as you tear through it.

9. Also feel the sensation of vacuum in your belly. If it is not there, visualize it.

10. Continue visualizing falling down the hole as you fall asleep.

11. Each time you wake up during the night, visualize falling down the hole again as you fall asleep. Also repeatedly affirm: "Tonight I will AP."

12. After a few rounds of awakening, visualizing, and falling asleep, you will feel a floating sensation as you drift off to sleep while visualizing. You will then be ready to exit the body.

13. Roll out of your body by rolling your awareness, as you would if you were rolling out of bed and falling onto the floor.

If you still are unsuccessful in astral projection, do not be discouraged. Get back on the horse and try again. It took me a few months of vigorous practice from the moment I discovered the possibility of astral projection until I achieved my first astral projection, but then, of course, I did not use this excellent technique. Each person has different strengths and therefore astral projection comes easier to some people; however easy or hard the ability to astral project comes, never forget that astral projection is a skill that can be learned and cultivated. Just keep at it and you will succeed. It is only a question of time until you can enjoy the worlds outside the physical.

Again, for many projectors, the largest obstacle to achieving a good state for astral projection is the lack of intensity in their visualization. No matter how hard they try, they can't get the visualization immense enough. The visualization does not give them anything back. It does not take on its own life as it should. The visualization turns into hard work and, consequently, the whole projection session is viewed as work rather than as fun, as it should be. The problem here is not that the projector lacks the capability to visualize properly. Everyone can visualize, because everyone has imagination. The problem is that the projector tries too hard.

Visualization is a game. It should not be taken seriously. If the projector takes it seriously, she shuts off the imaginary part of her mind, thereby blocking the mechanism of visualization. The cure for this is of course to visualize a place or event that the projector feels is entertaining and exciting. If you found your passions in the earlier exercises, you should have a good picture of what you think is fun. Just pick one of your passions and construct a visualization based upon that theme. For example, if you enjoy shopping, then this is your chance to go to the mall in your mind and buy all those things you can't afford otherwise.

Exercise: Third Try

1. Continue doing the exercise for astral projection each night until you exit your body.
2. For diversity, and for the sake of fun, replace the meadow with a visualized environment that you find fun and exciting. For example, if you like submarines, then visualize walking around in a submarine. If you like big city life, then visualize walking around in a big city. Let your creativity flow.
3. Be sure to touch things. Let nothing escape your imaginary fingertips. Imagine that the sensitivity of your fingertips has increased tenfold.
4. Continue the visualization and the affirmation "Tonight I will AP" until you fall asleep.

5. Each time you wake up, repeat the visualization and affirmation as you fall back to sleep.

6. When you wake up at your usual time, spend about two minutes reading about astral projection.

7. Go back to bed and repeat the visualization as you fall asleep.

8. When you wake up the next time, repeat the visualization and affirmation as you fall back to sleep.

9. As you fall asleep, you will enter a weird floating state.

10. Roll out of your body.

Simplified AP Technique

In the next journal entry I use my usual technique (the one explained in the previous chapter) minus the visualization and affirmation. It is a more on-the-fly astral projection technique, as it requires less preparation. I think this is an excellent technique. It saves us the effort of visualization. Astral projection does not have to take half a day of preparation. That has kept me from projecting once in a while: My usual technique takes too much time and its visualization takes too much energy.

Sunday, August 10, 2003
Easy Astral Projection

I read Seth: Dreams and Projection of Consciousness[13] *by Jane Roberts. Seth suggests the following AP technique: 1. Induce a medium trance in whatever way you choose. 2. Find the inner self. 3. Imagine this inner self rising upward. 4. There will be a moment when you feel your identity and consciousness definitely withdrawing from the physical organism. 5. Will yourself out in a quick motion.*

I think, "That will work, but it could take me three hours to enter the required medium trance, so I am going to do what I always do: go to sleep tonight and when I wake up, I will push myself out as suggested by Seth as I fall back to sleep." After all, the hypnagogic is a trance state.

Before going to bed, I wonder why I have not had an astral projection for more than a month. I feel like I am not progressing. I have hoped to develop my intuition and other faculties, but I feel my psychic development is stagnating. Then I look over at Barb as she sleeps peacefully. Her serenity makes me realize that my psychic abilities are evolving, but changing one's subconscious is a slow process, so it takes time. But I am progressing. I get some peace of mind from this conclusion. It is funny how progress only comes when we stop being impatient.

I finally fall asleep at 1 A.M., after staring at the ceiling for two hours. When I wake up in the middle of the night, I remember to push my awareness out. I push and I push, but nothing happens. I think, "Bah, this is not working," and decide to give up and go back to sleep.

I dream I am with a group of people. The mood within the group is very pleasant. I like being with them. Could this be a glimpse into my life on a soul level? There is also a teacher who instructs us all. After some time, class is over. As I leave for the outer dream world, the teacher tells me: "Now, do not forget to push your awareness out." I reply, "I won't."

When I wake up at 6 A.M., I remember my promise. I press my awareness outwards while keeping my attention by the ceiling, as if I am there, trying to look down at my body in bed. After a few seconds, my body just falls away. Funny, it does not feel like I am leaving the body as it usually feels. It feels more like the body is leaving me. Maybe it is falling asleep. I think, I can't believe how easy this is! My awareness is free from the body, but still attached to it. I have that familiar out-of-body tingling all over my awareness. I try to sit up a few times but can't break the attachment to the body. I try rolling out but can't do it that way either.

Then I think, when I roll out, I always end up in a self-created, illusory astral world. Maybe if I just command my way out, I will project closer to the physical, or somewhere similar to it. I command for a little while, but then I start recapping what I will do once I get out: Meet some spirits who can teach me the ways of the astral, and see if I can get closer to the physical plane. This recap is important, because I know that when I completely leave the body, the memories of daily life will be inaccessible unless I recap them right before the exit. But when I am done recapping, the astral projection state is gone and I am back in the body.

Although I did not manage to fully leave the body, I am very satisfied with this session. I have been taught a quick and easy projection technique, with the assistance of that teacher in my dream.

I recommend this simplified technique to any projector. It is less reliable than the technique described earlier but takes a lot less effort.

Choose whichever is best for your purposes; do they require reliability or simplicity? However, in order to use this simplified technique, you need experience in the hypnagogic state. As we use the hypnagogic as our exit trance state, we need to understand exactly when to apply each step in the technique. This experience is easy to acquire: Just be observant to what happens in your mind as you fall asleep each night.

Exercise: Simplified Astral Projection Technique

1. Before going to bed, tell yourself: "When I wake up during the night or in the morning, I will remember to try out the simplified projection technique."
2. Go to sleep as you usually do. There is no need for any special preparations.
3. When you wake up during the night, do not move an inch. Do not open your eyes.
4. Relax your body.
5. Relax your mind. Let it sink.
6. Focus your awareness in your chest.
7. Turn your attention to the air below the ceiling. Try to detect any movement or sound up there (this is just a diversion for the mind).
8. Pretend a part of you is already up there, while another part, the awareness in your chest, is close to the body.
9. From the part of you up by the ceiling, turn and look at the body below.
10. Make the awareness in your chest press outward and upward toward the part of you hanging out by the ceiling. Imagine that the two want to unite.
11. Stay by the ceiling, looking down at the body and pressing up from the chest simultaneously. Allow your body to fall asleep any time, but do not pay the body much attention.
12. If your little diversion was immersing enough, you will remain awake as your body falls asleep. You will then be released from the body.
13. If you are still attached to the sleeping body, apply an exit technique. Roll inside the body (do not roll out yet) in order to break the attachments. Try commanding, "Exit Now!" If that does not get you out, try pressing yourself out through the top of your head. As a last resort, roll out of your body.

The Reality of Astral Projection

After one's first astral projection, the question every person raised and educated in Western society would ask is: "Was it real, or did the astral projection only take place in my mind?"

The answer to that question is: Yes. It was real *and* it only took place in your mind. When we experience waking physical reality, we are not experiencing it directly. Instead, what we experience is our *perception* of physical reality. That perception only exists in our minds. We experience the perception of astral realities in the same manner. Therefore, both the physical and the astral take place within our minds.

The question itself is faulty. It assumes that what takes place within the mind is outside reality. The opposite is true: What takes place within the mind decides what reality *is* for that mind. What happens in your mind *is* your reality. Reality is something you *create* with thought and intent, not something that happens to you. In fact, it is very likely that there is no such thing as an outside world. It could be that anything that ever existed was created inside each one of us. Physical matter could be a product purely of the mind. Future research in quantum physics may point to this upsetting notion.

Whether you accept the astral as real depends on your beliefs. Reality is a subjective concept. Plenty of people believe the astral is unreal. Plenty of people believe it is real. Many believe the physical is real and some believe the physical is unreal. All views are correct. We have such difficulty agreeing on what is real and unreal because we try to push our beliefs upon each other. We are almost desperate to have someone else acknowledge that we have a sound understanding of reality. What we do not realize is that reality is subjective enough to incorporate all beliefs on the matter.

There is no official definition of the word *real*. We do not know how to tell a real object from an unreal object, other than subjectively. Therefore, the measure of reality must unfortunately be reduced to beliefs. It is quite simple: If you believe the astral is real, it is real. If you believe it is unreal, it is unreal. You can mislead yourself either way. Perhaps the healthiest approach is to retain a neutral view while still seeking more astral experiences. In time, your experiences in the astral will form your belief as to whether it is real.

As the physical and astral realities live within your mind, they will respond to your level of belief in them. If you believe in them as real, they will become important parts of your life. If you believe they are unreal, they will play smaller parts. Your beliefs govern your reality. Quite possibly, if you stopped believing in the physical as real, it would break into shards and disappear.

Within your mind, anything is possible. You do not need to categorize your experiences as real or unreal. Categorization may be more obstructive than helpful, because you would constantly be pondering whether what you are experiencing applies to reality. If you want to create a physical experience, just do it. If you want to create an astral experience, just do it. It is up to you whether you want to distinguish the two according to how real you believe they are.

Personal Challenges for the Projector

So, now you have seen the astral. Your beliefs will change little by little, as your subconscious acknowledges the experience. Your belief system will open up to make room for this new frontier. Some old beliefs will die and some will change. As they do, new doors will open for you. New possibilities of how to live your life will present themselves automatically. Quite possibly, your life will never be the same. Let this subconscious process take its course. Do not analyze your experience too much, but keep the memory of what happened alive.

Sharing Your Experiences

You now possess a knowing that many people do not. If you choose to share this knowing with others, you may find that they react with disbelief or even with resentment. Their reactions depend on the openness and flexibility of their minds. You might be serving them knowledge that does not comply with their belief systems. In their subconscious, they realize that the information you give them may upset their own view of reality, even shake their whole existence. They have worked for decades to build a good set of beliefs about how reality works and now you threaten to undo all that for them. Their belief system defense kicks in and forces them to deny, disregard, and forget what you tell them.

Out of fear of knowledge and the change it represents, their belief system defense wants to discredit and ridicule you so that they can brush you off. It may even force them to view you as a lunatic who needs psychiatric help. They might distance themselves from you or build a protective wall to prevent further upsetting ideas from reaching them. This is a natural reaction. They are afraid that you will upset their lives that they have worked so hard to stabilize. Simply put, they can't handle your version of the truth.

Their reaction of disbelief is understandable. When I first discovered astral projection, I was very puzzled. I had never heard of anything like it. Could it be possible that I had lived my whole life ignorant of something so fundamental to our being as the ability to traverse realities? If leaving our bodies were possible, surely my parents or someone close to me would have taught me how to do it. Or was it a secret?

A short while later, I realized that OBE was a delicate matter. You don't brag to your friends, "Hey, guess what I did this morning! I shed my physical body and visited the aliens on Europa, Jupiter's fourth-largest moon. They were having a barbeque—a vegetarian barbeque." If you do, chances are you will find yourself without friends, and possibly in a room with cushioned walls. This, I suspect, is the factor that prevents people from talking about it and inhibits the spread of astral projection knowledge.

You should know that you do not need to convince anyone else of what you have experienced. It is not your responsibility to convince others of your own new-formed beliefs (yes, your interpretation of your experiences is merely beliefs that mirror the truth in varying degrees). You may serve others your knowledge, but it is up to them to eat from the plate. Like the saying goes, you can bring a horse to water, but you can't make it drink. In fact, you *should not* insist on them partaking of the knowledge. That would be a violation of their supremacy.

They are powerful beings, capable of taking care of their own lives.

They do not need you to show them the way, because your way may not be their way. They do not want your knowledge because, however unlivable their lives may seem on the surface, deep down, they have everything under control. They are where they are because they choose to be there and they choose to be there for a reason. Who are we to undo all the hard work they have undergone to get where they wanted to go?

Ultimately, it does not matter whether or not they believe you. They will come to their own conclusions at their own pace, with or without your intervention. The choice of accepting or denying is a right all beings enjoy.

Sleep Habits

It is not only what you communicate that gets on people's nerves. The astral projection technique used here takes advantage of the sleep process. By using it, you gain invaluable knowledge of what goes on when we sleep, and with this knowledge comes a desire to spend more time in the sleep state. Consequently, you will find that you spend unusually long periods of time sleeping, projecting, or simply dreaming. Because of this, others will think you are lazy and even inconsiderate.

Sleep has lost its importance in modern society. Most people sleep only because their bodies need the rest. Beyond that, they consider sleep a waste of time. However, it is during sleep that we do our most important work. To say the least, sleep is a gateway to other dimensions, where we get inspiration and creative ideas that we can use in waking life. Society does not recognize this benefit of sleep. The only thing important in modern society is the efficiency and productivity of our waking time. It was not always like this, though. Native American people, for example, believed that dreaming is the real state of being and that waking life is a mere illusion or a pause from real life. There is no greater tragedy than the eradication of those cultures and the consequent passing of their sleep knowledge into the shadows.

Understandably, people conditioned by this belittling attitude toward sleep will want to "save" you from your "lazy" habits. Unfortunately, there is little chance that you can convince them of how much you appreciate sleep. They are not about to change their beliefs of day and night unless they have the actual experience of what sleep can give them. A belief is a dangerous thing when it does not grant others the freedom of choice. In any case, do not be offended by their persistence. Instead, understand where they come from and what beliefs about sleep they hold.

Conquering Fear

Did your projection scare you? If it did, that is perfectly normal. I have yet to meet a person who is not scared out of his mind when his sense of reality is tossed inside out. I, too, was terrified during my first short projection. In fact, I panicked.

Now, I must tell you that the fear you experienced can do much harm. As it is said, *we have nothing to fear but fear itself.* Projections are not harmful in any way. The evidence is that you projected and you are still alive and well. The only way you can get hurt is by allowing the fear to control your life. Besides, it does not make sense to be afraid of the astral projection experience. Why would you fear your capabilities, your own nature—your true self?

Thursday, January 25, 2001
Blocked by Fear

As I go to bed the night following my first astral projection, a pinching pain arises in my stomach. It takes me some time to figure out what causes it. It seems that my subconscious has associated the scary astral experience last night with the act of going to sleep. It thinks that if I begin to fall asleep, I might have the same experience, which is *something it wants to avoid. Consequently, my subconscious inflicts pain to keep me awake. This is unacceptable. I can't stay awake forever.*

I command my subconscious to eliminate the new rule. I explain that there is nothing harmful about the experience. The proof is that I came out unharmed. I also tell it, in a less than polite way, that I want more astral experiences and that whatever it comes up with will not stop me. I tell it that it is bringing not only me down, but also itself with its stupid rules. What do you know: the pain instantly disappears.

Exercise: Affirmations

To get a handle on the fear, play the affirmations you recorded in the Affirmations chapter in the background throughout your day:

"You are an unlimited being."

"You can do anything you put your mind to."

"You deserve an infinite number of AP experiences."

"You observe everything that happens in your mind during sleep."

"Tonight you will AP."

"You are connected to everything."

"Everything is connected to you."

"The mind veil is removed."

"The universe takes good care of you, whether you are with or without your physical body."

"Face the direction of the universe and follow its flow. Trust that the universe is going in the right direction."

If you experienced fear during your first projection, your subconscious will probably build up a good defense against further attempts to project. The defense is for your protection, or so your subconscious believes. You must consciously deal with this defense. It may even produce physical pain if you attempt to project again. In my case, it produced a pinching stomachache. If this happens, just relax and acknowledge that the pain is created by your subconscious and that there is nothing wrong with your physical body.

If you give in to the fear and stop practicing astral projection, the fear will root itself more deeply in your subconscious as time goes by. If you quit astral projection, you invite fear to govern your decisions for the rest of your life. In a few years, the fear of the body exit will be a substantial part of your life. By then, it will be very difficult to dissolve. Therefore, the best time to deal with the fear is now, before it gets out of hand. Get back on the horse immediately—that is, continue practicing astral projection despite all fears.

Exercise: Dispelling Fear

Before your next astral projection session, do this fear-dispelling exercise again:

1. Close your eyes.
2. Relax your mind.
3. Move your center of thought to the center of your chest.
4. Create a small pearl of love in the center of your chest.
5. Let love beam out from the pearl in all directions.
6. Let the love bathe everything around you.

How do you feel? Have worries and fears subsided?

Psychic Side Effects

Since I started practicing astral projection, weird things have begun to happen. It seems the more I practice, the more my subtle senses develop, opening me to intuition and similar abilities.

Monday, June 25, 2001
Clairvoyance for Lunch

I am making lunch. I get a plate from the cupboard and a thought pops into my head: "If I drop this plate, it will shatter on the floor." The thought feels like mine. The weird thing is that there is nothing leading up to it: Suddenly, the thought is just there, uninvited. I put some food on the plate and heat it in the microwave oven. When I reach for the plate in the microwave oven I think, "I better hold the plate with both hands, or I might accidentally drop it to the floor." I am worried about dropping the plate and I can't understand why. Then I think, "What is wrong with me? I am not going to drop anything. I never drop anything!"

On my way to the table, the plate breaks in two (the heating process probably caused a crack in the ceramic), and the food falls to the floor. I now have a piece of plate in each hand and a dumbfounded expression on my face. I am partly amazed by my thoughts prior to the accident, partly disappointed that my food is spoiled, but mostly I am angry because I did not listen to my intuition.

Sometimes, a window to another world opens up. You get a glimpse, a brief taste, of a world that is beyond the comprehension of the rational mind. Whether this is the home of our souls, I do not know, but I know it is accessible, and the only thing preventing us from venturing into that world is our limiting belief system. When we make contact with that world, the rational mind starts explaining what it sees in conventional terms, and when it can't explain what it sees, it denies the experience and closes the window to that world. In time, and with practice, subtler parts of our intelligence will replace the rational mind in this interaction.

Monday, November 12, 2001
Bright White Light in My Room

I wake up early in the morning. The room is dark. Still in bed, I clear my eyes of the junk that has gathered during the night. Suddenly, there is a flash of bright, white light. It lasts for a second. It looks like the beams from a car headlight, but with a wider spread. The light source must be inside the room, because the curtains are closed and there is no sound from a passing car.

Afterward, I wonder what the flash meant. Perhaps some entity wanted to show that I am not alone. Or maybe I saw beyond the physical world for an instant and my ego closed it down when it discovered what I was doing. Or maybe it is supposed to trigger a memory of something I have to do. Or maybe there is something wrong with my eyes or brain.

Monday, November 12, 2001
Seeing through Closed Eyelids

A few days ago, during an attempt to OBE, I could see through my closed eyelids. I did not reflect over it at the time, because it felt natural. I could see the ceiling through the darkness.

Whether the physical eyes or the astral eyes were in use remains unknown. It did not seem at the time that my awareness was removed from the physical body, which makes me think that either a nonphysical faculty of vision is available from a waking state of mind, or our physical eyes are capable of much more than we have so far discovered.

Sunday, December 9, 2001
A Guide's Thought

I turn on the computer and go to the bathroom. Then I remember that I always have to turn on the monitor before I turn on the computer or the monitor will be unsynchronized. I think, "Oh no, now I have to reach over and detach the monitor cord and then plug it back in to get the monitor working properly. What a hassle." Then I hear a thought, "It may be less work than you think." I figure that could be one of my guides telling me not to worry, so I do not worry. When I return and turn on the monitor, it works perfectly.

One day while apart, Barb and I decided that I should astral project over to her house. Although I did not have a successful departure of the body, I did succeed in perceiving her bedroom correctly when I visualized floating inside it. Below is an excerpt from an Internet chat the following day.

Thursday, January 17, 2002
Remote Perception

Barb: You were supposed to come here last night.

Magnus: I was there, but I was still awake.

B: Really? Do tell!

M: You were awake too, I think.

B: What was I doing?

M: You were on your back, not on your side?

B: I was on my back. I usually sleep on my tummy, though, but I was 'sucking' you in.

M: The cover was under your arms, not all the way to your chin?

B: Yes!

M: I first got the impression you had an army of pillows under your head. Then there was only one. White.

B: Oh my god, yes! There was an army of pillows, but I moved them. Started to get a headache. What else? What did you do? See, hear, and feel?

M: I floated above you for some time, then rested next to you. You turned and looked at me at one time.

B: I had my arms up/palms up, and I felt you, mostly to my right . . . or, strongest to my right. Did you lie down, to my right?

M: I lay down first on your left side, then on your right side, because it was easier (to visualize) for some reason.

B: Easier because that is where I wanted you, and at a deep level, you knew that. I felt you . . . someone . . . brush the hair away from my face.

M: Hey, I did yank your hair. Hard! And I might have brushed it, too.

B: *It didn't hurt, but I felt it, very much. Why hard?*

M: *Because you weren't responding to the brushing. Could you describe your haircut?*

B: *Not much to describe, really. Long, almost to my bra strap. Almost one length, blonde, semicurly.*

M: *I got the impression it was in a knot or something.*

B: *It was actually, pulled back, clipped back in a "comb." But later, I pulled out the comb. Too uncomfortable to sleep in.*

M: *I thought your TV was at the foot of the bed?*

B: *It is.*

M: *(Mounted) on the wall or on a table?*

B: *Table.*

M: *Good. A funny thing. I left you and came back a few times. Twice, I stepped into someone else's bedroom. It was embarrassing.*

B: *Where they . . . in a . . . compromising position?*

M: *An old couple was lying in bed. They were reading, I think.*

Saturday, June 1, 2002
Lucky Pennies

Barb and I are out walking. We find a penny on the street. Barb says, "We found one penny the other day, and one now. They are lucky pennies, but only if you find them with their tails up. Three is the magical number." Then we walk on, turn a corner, and find a third penny on the street! This one also has its tail up.

May 2003
The Dime

Barb and I are broke again. All we have is a handful of change. We go into a thrift bread store. They have a deal, five loaves for three-something dollars. When we get to the register, we find that we are seven pennies short. How embarrassing. Barb goes out to the car to look for change under the seats, but there is not much chance of finding anything, since we have already cleaned out every penny from the car. For no apparent reason, I turn my head down to look at the floor and find a dime just lying there, staring up at me. That dime was not there before! Humbly grateful for this gift, I pick it up and pay for our daily bread.

Sometimes you pick up information about future events with your subtle psychic senses. Often you do not know how or where you got the information. It seems as if thoughts just pop into your mind, without cause. But of course, there is a cause, and that cause is the fact that we are capable of sensing the world around us in many more ways than we conventionally think.

Friday, September 6, 2002
Premonition

Barb, Jazz, and I walk in Lewisville Park, Vancouver. I smell berries. I stop and search but find none. Darn it, I so wanted some berries. We continue down the path and come upon berry bushes! Then, after stuffing my mouth full, I get the urge to spread my arms and imitate a propeller airplane. "Brrrrrruuuuaaaooooom!" A few seconds later, a propeller plane flies over our heads. As we drive home from the park, I make a remark that the clouds look just like they do in The Simpsons *cartoon. A second later, someone on the radio mentions Ralph from* The Simpsons.

October 2002
Precognitive Dream

I dream I visit a gypsy-like fortuneteller. She tells me that I will go to another city where I will meet a woman, whom I will recognize by a tarot card that she will give me. The woman will also tell me something that I will not believe, but which is true. . . .

Four months later, Barb and I have moved to Tucson, Arizona. We had not planned the move at the time of the dream. One day, we meet a homeless woman who has been kicked out of her Native American reservation by the tribal leaders because she got a restraining order against her abusive Native American husband. Now she is begging at the intersection with her two kids for enough money to stay at a motel. Who would kick children out of their home?

The woman, whose name is Sue, tells me about chem-trails in the sky. Supposedly, some of the people in charge are knowingly polluting the air with radioactive substances and other poisons. I am unsure what to believe. Why would they poison their own population? Who would do such a thing? How do they sleep at night? I must admit though, that what I thought were jet contrails are suspiciously well distributed across the sky, parallel and at right angles to each other. They linger for hours, whereas regular jet contrails are washed away by the wind in mere minutes. These trails are spread by what looks like military aircraft. I have never seen a commercial airliner do it.

When the TV news discloses that Tucson kids are afflicted with cancer worse than that found in the rest of the country, I don't know what to believe. Could the cause of this cancer be the radioactive chem-trails?

Sue and I find a common interest: Carlos Castaneda. Before we part, Sue gives me his last book, The Wheel of Time.[14] *Imagine my surprise when I discover that its cover looks like a tarot card.*

CIRCLE 3

"Mind" Your Step

*Experience how your mind affects the astral
and learn to harness its creative powers.*

It is always strange to realize that physical reality has that
little hold, comparatively speaking, that you can slip out of it so
easily, that it is more like bright transparent cellophane than
solid wood or rock. You can go in and out of it, through it and
back, without leaving a tear. Yet the world is so smooth and
unseamed when you're in the body and focused there.

—Jane Roberts, *Seth: Dreams and Projection of
Consciousness*[15]

Welcome to Circle 3 of *Astral Projection and the Nature of Reality!*
By now, you should have had at least one astral projection, so you will
have no problem relating to the topics I will now discuss. In this Circle,
we will explore the nature of the astral. Up until now, I have deliberately
avoided describing my view of how the astral looks and works, because I
did not want to create any expectations on your behalf. Expectations
severely affect one's perception and interpretation of astral experiences.

However, it is now time to investigate what happens during an astral projection. In order to become skillful astral projectors, we need that knowledge. Remember to form your own understanding of the astral based on your own experiences. Take what you can from the topics discussed in this Circle, but only if fits into your personal experience.

Needs for Growth

Our astral environments are extremely individualized. Some astral projectors report seeing worlds similar to our own, while others tell of worlds inconceivable to our rationality. Some meet regular types of people, while others run into angels and goblins. The variety of experiences to be had in the astral is baffling. As humans, we are trained to think in physical terms, so we ponder this astral vastness. If we are unfortunate, we arrive at the conclusion that the astral is not a real place, only a figment of our imagination; if we are fortunate, we conclude that the astral is not physical and therefore can't be comprehended in physical terms. Therefore, the words *real*, *place,* and *only* do not apply in the astral.

The Meta-World

Considering all the objects and thoughts that appear in the astral, the astral must be a *meta-world*: a realm in which worlds are created and destroyed in the blink of an eye or sustained for an eternity, each world having its own unique objects and creatures. A simple thought, coming from any consciousness, causes a new world to pop into this meta-world. Thoughts also design creatures and objects that appear in this new world. Perhaps even our physical universe has its roots in the astral, created by an initial astral thought and maintained by the thoughts of all entities living in the physical.

The reason why astral projectors report different encounters is that what they have seen is what they themselves have created. The astral, being a meta-world, will create or attract anything a mind intends to see or otherwise experience. From this theory, we can see our importance as creators in the physical and the astral.

Our state of mind shapes our thoughts, which in turn form our current world. Following this idea, we come to this simple rule: Change yourself, and your astral, dreaming, and physical environments will change. The mind of an incarnate human is complex, containing several layers of conscious and unconscious intentions. Each of these layers has a different idea of what is in our best interest; consequently, each has different ideas of what it wants to see in the astral, or anywhere, for that matter.

The Attractor

For the novice projector, a part of the mind that resides in the subconscious often becomes dominant and takes over the role as the creator. This happens naturally. We are so used to letting the subconscious guide us in the physical—it guides us when we walk, run, drive, or do anything we consider automatic—that we do not question the fact that it also tries to guide us in the astral. One part of the subconscious knows very well how to handle the astral because it spends most of its time there. Unfortunately, this is not the part that takes charge.

The part of the subconscious that takes charge is something I call the *attractor*—a part of the mind that attracts or creates the exact situations you need in order to further yourself as a spirit. Its motivation is divine intention, adhering to our primary goal as a spirit to evolve through experience. Therefore, what we see in the astral is what we *need* to see, as deemed by the attractor. For example, if the attractor deems it necessary to put me in a life-threatening situation so that I may realize that my time on planet Earth is too precious to be wasted on a job that makes me unhappy, then it will do so when it gets an opportunity. There are plenty of opportunities for that in the astral, because anything can be created there.

Perhaps it will create a fire-spewing dragon or a banana with a grudge. The possibilities are endless. What it chooses to create for me to encounter depends on what kind of person I am and what I need to experience at that given moment. It will be unique in the sense that the attractor in other people will create something different, more in line with their personality.

Of course, the attractor does not have to create a life-threatening situation. Each person has a plethora of obstacles to freedom that she needs to recognize and understand, and the possibilities to recognize them in the astral are as endless as the variety of objects that can be created.

The attractor is active also in the physical. You have no doubt noticed that situations arise and people appear just when you need them to. Perhaps once, when you were on your last dime, you happened upon a lottery win or a person offered to loan you money. Or perhaps this bully back in school tormented you, and now that you look back on it, you realize that the torment was exactly what you needed at the time to grow as a person. However, the physical is a slow-changing world. The time it takes to manifest a bully in the astral is many thousand times faster than in the physical. That is why I call the astral "the Freeway of Personal Growth."

Growing from Nonphysical Experiences

The dream world also manifests objects very quickly. As does the astral, it offers opportunities for spiritual growth. What is interesting about dreams, however, is not the entities you encounter or the specifics of the situations, but *how you react* to those situations. The attractor is very quick to put you into dream situations that show you what you need to work on in order to conquer your next spiritual obstacle. How you react to a situation in the dream world is approximately how you would react to a similar situation in the waking physical. Think of the dream world as a laboratory where behavior that would not do in the physical is tolerated. If you, after waking up, deem you have behaved poorly in a dream, then you know what needs attention within you. (Do not beat yourself up over it, though; you can never hurt anyone in a dream.) And all this is thanks to the attractor!

As we gain more astral flight time, we learn how our minds affect the astral, and eventually we stop relinquishing control of creation to the attractor. Another way to put it is that the will to actively explore grows stronger than the will to passively learn, which is the way of the attractor. There are plenty of wonders to experience in the astral, and we do not want the attractor getting in the way as we go exploring those things.

There are an unfathomable number of worlds in the astral. If we categorize these worlds according to their life span, we can say that there are two types: transient and persistent. Transient worlds are short-lived, temporary worlds in which you can create anything. Objects appear and disappear at the whim of your thoughts. Persistent worlds exist before you project to them and remain after you leave them. The objects have a longer life span.

In a typical transient world, you are the only inhabiting being. As such, the world will respond to your intentions alone. A persistent world may be inhabited by millions of beings. The appearance of the persistent world is held in place by the intentions, beliefs, and thoughts of the inhabiting astral beings. The sheer number of thoughts spent on the world perpetuates its existence. If one being stopped thinking of the world, there would be several million more beings to continue thinking of it. This is why it is persistent. If all inhabiting beings stopped thinking of the world, it would become transient.

The transient and persistent worlds are superficial in that they are controlled by thoughts. The objects within them are merely thought-forms. Deeper levels of the astral are not so easily affected. These make the foundation upon which the superficial worlds are created. It is very difficult to reach the deeper levels unless you understand exactly how superficial worlds respond to your thoughts.

Without that understanding, our exploration will be hampered as we get entangled in the superficial objects our mind creates for us. In time, we will gain control over our mind, thereby ceasing the creation of superficial objects. Then we will have no problem spotting and reaching the deeper levels of the astral.

Taming the Mind

As mentioned in the previous section, your mind is the director of your astral environment. Anything you can conceive, you can create. The bad news is, the subconscious mind is a master of conceiving everything from breathtaking beauty to horrific nightmares, and it does this continuously unless you tame it.

Exercise: Stopping the World

1. Close your eyes.
2. Stop thinking for a minute. Do not try to silence the individual thoughts. Instead, stop the entire thought *process*.
3. Sit in a complete void for one minute.
4. In your current state, you have complete control over your mind.
5. Repeat this exercise every day.

Astral Replicas of Physical Spaces

When we are released into the astral, we often initially find ourselves in unknown waters. We may react in confusion. Consciously, we query our usual physical senses for information, which is the same thing as asking the subconscious to tell us what our surroundings look like, since our senses are managed by the subconscious. The subconscious then reaches out into the surroundings and finds that the eyes, ears, and tactile senses are not working.

The subconscious can't make sense of the situation, and it informs us of this. The subconscious definitely does not like being confused, so it may encourage us to panic. Now we consciously have a choice between panicking, getting scared, trying again to sense the surroundings, or keeping cool heads and trusting that things will work out.

We will probably choose one of the first two alternatives (panic or fright) during the first few projections, but when we finally manage to control our fears, we will be more in charge of the situation. We will then begin to stubbornly insist that there *must* be some sort of surroundings to be sensed. Since we have become used to a constant input from our bodily senses, we automatically expect this service even when we are traveling outside the physical realm. We can't accept that our physical senses have stopped feeding us with information.

What happens next is key to knowing the ways of the astral. In our hunt for clues about the surroundings, our imagination will pick up the slightest conscious or subconscious thought and search very hard through our memories for any associated memory that describes a physical space. When it finds one—and it always does, because our minds are packed with memories of physical locations—the imagination will create this space as an astral environment for us. For example, when projecting, if we have a subconscious thought of the physical room from which we projected, then our subconscious mind will create an astral replica of that room for us to experience. As a result, our subconscious mind is no longer confused, because the cause of the confusion, the lack of sensory input, is eliminated. "Excellent solution!" says the subconscious. However, this may not be what we want, since our conscious mind will be very confused as to whether the surrounding space is the physical space or an astral replica of the same.

The astral offers no resistance in this act of creation. The astral replica will be amazingly detailed and it will feel just like a physical space, with the exception that we can float in the air, walk through furniture and walls, and consciously create any additional objects we desire. In the astral replica, it will seem like our physical eyes and ears are active, but this is just a way for the subconscious mind to feel comfortable. The physical senses are still in the physical body, where our awareness is not.

Saturday, November 30, 2002
A Noisy OBE

I regress in memory in search of anything that might resemble an alien abduction or a mind screen memory covering such an experience. I find nothing, but as I begin to slumber my subconscious starts dialoguing with an other-dimensional alien. I do not reflect on the oddness of the event, because only my rational mind, which is about to fall asleep, views it as odd. The discussion continues for hours and I am never actually asleep, but dangling in the hypnagogic state.

I wake up briefly and decide to have an out-of-body experience. I do something weird with my mind. I do not know how I came up with the idea, but it feels like the right thing to do. It feels like I am pulling my awareness, as if it were chewing gum, out the back of my head, leaving my head tingling. My awareness slings back into my head.

I can sense that there is another person present. I assume it is Barb. I want to help her get out of her body. I think to her, "Let's get ahead of time." I accelerate the flow of time through my awareness (don't ask me how I did that). Time now flows faster than normal. It even flows faster than my body can handle, which falls behind. I experience events that will happen to the physical body several seconds in the future: A dust particle that has not yet fallen lands on my chest. I feel a muscle spasm I have not yet had.

My awareness is askew from the body, this time askew in time, and a slight roll makes me fall out of my body. I am floating. I try to remember what I planned to do while out of my body. I evoke a recollection procedure that is somehow managed by a part of me still residing in the body. Consequently, I regain feeling of the body and begin bouncing between my projected awareness point and the body. I remember I planned to visualize a song to see if it comes alive in the astral. I think a few tunes, but they do not turn into anything self-sustained. They are just plain tunes.

I float into the room but can't remember that I projected from the cabin. I have no idea of what the room is supposed to look like. Therefore, I can't create an astral replica of the room like I usually do. I feel awkward. I am so used to being somewhere that being nowhere causes me to feel lost and confused. This is not bad news at all, although I do not realize it at the time. I have turned the subconscious procedure of creating my astral environment into a conscious effort. This is an extraordinary achievement, for me at least. The power of creation is at my conscious disposal. This can only mean that I am beginning to master my mind.

I choose to create the Vancouver studio, because I suspect I projected from there (which I did not). I can't remember what it looks like. I lived in it for six months, but currently, I have no recollection of what it is like. This memory block must have something to do with the projection mechanics. I think there should be something that looks like a bar, and sure enough, I soon crash into, and through, the solid astral matter of a wooden bar. There is no bar in the physical. The simple act of guessing that there is a bar created the bar in the astral.

I get the idea that if I make enough noise, Barb will hear it in the waking physical world. This will be a good experiment to see if astral sound travels into the physical. I float into the kitchen and start opening and slamming shut the refrigerator doors. Obviously, I do not remember the physical placement of the fridge, because it has never been in the kitchen, but I do remember that is has a double door. This makes me wonder why some memories are accessible in the astral while others are not. I make terrible noise as I repeatedly slam the fridge doors. I make so much noise that the Barb sleeping in my little astral world wakes up and yells, "Shut up!"

I come to in my physical body. My physical shoulders are moving as if they are still slamming the doors. I realize that I am in the Arizona cabin, not in the Vancouver studio. Barb wakes up shortly after and when I ask her, she tells me she has not heard any noises in the physical nor in the dream world.

During this out-of-body experience, I had a nauseating fear. It is very rare for me to be scared during a projection. The fear stems from my fear of, should it ever occur, finding an alien physically present in my bedroom at night. It is an event I desire and fear at the same time. I returned from the projection on the brink of terror, but managed to dispel the fear with the aid of love. I still checked every corner of the cabin.

When we have been through the automatic procedure of creating an astral replica of a room a few times, we realize that the astral surroundings that imagination has created for us, in spite of their convincing look and feel, are not an actual physical space, but an astral replica of that physical space, created from our memories of that space. We might call this astral replica an illusion, but then all astral worlds that are created in the same manner must also be illusions, including the physical world. Then most of what we know of Creation is an illusion. Consequently, the word *illusion* loses its meaning. What remains is a set of worlds that simply *are*. We can no longer classify them as real nor illusory.

Once we realize that what we are traveling through are astral worlds created by our own subconscious mind with the help of imagination, we can tame the subconscious and nip the automated creation of astral environments in the bud. We can do this simply by understanding how the subconscious works and will it to cease creating astral replicas. When this is accomplished, we will simply project into an astral void. This is the meta-world that surrounds the astral worlds. From there, we can freely explore any astral worlds that other beings have created or investigate the deeper levels of the astral.

However, taming the subconscious may not be so easy. There are ideas and thought patterns that just will not yield. They get in the way of reaching the astral void. If this happens, we must regress through memory and time to find the cause (often a trauma) of the obstructive thought patterns, so that we can heal them. In a manner of speaking, we must clean our own astral home before we can visit the astral homes of others. This healing frees us not only in the astral, but also in our physical lives, which become clearer and freer.

Addictions

When I hear the word *addiction*, my mind displays images of people smoking a pack of cigarettes per day or an unfortunate person forced to live in the street because he has to spend all his resources to satisfy his craving for narcotics. But addiction does not have to be that severe. An addiction is simply an urge or craving that our conscious mind is unable to resist, let alone control. As such, we have to build a complex system of beliefs surrounding that addiction. These beliefs help us prevent the addictive behavior from interfering with our lives, while at the same time we do not have to deal with the addiction. The trouble with this solution is that these beliefs complicate our lives and prevent us from being who we truly are.

Addictions come in many shapes and sizes. They may be a craving for chocolate or a fixed idea of how we are supposed to interact with other people. Only our creativity limits the form and severity of an addiction. In any case, no matter how small an addiction is, it can give us trouble in the astral. The astral is very sensitive to what goes on inside our mind. If anything is out of control in our mind, then our astral surroundings and our astral behavior will be out of control. However harmless an addiction may seem in the physical, it can cause us serious problems in the astral.

We aspire to travel with as few obstructions as possible, but addictions represent obstructions. When traveling in the physical, we use moral and social beliefs to suppress addictive cravings, but in the astral, we do not have that luxury. In the astral, we are like open books, unable to suppress any part of ourselves. Therefore, we need to deal with our addictions before we can venture unhindered in the astral.

Exercise: Identifying Addictions

1. To determine whether you have an addiction, list all the possessions and accomplishments you feel are important in your life.

2. For each of the items in the list, ask yourself:

   a. "Do I feel I must have/do this?"

   b. "Do I feel that if I do not succeed in this venture, I will not be able to stand the outcome?"

   c. "Do I feel that whether or not I have it/succeed, I will still be as good, happy, valuable, and precious as I am now?"

   (Indicators recommended by Ken Keyes[16])

   If you answered yes to questions a or b, and no to question c, then you have an addiction. In that case, mark that item in the list as an addiction. Do not fret. You are doing great. You are taking the first step to becoming a freer you.

Realities and Beliefs

It might be helpful to think of astral projection in terms of a reality-filter model, as described below. I devised it in order to understand what happens in our mind during projections. It is merely a model and so does not necessarily mirror the exact truth (if there is such a thing) of what happens.

The Function of Beliefs

As we project our awareness to a place in Creation, that place becomes our reality. There are a vast number of places that can serve as realities. Their natures can be categorized as physical, astral, mental, and other ways of being, most of which we have yet to discover. When one has projected to a reality for a long time, one begins to understand how that reality works. The subconscious then begins to draft rules on how to interact with that reality. These rules are nothing other than beliefs and are part of a person's belief system, which dictates (and limits) how one behaves in that reality. A belief helps us interact with a reality, yet it limits us by preventing us from seeing other possible ways of interacting in that reality.

Removing a belief has some strange effects. For example, since we have projected to the physical for as long as we have, our subconscious has built a set of rules that tells us how to interact with gravity. These rules can get complicated. If an entity unfamiliar with these rules were to project into a physical reality, it would probably be surprised when the planet tries to suck it to the ground; bystanders would have a good laugh at its fumbling movements.

The subconscious also makes up rules about how to act toward other beings. We call these moral and social rules. If that same novice entity were to project to physical Earth, it would not understand how to interact with people and might even, without understanding it, hurt them. This is why some possessive spirits appear to be so inconsiderate in their acts toward other people.

Circumventing Beliefs

As we project away from a reality, we may circumvent some of our beliefs belonging to that reality. For example, if you project to an astral reality, you might do things there that are considered harmful in a physical reality. You might engage in sexual or violent acts and not feel bad or guilty about it until you return to the physical. This is because you have circumvented your moral beliefs. You left your morals in your physical reality (see figure 6).

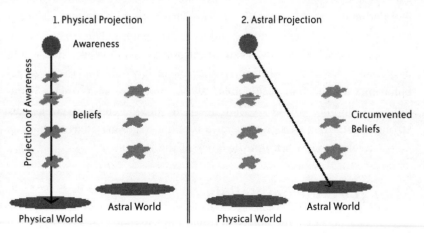

Figure 6. A projection into another world may circumvent our beliefs about that world.

In Jane Roberts's *Seth: Dreams and Projection of Consciousness,* Seth, a channeled spirit, says: "Using the third form [according to Seth, a projection can take one of three forms, where the third form is the most vigorous], there could be a tendency for you not to recognize your own physical situation [i.e., you completely lose touch with your body and the physical reality]. It would be difficult to carry the memories of the present ego personality [and its morals] with you."[17] I do not yet know why we can't bring the ego with us during the projection. Until we have explored more of our nature, we will have to be content with the fact that leaving our egos behind is an integral part of projection mechanics.

Because of this split from the ego, urges that previously were suppressed by moral beliefs in the physical can break free and run amok in the astral. This may hinder you in your travels, because there is nothing worse than being a victim to your own urges. Likewise, a possessive spirit's urges can run rampant in the physical. A possessive spirit circumvents its moral beliefs when it possesses (projects into) a human body. It can't resist harmful acts if such urges are present, and it does not feel bad about them, because it is the belief that the acts are bad that makes the spirit feel bad, but in spirits that belief is absent.

As we project back to the physical reality, the circumvented moral beliefs kick back in and we feel remorse for our astral acts and perhaps even shame for our urges. The belief that those acts are bad makes us feel bad about having done them. The cure is then to remove the urge by finding its cause and understanding its mechanics. The cure is *not* to reinforce our moral beliefs, as some religions seem to think. That would only cause the urges to grow stronger, which would make our astral behavior even more unpredictable. All our urges are simply signs pointing at something within us that needs attention, and they will grow stronger until they have caught our attention. Urges are there to help us help ourselves. They are not the work of the Devil.

Thought-Coloring Beliefs

Consciousness is the ability to think, not the thoughts themselves. In a tiny spark of Creation, a thought is born out of your consciousness.

The thought is a pure intent. On its way to your conscious mind, it has to pass through a number of beliefs in your subconscious. Each belief is like a filter that colors the thought and gives it direction. The filters are adjusting the thought so that it will apply to your current reality. When the thought finally reaches your conscious mind, it has lost its original purity. (However, you can still sense the purity by listening to the space *between* thoughts.) It is now a representation of your beliefs regarding its original intent. The thought will move your mind into a state decided by your belief system unless you consciously and firmly control the thought and critically scrutinize it.

When you have consciously acted upon the thought, the thought leaves the conscious mind and slips back into the subconscious. Depending on how you acted, your subconscious mind reinforces the beliefs to either encourage or discourage future thoughts of similar context. The thought is a result of the belief system but also serves as feedback for it. If you did not consciously question the thought, or act in an opposed manner, the subconscious would assume that the thought is acceptable within your current reality.

The reasoning of the subconscious mind is that if the thought passed through the belief system and the conscious mind without incident or any objections, then the belief system is proved accurate and well-adjusted for functioning within the current reality. The reasonable thing to do then is to strengthen the belief system, rooting beliefs more deeply, in order to promote similar coloring of thoughts in the future. If, on the other hand, the thought met with trouble—for example, if the movement of a hand guided by the thought caused a vase to fall to the floor and break—then the belief system will be reinforced negatively, causing such thoughts to appear more seldom in the future. You can see now the value of being able to criticize your own thoughts and beliefs.

Astral Sex Urges

I will now share some intimate details about the contents of my sub-conscious mind. I do this not for enjoyment, but to illustrate how severely addictions can cripple our astral explorations and get in the way of the things we want to do. I know this chapter will help many interdimensional travelers. Even if your addiction is not of the same nature as mine, surely there are similarities: something that all addictions have in common. I am convinced that there is a common cure for all addictions.

Wednesday, October 10, 2001
Astral Sex

I am reading William Buhlman's Adventures beyond the Body.[18] *He uses the following OBE technique: As you fall asleep, visualize being in a remote but familiar place. To try it, I pretend I am in my parent's living room, as it looked 14 years ago, when they used it as a bedroom. Before I fall asleep, I tell myself, "I want to have an OBE tonight," and, to my delight, another part of me replies, "Okay."*

I fall asleep and wake up an hour and a half later. My body is numb. I immediately recognize the state as perfect for OBE. I let my mind sink quickly into a relaxed state. I think, "OBE now!" and am surprised to see it work when I sit up in my bed and sense my physical body is still lying down. I do not roll out as I usually do, maybe because Buhlman says to sit up in his book, or maybe because the technique does not require rolling. The Buhlman technique is much easier than what I usually do, which is putting my body to sleep, letting my mind drift toward sleep, and hoping I will pop out before I fall asleep.

I float in the room for a few seconds. I can't see and I think I have to open my physical eyes in order to see. I open my physical eyes, but I only see the ceiling over my bed, where my body is. At the same time, the projected part of my awareness is by the bookshelf, although I can't see it. I close my eyes. I think, "Clarity now!" and my astral vision is working. Then I think, "I want to meet Richard!" (Richard is one of my spirit guides, and a very good one at that.) Nothing happens. In retrospect, I suspect that I was at too low an energy frequency to see him. My body awareness increases and I find myself in bed again.

I relax my mind again and sit up. I float out into the room and through the wall. A little old lady is inspecting a young tree (which is not there in physical reality) on the lawn outside. I fly past her and notice that the park outside is full of people. Many are having picnics. Some can see me as I fly over their heads. They turn their heads to look at me. Others can't see me. I have the feeling that some of these people should not see me flying, because then they might discover too abruptly that they are not living on Earth anymore. Is it just my imagination or are these people dead? If they are, they don't seem very upset about it. In fact, everyone seems to be having a wonderful time.

I think I am holding a good altitude, but suddenly I crash into a woman having a picnic. I think, "That must have hurt like hell!" My mind starts racing to come up with some way to apologize that will be acceptable to these people, but she does not even seem to have noticed the impact. Nor does she notice me.

I am enjoying this. After all, I am doing something that none of the other people can. It is getting to my head. I am fast and I am invisible. At some point, my rational mind goes to sleep and my primitive drives take over.

I fly over to some campers. I crash into their tent. This flying business is tricky. Then I notice a young woman leaving the campers. There is something special about her. Something about her intrigues me. I fly over and see she is disappointed and angry. She has been in an argument with one of the campers, who I sense is her previous boyfriend. By now, my primitive mind is in charge. There is no guilt or shame in what I do, because those parts of my subconscious mind are asleep. My sex drive takes over.

She has a great body. I squeeze her breast and it is softer than air. I say without hesitation, "I want to have sex with you. Now." She says no at first, but then she says, "Okay, but I have to go home and change first. Then we can go listen to the band and then we can have sex." I agree. She leaves for home. In retrospect, I hope she and the other people are just dream characters, because my moral beliefs make me think I am making a complete ass out of myself.

Darkness falls over the park. I float over to the building where a band plays. I float past the long queue of people waiting to get inside but am stopped by a doorman. He is an old friend from my youth, though still alive. He checks my arms for the club stamp. I try to create one with my mind, but it does not turn out anything like the club stamp. He says that since they will be closing in ten minutes, I can't enter without the stamp. I say, "Fine," and simply float through the wall to where the band plays. Sometimes it is good not to be solid. The band is divided onto two stages, with the audience in between. The setup is very cool. I wonder how they manage to prevent feedback in the microphones. After a while, I see the doorman and some other gorillas making their way through the people on the dance floor. They are coming for me. Not wanting to get thrown out, I decide it is best to leave through the wall.

I meet the woman outside. She has changed into an extremely short skirt. My god, she looks good! I tell her that they will close in five minutes, so we might as well skip the band. She agrees. We go to a secluded area in the park, which coincidentally has a bed next to a pool. We have sex. I am quite sure I can have a physical orgasm, but I do not want to, because my girlfriend is lying next to me in the physical bed. I figure it is better to move my physical body off the bed first. I move back to the body instantly. I try hard to move my body, but that does not work, since it is asleep. But then, effortlessly, I move off the bed. I think it is my body moving off the bed, but I am mistaken. I am not in my body. In all this confusion, my body wakes up and I am back in bed.

I relax my mind and sit up out of my body. I float down to the floor and stand up. I think, "Clarity now!" My vision is crystal clear. I have never seen this well in my whole life. First, it looks exactly like my room, but then things start to change. My bed is suddenly at the opposite wall. There is only a small window, instead of two large ones. I think, "Hey, this is not a bad way to arrange the furniture. There is a lot of open space." But then I notice that my computer and some other things are missing, so maybe it is not a winner after all. I am pulled back into my body. An hour and 30 minutes has passed since I first exited the body.

This projection left me in awe. The sexual climax was something out of another world. It was not merely two entities coming together. It was two entities sharing the same energy, melting together to form a bubble of ecstasy.

Back from the astral, my moral beliefs kick back in. Is this cheating? Guilt weighs heavily on me. When I was in the astral, guilt never crossed my little mind. It seems the part of my mind in charge of guilt and loyalty is offline while I am in the astral.

The astral woman could have been a separate astral entity or simply a creation of my imagination. I can't tell the difference. Is the mind able to create such an experience without the help of an external entity? I am amazed by it, but I am even more amazed at my uncontrollable urge to have that woman. I could not restrain myself. I was like a wolf that had picked up a blood trace, completely at the mercy of my primitive instincts.

It could be that I, in the physical, have the same strong urge to mate but am successful in suppressing it with the help of social and moral beliefs—the same beliefs that seem to have gone out the window the moment I exited my body.

Monday, November 12, 2001
OBE

I wake up in the middle of the night, feeling alert. I am angry because of something I have dreamed, but I do not remember what. There is something about my state that tells me I can have an OBE, so I roll inside my physical body and am thrown out. I fall to the floor. I move fast because I am angry, not knowing why. I can tell by my state that I will not be able to stay out more than a few seconds.

I float through the door, across the corridor, and through my neighbor's door. There is a red light filling her room. How odd. The room is not shaped as in waking reality. I am beginning to feel drawn to my physical body, so I quickly roll to get free. My sex drive takes over again (sigh). My neighbor has a friend in her room. I am preparing for sex when I am pulled back to my body.

Once again, my sexual urge took over. I am beginning to realize that this urge is a serious obstacle. Astral sex is good in all respects, but this is not about sex. This is about the ability to exercise self-control in the astral, or in any unknown realm for that matter. In order to travel freely, I *must* be in charge of every part of me. After all, I want to spend my time in the astral finding answers to what we are and what reality is, and in that regard, sexual urges are a nuisance.

Sunday, April 14, 2002
OBEs as Tests

I wake up in the morning after a night of partying. I mean to drift back to sleep, but my body goes numb and my awareness shifts. After a few seconds, I am able to roll out of my body. I have no sight, so I tune into the imagination in my heart chakra. I can hear my girlfriend tapping her keyboard under the bed via my physical ears. I float down behind her. (In retrospect, it is silly that I still think the concept of space applies out of body.) Commotion pulls me back into my body. I roll out three times.

Suddenly, I can see. I am in a small room. A white and a black woman are lying on their sides on the floor, propping up their heads with their hands. They are naked; how nice. I get the impression that they have been waiting for me. My overactive sex drive makes me float over to them and have sex with them. The white girl disappears, so I continue to have sex with the black girl. She smiles joyfully as we get intimate.

As I am pulled back into the body, I realize that this is a test. It is an exercise in self-control, set up by my guides. The girls are bait. The purpose of this test is obvious: I must gain control over my sex drive before I am allowed to venture further into the astral. It is clear that I can't travel where I want until I can control my drives. In the future, whenever I feel the sex drive taking over, I will tell myself that I can have sex later, but not now. As I realize this is a test, I ask my guides to give me another chance to go out of body, but I fail to get back in the right state.

The tests during OBEs mirror my weaknesses in the physical world. It may be easier to deal with the problems in the astral because they are much more obvious there, and guides help me set up effective tests and learning aids.

Something is effectively preventing me from venturing farther into the astral. I suspect that I am surrounded by astral guides who know more about my sexual urges than I do. They encourage my subconscious to set up situations where I am able to experience these urges as purely as possible, without any moral restraints. The purpose is clear: to understand how the urges work and how they affect my physical and astral lives. I have been given a great opportunity for personal growth.

The part of the astral into which I have ventured is a laboratory where any behavior is acceptable and the consequences are mild. Similarly, physical reality is a laboratory where we can learn more about ourselves. It is a game stage where we try out new experiences. Consequences are mild because physical life is short. In the deeper astral however, in the domains of our true nature, actions really matter. There you need superb control over your mind because bad behavior may have grave consequences.

I start to invent ways to manipulate my mind in order to prevent my sexual urges from being triggered. After some trial and error, I find that postponing the urge works best. Typically, as soon as I exit my body, I tell myself, "I do not need to have sex right now because there are plenty of opportunities to have sex later, after I have finished what I set out to do."

Exercise: Playing with Fire

1. Close your eyes.
2. Relax your mind.
3. Consult the list of addictions you compiled in the exercise "Identifying Addictions." For each addiction do this:
   a. Visualize yourself surrounded by people or objects (concrete or abstract) that match the preference of your addictions.
   b. Visualize the objects so intensely and in such detail that they normally would trigger the urge of the addiction. In my case, since I am addicted to sex, I would visualize persons of the opposite sex coming on to me, but this of course may not be the preference of your addiction.
   c. Tell yourself: "I have more important things to do. I do not need to give in to my urge right now. I can do it as much as I want *later*. I will be just as fine, I will have just as much fun, if I choose *not* to do it right now."
4. Do you feel you have an upper hand on your addictions now? Be proud of yourself for your level of self-control.
5. Remember what you did in this exercise. If you feel your addictions taking over anytime in the astral, simply execute step c to reinforce your self-control.

However, postponement only provides temporary relief. What I need is a permanent solution that puts me back in the driver's seat of my astral travels. In my efforts to find a permanent solution, I affirm to myself that "I don't need astral sex." Then another part of me replies, "Yes, you do need it." A third part of me finds out that I have been lying to myself and a fourth part of me starts laughing hysterically.

Obviously, I do need sex, but why? My urge in the astral goes well beyond a reasonable instinct to further my genes and preserve the species. There must be something else lurking in my subconscious.

Causes of Addiction

Tuesday, May 21, 2002
An OBE from a Dream

During the day, I hold two crystals in my hands. As I inhale, I draw energy from the crystals into my arms. Sometimes, I push the energy all the way out through my feet.

As I drift off to sleep later that day, I visualize I am in a forest. I touch trees and leaves. This is from Buhlman's OBE technique. Simultaneously, I turn my eyes and attention to the area between my eyes. I repeat, "I will OBE tonight," over and over. It is difficult to do all three things at the same time, but not impossible. The visualization falls apart all the time. Each time I resume visualization, I find myself in a different forest.

One time I find myself in the place of home, where I am totally content. It may be a place in another reality or in another life, perhaps on another planet. There is a green bush with great energy. The surroundings shine with fulfillment and joyful energy. My subconscious violently pulls me back after a few seconds, as if I am not meant to see the place of home. Perhaps my subconscious is afraid that the memories of that place will empower me, the soul.

Three hours later, at 5 A.M., I dream I am in a group of people driving a jeep through

209

a desert-like area. We are hiding from Lucifer. We do not want him to judge us, because we know that if he did, we would all go to Hell. We hide behind a hill. We see a mother with twin daughters. The daughters drive their feet into the ground as if they were drilling for oil. They start breathing heavily. Their mother sighs; she does not believe in what they are doing. They insist that breathing water is the best way to contact good spirits. Somehow, their act of breathing pumps water up into their feet and out through their mouths. In retrospect, I suspect the "water" is more a kind of water-like energy. I think this part of the dream is meant to teach me some things about energy control by means of breathing.

We drive off. Suddenly, Lucifer spots us. We are terrified as the Earth sucks us into its bosom. We find ourselves escorted by heavy guards through a light green subterranean corridor. We are going to the place of judgment. The corridor is warm and comfortable. I think, "Well, at least it is warm down here." Then I think, "Hey, I don't believe in the Devil!" This breaks the dream, as if it can't survive without my beliefs. The corridor breaks into pieces and I fall through the floor.

I find myself in a void. I have that tingling sensation of freedom and adventure I always get during an OBE. I find myself floating over my bed in an astral duplicate of my old bedroom. My mind must assume out of habit that I am still in Sweden, because in physical reality I am in Vancouver. I float down to the floor. I am blind. I command, "Clarity now!" a few times. I can see with extraordinary clarity. I run my hand along the side of the bed. It feels as real as in physical reality. I think of what I want to do. My sexual drive takes over. (In retrospect, I regret not having stated a clear goal for this travel.) I decide to go upstairs into some women's room and watch them sleep. After all this training, I still believe I am in physical reality, when I am really in an astral arena of my own mind's creation.

I float through the door. There is more resistance than usual, but I push through the wood. I expect to enter the corridor but end up in an old dusty emergency staircase instead. I feel I have been in that staircase before, perhaps in another OBE or dream. I float up and enter the second floor corridor. I turn right and enter a room. People are resting in sleeping bags on the floor. They greet me as I enter the room. A copy of me is already there. My brother massages that copy's feet, which is odd. He would never touch me and even more unlikely give me pleasure. Nobody reacts to the fact that there are two of me in the room. I sit down next to the other copy of me.

I get bored fast. My sex drive takes over again. I spot a familiar girl in the room, someone I knew about 12 years ago. She was notorious for her large breasts. I float over, grab her right breast, and kiss her. Everyone in the room is surprised and stares. She has a surprised look on her face. I can sense that she is offended. I grab her left breast and kiss her. Same *reaction. This breast is smaller, so I decide to return to the previous breast. I am pulled back to my physical body. I wake up in Vancouver. I lost to my sex drive again. Damn it.*

I went through the door with the intent of looking at women sleeping in their beds. This is an old teenage fantasy. Unlived childhood fantasies seem to linger in the subconscious, in the shape of compulsive addictions. How do I resolve them? By regression. I should look into childhood fantasies and maybe live out a few. Then I will gain conscious control over them. They are only dangerous when they are hidden.

In an effort to understand my seemingly unreasonable emotions and addictions, I decide to venture into my childhood. As if by accident, I happen upon a Rapid Eye Technique designed to release old memories, which I perform after some small adjustments (see the next exercise).

Exercise: Rapid Eye Technique

1. Before doing this exercise, make sure you do not have any appointments later in the day, since information (including suppressed painful memories) will be flowing into your awareness from your subconscious. You should also arrange for a close friend to give you emotional support when the memories surface. All your friend has to do is listen, preferably nonjudgmentally, to your story. The purpose of having your suppressed memories surface is to process them and release the pain tied into them. Sometimes just talking about them helps immensely.

2. Mentally detach from your current life situation. Your current situation is highly connected to your addictions, because to some extent, your addictions have led you to where you are today. It is easier to work with addictions when you are away from their playground.

3. Record the affirmation: "You are free from all feelings of disgust, dishonor, shame, guilt, fear, and pain. You are free from all feelings of abandonment, being unloved, oppression, sadness, and grief. You are free from all feelings of not worthy, not good enough, not having enough. You are free from all feelings of escaping, forgetting, suppressing, and denial." If you can record it on a computer, then you can loop it when you play it back. Otherwise, record the affirmation about five times in a sequence.

4. Get a one-foot stick.

5. Turn your eyes slightly upward to a spot between your eyebrows.

6. Blink your eyes very rapidly.

7. Wave the stick in front of your eyes, very fast. Try to follow the end of the stick with your eyes, but keep blinking. This step is designed to imitate the rapid eye movements of a sleeping person. It opens a door to your subconscious, making it easier to deprogram. Wave the stick first from side to side, then up and down and any other way you feel has an effect on the veil to your subconscious.

8. While following the waving stick with your eyes and blinking, listen to the recorded affirmation in the background. You do not have to listen actively. Your subconscious will get the message even if your conscious does not pick it up.

9. In the rapid eye state, your subconscious accepts the affirmations without question. Most of us have beliefs telling us we are shameful, but as the affirmation "You are free from all feelings of shame" is accepted by your subconscious, that belief is no longer valid. The belief was formed a long time ago from situations that "prove" you should be ashamed.

   Because the memories are painful, they are stored in a suppressed state in your subconscious. These painful memories would interfere with your daily life, so the belief holds the experience they represent, minus the pain. As the belief conflicts with the affirmation, the belief is put into question. From the conflict, the subconscious has a need to remold the belief. The belief has been proven incorrect; in order to make it more correct, the old painful memories must be brought to the surface and once more be processed, to provide a base of experience for the improved belief.

   The good news is, as the memories surface, you have a chance to consciously process them, thereby deciding how the belief will be reformed. You can, for example, view the memories from a positive point of view, encouraging the forming of the belief "I am shameless."

10. Starting a few hours later, these painful memories may continue to surface for days. Do not attempt to deny or ignore them. Experience them, describe them to a friend, or write them down in your journal.

11. When you are done describing the memories, release their importance. They have been suppressed because they are important to you. Now that you have worked through them, you have partaken of their purpose, and so they have outlived their importance. In the end, keep only the memories of good times and the laughter.

After the exercise, I often feel angry, but without apparent cause. Everything annoys me. Later that night, the dam holding all my suppressed emotions crumbles. I am overcome with sadness, pain, and lots of self-pity. I cry my eyes out. Luckily, Barb is there to support me. With her help, I manage to view the emotional discharge as a cleansing rather than a breakdown. The memories my subconscious has fought so hard to suppress (in its attempt to protect me from their negative effect) are now in the open, easily accessible. They flood into my awareness.

At first, they make me terribly depressed, but after telling Barb about their every little detail, it feels like I have finally processed them, and I am greatly relieved. A weight has been lifted off my shoulders, a weight that my subconscious had decided I must carry because it deemed I was incapable of handling the memories. I feel freer, less controlled by my subconscious. I also feel more energized, because the energy used to suppress the "harmful" memories is now freed up and at my disposal.

The next day, propelled by the momentum of memory release, I write down everything I remember from my birth to present date. Even though I can only remember about five percent of my life, I manage to see a pattern in certain repeating situations and how I react to those situations.

Exercise: Life Review

When you feel the memories being released by using the rapid eye technique, write down everything that you remember from this lifetime.

I find in my life a repeating pattern of situations in which I attempt to get attention from other people, mainly of the opposite sex. My need to be noticed and, above all, liked and accepted is stronger than anything. During my teens, I felt disliked by people and devised ways to get into situations that presented more opportunities for being liked.

My subconscious had, little by little, increased my desire for sex. It figured that with a more powerful sex drive, I would be more likely to seek such situations. An act of sex would be undeniable proof that I was liked (at least by my partner) and it was this proof that my subconscious desired. My need to be liked would then be fulfilled. The transformation from a young boy who felt people around him did not like him enough to an astral sex maniac took place in the subconscious, and so subtle was the change that it had become a self-created second nature.

Each time my sex drive was inflated, another part of me reinforced my moral and social beliefs; after all, I had to function in society in spite of my growing sex urges. This battle between moral beliefs and primitive drives was fairly balanced until one warm spring day when I left my body. I brought the sex urge into the astral while, for some reason, which I suspect has to do with the mechanics of astral projection, leaving my moral beliefs behind. My need for sex became apparent. The balance between the sex drive and the holding-back moral beliefs was upset. The bubble burst and the subconscious's bluff, the game of desire and manipulation, was called.

Healing Addictions

Sunday, June 2, 2002
Causes of Sex Addiction

I asked for help on my sexual urges in the astral a week ago, and the help just arrived in the form of an insight. As I look back on my childhood, it suddenly dawns on me: Sex has become a way of getting love, approval, and respect—the very things I felt I lacked in my childhood.

Think about it—it is only logical that the person who has sex with me feels love, approval, and respect for me. The need for these things is so strong that, when they are not met, I go after them aggressively. I do this by multiplying my sexual urges until I am incapable of resisting them. They take over. I am defenseless against the sexual urges. All of this happens subconsciously. I will never be able to satisfy these needs until I realize I already am loved, approved, and respected. Until then, my sexual urges will remain uncontrollable in the astral.

The Motives of Addiction

Now I know why I repeatedly end up in astral situations and environments containing sex: My subconscious is bent on getting sex as a

215

means to feeling liked and appreciated. I do not fully understand why the subconscious would go to that length just to be liked, but I do know that all humans have the need to be liked. We need to feel liked in order to bloom as individuals. It is a fundamental human need.

Wednesday, June 12, 2002
Visualizing a Break-In

I dream I am in my parents' house. I am some sort of agent in an undercover operation. My colleagues are with me. We are spying on a neighbor. We suspect he is involved in organized crime. We get in our car, in case we have to tail them. The driver is about to park on the street. I know the neighbor will discover us if we park there, but the driver thinks it is safe. We argue for some time. I end the argument with "You will not park here."

We continue down the street. We park in somebody's driveway. We think the people who live in the house are on vacation. The suspects are driving our way, so we run into the garage to hide. Used packaging material is scattered across the floor. We sneak into the house. We are moving up a stairway when we hear someone in the house. Barb makes some noise in the physical and I wake up.

I visualize being back in the dream house. During my childhood, I always wondered what that house looked like from the inside. It was the most luxurious house in the neighborhood and I assumed rich people lived there. I sneak up the stairway. I am alone now; my fellow agents are gone. The visualization is extremely real. I am not the least connected to my physical body. I touch things and the texture is real. I am sneaking around in someone's house and it is exciting. I reach the end of the stairway. I want to explore all the rooms. I start in the living room. I look at a wall. I can see and touch the wallpaper. I make the wall wobble like liquid. It is a very cool effect.

I am about to enter a room. I think of going right through the door, but then I realize that I might end up anywhere my mind takes me (sometimes I end up in weird places after moving through walls or floors). I decide to open the door instead. I enter the room. It belongs to a teenager. There is a lot of schoolwork and other projects on the desk. There is also a very old computer. A label on it says "C-kit" or something similar. Lots of red silk nightgowns hang on a wall. I realize a girl lives in the room. I had assumed that a boy lived there, because of the computer and other technical stuff on the desk. I am positively surprised.

I leave the room and see an older woman in another room. She must be the mother in the house. She is wearing tight white pants and a reddish blouse. Her legs are rather fat and her breasts are large. Her body is not very attractive, but there is something about the energy she puts out. I can tell she is a very good-hearted person. She enters the living room and somehow senses me. She asks me something like, "What it is like to be discarnate?" I reply something I can't remember. Then she asks if I had ever killed anyone when I was discarnate. I say, "None that I know of." Then I try to scare her by roaring and charging. I am only joking and her giggle tells me she can sense that. I kiss her.

I want to have sex with this woman. I think about it for a while. Is this yet another urge caused by my sex addiction? I do not think so, because she is very different from all the other "temptations" I have encountered. I am attracted to her personality, not her body. Shortly thereafter, the visualization ends.

I wanted to have sex with her, but I did not feel I had to. This must mean I am overcoming my sex addiction. The reason I could explore the house as freely as I did means that I am allowing myself to explore more. The risk of getting caught up in sex scenes is lower, which gives me better opportunities to explore. Additionally, the fact that her body was not sexy means that my mind does no longer feel it is necessary to create sexy women for me. This gives me a more accurate perception of the things I run into in the astral.

Being liked, appreciated, and accepted are names for *being loved.* Ironically, during all those years I was looking for sex, I was really looking for love. In fact, all addictions are just tools invented by the subconscious to attract love from other beings. A young student who can't behave in class is addicted to misbehaving or addicted to always getting into trouble with his peers and teachers. This student is subconsciously setting up these situations because he wants attention, and there is no more effective way of getting attention than causing trouble in class or pestering his classmates and teachers. The student thinks that he can't get love unless he has attention. In his subconscious, attention is nothing other than love, and that is what all people crave. There is nothing wrong with a troublemaker, except a perceived lack of love.

Addiction is not caused by a chemical imbalance, but an emotional imbalance. An emotional imbalance may cause a chemical balance, not the other way around. The chemical imbalance, in turn, gives rise to cravings. In other words, all addicts, from the caffeine gulper to the heroin pincushion, have in common an unsatisfied need for love. Satisfy their need for love and their addiction will dissolve.

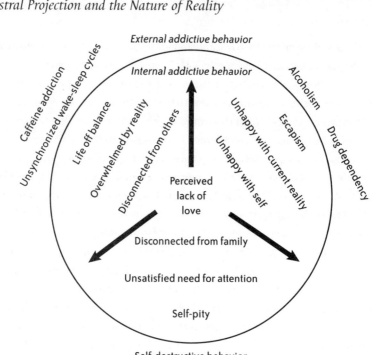

Figure 7. The inner cause of addiction.

Universal Love

Coincidentally, during an astral exploration, I sensed without a doubt that there is a living consciousness I can only describe as (because of the inadequacy of human language) the universe. It is built up by all individual consciousness in the universe, although not limited to the *physical* universe. What's more, during this astral exploration, I was shown that the universe loves each and every one of us in abundance and takes good care of us. I may sound like I have been brainwashed by institutionalized religion, but this is not the case. I know the universe loves us because I have seen it, not because of what someone else has written, and I encourage you to see the same.

There is no need to feel lonely, because none of us is ever alone. In fact, when you come to understand the universe, as I am sure you will during your astral projections, it is impossible to feel lonesome. Likewise, there is no need to feel unloved. The way things are arranged, all beings in the universe love you, whether they know it or not. If we all did not love each other, the universe would fall apart and crumble into nothingness. The universe lives and breathes by the intention to create, and the only reason we create anything is that we love what we have created and will create.

Ponder this: Currently, humanity has the weapons to blow up the Earth at least 20 times over. But even though the wars are evidence that we do not like each other, Earth remains intact and the human race survives. Why have we not blown ourselves to smithereens yet? With a few exceptions, we do not wish to destroy one another. Why not? Are we afraid of reprisals? No, we refrain because we love one another. If we did not love one another, we would have wiped out ourselves a long time ago.

That person who hurt you yesterday did it because he was lost in his own ignorance, but that does not change the fact that he loves you. Likewise, you too love all other beings in the universe, even if you do not acknowledge it. Some people feel that certain beings are not worthy of love and, although it is completely okay to feel this way, it does not change the fact that love is there. If you look deep enough, you will find that you have love even for your worst enemies.

So, if there is so much love in the universe, why do we feel so unloved and lonely? Well, before we can feel loved, we have to *realize* that we are loved. As an analogy, we could stare at a beautiful painting all day, but what good would that do if our eyes are closed? By realizing that we are already loved (by the whole universe), we immediately satisfy our fundamental need for love and being liked. The subconscious will then not have any need to invent any sort of addiction, since the purpose of addiction is to attract love. We then become free of addiction, which in turn means that we can travel through the astral unhindered by urges.

Exercise: Lovely Guidance

1. Close your eyes.
2. Relax your body and mind.
3. In a crystal clear thought, not necessarily directed to anyone in particular, ask for an experience that will help you discover to what extent you are loved by everything and everyone in the universe.
4. This experience might take up to a week to manifest, so don't hold your breath.

The reality of universal love also solves personal traumas. At one point or another in our lives, we all feel shocked, hurt, or violated. The downside of being a person is that we take things personally. We are quick to assume the role of the victim. We are so immersed in our role in events that we can't see the big picture, the cause and effect on a universal level.

Every painful thing that has ever happened to you was done out of love for your growth. The goal of the growth is to realize that you are loved by everything in the universe. Pain has been inflicted on you by those who love you, because they love you. Strangers inflict pain, too, because they love you. In this light, past hurts are not hurts, but loves. Past emotional damage is not damage, but healing. Likewise, what you did in the past toward others, intentionally or not, you did out of love for them—a love living in such a hidden part of you that you may not have been aware of it at the time. You may think you hurt someone, but what really happened was that that someone attracted the experience of hurt because he needed it in order to grow. Because of your love for that person and her growth, you supplied the hurt.

Therefore, do not feel guilty or ashamed for anything you have done or feel hurt by other people. Why would you feel bad for growing? This is the implication of universal love. If you accept this love, all your past traumas and hurts will be healed. (I will be passing the donation bin around now.) Then you can drop your old emotional baggage, because it no longer serves a purpose. It did serve a purpose at one time, and that purpose was for you to realize that the whole universe loves you.

Road Signs to Growth

As mentioned, the best way to prevent yourself from going astray in the astral is by solving your addictions. Ironically, the "going astray" itself is trying to assist you in doing just this, that is, solving your addictions. It shows exactly what your addiction is so that you can solve it. Your waking reality is trying to show you the same thing but, as mentioned before, things manifest faster in the astral than in the physical. Cause and effect are often so far apart in the physical that it is very difficult to see what causes what and why. But luckily, thanks to your skill in astral projection, you now have the ability to identify the nature of your addiction by letting your addictions play out in the astral.

Saturday, June 22, 2002
Solution

I take two kava-kavas for relaxation (this is the first time I take kava) and put some relaxing lotion on my wrists before I fall asleep at 11:30 P.M. Barb puts quartz crystals around the bed. I dream that some guy and I are lost in a dry forest area. Perhaps we are hiding from someone who is chasing us. We find a bird's nest. As we are starving, I decide to pick two eggs from the nest. The other guy thinks it is a shame to take the lives of two birds. I think so, too, but I have to in order to survive.

Later in the dream, I am sitting by a railroad crossing with a group of people. We are doing something important, but I can't remember what. Perhaps we are shooting a movie, because the actor Dan Aykroyd is there. Or perhaps we are just directing cars safely across the railroad. There are a lot of cars. Have they come to get a glimpse of the shoot?

Suddenly, an electrical storm moves in. Dark clouds form above our heads. We see a small jolt of blue lightning in the clouds. Then it explodes and shoots down onto the railroad track as a big lightning flash. I can tell that this is no ordinary thunderstorm. The flashes behave almost intelligently. We decide we have to get out of there fast. Someone shouts, "We have to leave, now!" I am just about to leave, but then I think that it would be interesting to stay and see what happens. I know somewhere in the back of my mind that this is just a dream.

A second blue streak forms in the clouds. It shoots down right next to me! There is a big crackling sound as it demolishes the railroad car in which I am sitting. The lightning bolt divides into branches and one hits me. I feel its blue energy penetrating my chest. Everything pauses. Time slows down. I get flashbacks. I am in my mother's womb. I see a baby's face and its black eyes. Is this my twin? Did my parents have twins and never told me? Or is the face I am looking at mine? Am I dying? I know I am in a dream, but can you die in a dream? I don't want to die, so I decide to pull back to my dream avatar, the one lying motionless by the railroad track. The flashbacks stop.

The dream turns into an astral projection. I get entangled in sex games. I enjoy the freedom of creating these sex situations. Then a spirit guide moves in and tells me to stop the sex pleasures because he has to talk to me. In spite of this, I continue for a bit. After a while, I realize I do not need the sex. I realize that I would benefit more from exploration. I stop the sex games. I am proud of having that sort of control over my thoughts.

I find myself in the garden of an orphanage. There are apple trees and a green lawn. I see many happy children living in the orphanage. The guide is next to me. I ask him, "If you are a spirit guide, what is my next step in life? What should I do next?" He laughs and says, "Your life is what you make it. You create it as you go along. There is no set next step."

I am blown away by this realization. Life is not preplanned! I feel free, relieved from the concepts of destiny and fate. We talk for a while. Then I move down the street. At the corner, two girls from the orphanage are playing UNO, the card game. I join. I have to pick up a lot of cards and realize I can't win. Without a chance to win, there's little reason to stay, so I bid them farewell and move down the second street.

This street has a long line of shops. I enter one shop, which I feel I have been in before, perhaps in a dream. I find the computer game section and search for games I might like. There is a buccaneer game titled "1720." As I float around in the store, a few people look at me and ask me if I am okay. I know that because I am a visitor to their realm, I look pale and a bit transparent to them. I tell them I am fine. At one occasion, I make an "Oooooo-ooo-oooooo" sound, like a spooky ghost, and to my surprise, someone else replies with another "ooooo-oooo!" I think the ooooo-oooo must be coming from the physical reality around my body. (Later, after waking up and asking Barb, she tells me there were no sounds from my physical body or hers.)

I find a big red paper package containing the Ejay hip hop kit for 390 Swedish crowns, which apparently has everything you need from composing music to burning CDs and printing labels. I am familiar with Ejay but have not seen such a complete kit in physical reality. I look over my shoulder to make sure no store employee is around and then I open it. It contains lots of paper CD cases. They have the text "Lice MT" printed on them. That must be the brand name.

As I am coming out of the projection, I have a vision of Barb's car being towed away by the police. The car has animal droppings in the front passenger seat. Then I'm fully awake in my bed. The projection lasted more than an hour.

Note added August 1, 2003: April, ten months later and three states away, and Barb's car stalls in Tucson. Some Oro Valley police officers are nice enough to stop and try to help her (kudos to the cops in Tucson). When they investigate the engine, they find a little mouse nest built on top of the battery (we knew there were mice in the car, but we thought we had evicted them all) and accompanying mouse droppings in the front passenger seat. After the cops give up and leave, we tow the car to the nearest auto shop.

Further Healing

To recap, there are two reasons the mind creates objects of addiction (for example, a sex object) in the astral: 1. The addiction object gives the mind temporary satisfaction, and 2. The object alerts you to the addiction so that you may solve it (if you choose to). The mind wants to be free of addiction.

This and the previous chapters demonstrate the importance of working toward an open and free mind. The perception of a lack of love creates trauma. The trauma may be something quick like a car accident, or it may be a complicated family issue remaining unsolved for several years. Naturally, if your father smacks you on the head every weekend, then you will think that he does not love you. The perceived lack of love creates a trauma. In spite of the abuse, your father may love you very much, but this does not matter: It is what we *perceive* that causes trauma, however close or far that may be from what actually happens.

Traumatic memories are, for the sake of your sanity, hidden in your subconscious. That is why it is so tricky to find the cause of addictions. In time, the subconscious forms an addiction from the traumatic memories. The addiction is specifically designed to get back the love you feel you lost during the trauma. When you realize you already have that love, the addiction may dissolve.

However, in severe cases, the addiction may persist, although diminished, for addictions are as hardheaded as humans are. As long as the memories of trauma remain in place, there will be a fire to keep the addiction going. Therefore, memories of traumas represent obstacles. These create limits to our astral travels and our lives; that is, until we consciously take charge of the healing process and bring the memories to light.

In order to heal an addiction, we need to explore the memories of a trauma and understand how they relate to our current addiction. This may take a great amount of effort but is well worth it. After we have found the cause, the addiction will probably disappear because the moment we understand the addiction it loses its purpose, which is to alert us to the presence of trauma, just like understanding the causes of wars brings peace. The addiction only has power over us as long as it is in the subconscious. Once we consciously observe the addiction and its cause, it ceases to function.

When we solve an addiction, we have not only solved an inconvenience but also grown substantially. Finding and solving our addictions is the fastest way to accelerated learning and spiritual growth. Sometimes, solving an addiction is even essential to continuing life. Addictions may even be essential for the survival of the human species. As long as we deny that we as a species have issues to resolve, we will continue to destroy the planet that sustains us, thereby digging our own graves.

As I mentioned at the outset of this discussion, I do not include these chapters merely for enjoyment. This sort of self-healing is of immense importance to all of us. Addictions play a big role not only in the astral, but also for our whole personal growth. They are like alarms, shouting: "Hey, we have a problem here that needs fixing ASAP!" If addictions were never formed, we would never suspect that we carry traumatic scars that need healing. Of course, the same effect can be achieved by denying the existence of the addictions and pretending that all is well.

A mind can't evolve as long as it denies the existence of painful memories. We can't evolve spiritually unless we dare to face every part of ourselves. In the dark side of our nature as human beings, where pain and sorrow hide, in the very place we dread to look, lies the key to bliss and beauty. When we dare to face that dark side and bring it into light, we are ready for a better life. But to take that first step—to confront the very things that are hidden *because* they are too painful to confront—is among the most difficult things a person can do. It is the ultimate test of will.

Ultimately, the choice comes down to living to avoid the pain or living to resolve the pain. We can choose our attitude. If we seek to avoid pain, we may have good lives, but we will not be able to grow. We would be living in denial, pretending that the traumatic memories are not there, and we would accomplish nothing in terms of spiritual growth. In the second case, can you imagine living without pain from the past, without sorrow in the now, and without worry for the future? Think of it this way: When you have conquered your fears and pains, the fears and pains will be no more. You will be free at last.

Exercise: An Invitation to Your Subconscious

1. Tonight, as you lie in bed, invite the memories of old pains to surface. Anything you fear to experience again, anything you feel bad about having done, and anything you wish would never happen again.

2. When the painful memories surface, experience them. Let them play out. Do not suppress them. Do not attempt to keep them back.

3. Experience only. Be an observer. Do not interfere as they play out. Do not try to figure out why they are still with you, how badly you performed, what you should have done instead, or how you are going to prevent similar situations from occurring in the future.

4. When they have played out, which may take hours, sit back and enjoy the peace. You did well.

5. Try to intuit what the memories just played out were about. What are they trying to tell you? They are still in your subconscious for a reason. They are there to tell you something about yourself.

6. What they are trying to tell you does not necessarily have to be anything bad. In fact, the nature of these memories is that they seek to point out good things rather than bad. They only reference bad things to get your attention.

7. Do not overuse your analytical mind, as it has no idea why the subconscious acts the way it does. Instead, use your intuition.

8. Intuitively feel how the memories relate to your list of addictions. Is there any addiction that is designed to prevent acts such as those committed by you or someone else in the memories? If so, those memories may be the cause of that addiction.

9. Understanding what the old pains are about may take several weeks. Do this exercise as often as you can handle it without getting depressed. Each time you perform this exercise, you understand a little bit better what goes on inside you; each time you do it, you become a little freer and feel a bit better.

There is no question that spiritual evolution is the most rewarding pursuit in life. The evolution of the mind should be our number one priority. All the prophets have said it, and the established religions are supposedly created solely for that purpose. But you do not need religions or gurus when you have addictions, for addictions are teachers in themselves. Believe it or not, your addictions are there to help you. They are steppingstones, pinpointing exactly what your next step should be. Without their help, you would not have experienced the spiritual growth the previous exercise above can help you achieve.

The next thing you should do, as a gesture of tying loose ends together, is to get at whatever caused the trauma in the first place. If a lack of love created the trauma, then realize that you are already loved by all consciousness and that you need not seek to be loved. If the addiction was created because your mean big brother stole candy from you when you were young, then for God's sake, go get lots of candy just for yourself.

Clarity Now!

If you happen to project into an astral area in which you can't see (i.e., no visual input), you can use commands like *"Clarity Now!"* or *"Clearer, clearer, clearer!"* Visual input will commence immediately. It will seem like your eyes suddenly start working after a time of blindness. Suddenly, you are able to see what lies around you.

Exercise: "Clarity Now!"

1. Project into the astral using one of the techniques described in the previous Circle.
2. If you already have visual input, go somewhere where you have none. Floating down through a floor or a wall sometimes causes me to lose vision.
3. If you find you have no visual input, command *Clarity Now!*
4. After your command, you should have plenty of visual input. If not, command *Clearer . . . clearer . . . clearer!*

Your Creative Powers

If you project into an already existing astral world, that world is what you will see. But if you project into an astral void, before you command clarity, there is nothing to see. That is what gives the impression of blindness. When you have no visual input, it is safe to assume there are no objects of any kind to see.

Your command for clarity then causes a world to spring into existence out of nothingness. The command *Clarity Now!* is not a command for your astral eyes to clear up, although it was originally designed for that purpose. Instead, the command is a direct order to your subconscious to inform your conscious mind of your surroundings. Eager to comply with that command, the subconscious reaches out and senses nothing, because, after all, you are in a void. Confused by this situation, the subconscious tries to make sense of what surrounds you. For us physical beings, the concept of *void* is inherently difficult to grasp. We are so used to having objects around us to look at and touch at all times, we do not know what to do with ourselves when we find they are not there.

The subconscious thinks to itself: "I know I exited the body and all that, but this is still mighty strange. I can't understand where I am. Hey, my last whereabouts was my bedroom, so maybe I am still there?" That brief thought is all it takes to actually create an astral world that resembles your bedroom down to the tiniest detail. The subconscious runs through all its memories of your bedroom, in order to decide whether you really are there. It tries to compare the memories' expectations of what your room looks like to your actual surroundings.

Ironically, in doing so, the subconscious also creates an astral counterpart of everything in the bedroom. This process only takes a few milliseconds. Suddenly, you can see your bedroom, but only because you just created it out of nothingness, not because your astral eyes started working. There was never anything wrong with your eyes.

Wednesday, March 21, 2001
An Attempt to Verify an OBE

I go to bed at 3 A.M. The alarm clock wakes me up at 7:15 A.M. I relax for 30 minutes or so until my body is asleep. My mind drifts toward sleep. When I am close to sleep, I attempt an out-of-body experience and succeed. I pop in and out of my body about ten times. The attraction to my body is so strong that I can only stay out ten seconds at any time.

Everything looks just like it does in waking reality, except everything is vibrating slightly. The colors are sharper and the textures of the furniture are more intense than in waking reality, but that is to be expected since I am not using my dull physical senses.

I have prepared a little test that will verify that I am really floating outside my physical body in physical space. I have placed an unread brochure on my desk, with the text facing the wall. If I can read the text while out of body, I will be convinced that the OBE is real. (Note: This took place back in the "old days," when I still believed the physical was the only true reality.) I float to my desk.

When I get to the brochure, it has fallen over, and I can't read the text. I figure someone passing by must have blown the brochure off the desk. I am angry that such a simple event has ruined the experiment. My efforts to go out of body seem to have been wasted. (After I wake up, I check on the brochure. The brochure is standing up, as I left it. Apparently, I had not been OBEing in my room. Either I had been OBEing in a dreamlike astral duplicate of my room, where my mind had made the brochure fall over, or I had dreamed the whole thing. It did not feel like a dream, though.)

In one "outing," I float downstairs into the basement. A neighbor is doing laundry. The only problem is that in waking reality, there is no basement in the house. In another episode, I float through the ceiling to the upstairs neighbor's room. In a couple of others, I turn around and look at my body. I see my body lying in bed, rolled up into fetal position. In waking reality, I know the body is stretched out on its back, because that is the body position I most commonly use before going out of body.

When we realize that by wanting to see a place in the astral, we create a *replica* of that place instead of moving there, we gain control over our minds and consequently over our astral travels. By consciously understanding the process of creation in the astral, the subconscious realizes that what it is doing (creating replicas) is not what we want. Walking around in a world of your own creation can be nice, but in most instances, it only diverts us from what we want to do. The subconscious then changes its way of functioning. Consequently, *Clarity Now!* stops working. After that happens, astral replicas will not trick us into mistaking them for the real places (if there are such things as real places).

The way the subconscious changes its performance also affects our physical lives, even though most people do not command *Clarity Now!* in the physical. We are then able to see things we could not before see. The physical is very similar to an astral world in many ways. We create our surroundings with the help of the subconscious mind in both the physical and the astral. When we change the way we create in the astral, we change the way we create in the physical. If we manage to suspend the act of creation in the physical, if only for a few seconds, we allow other things to appear in its place, things we know in modern society as paranormal effects.

Astral Senses

You might wonder why eyes, being physical senses, work in a non-physical environment such as the astral. Visual input can be provided by a plethora of senses, among them our physical eyes and what we call imagination, for lack of a better word. Apart from fabricating objects, imagination is capable of seeing things the physical eyes can't and making the visual input come to life. The physical eyes, on the other hand, are crude equipment, supplying us with only raw visual information. We have to use our imagination to fill out the missing information. When we interact with the astral, we fully engage the visual mechanism in the imagination because we did not bring our physical eyes.

All other physical senses can be replaced by imagination. For example, a previously sighted blind person still sees pictures of objects and emotions in his mind. A previously healthy disabled person still experiences the feeling of walking around in his mind. A colorblind person still senses the difference between colors.

The result is that when we project away from our physical senses, as we do in the astral, the sensory input provided by the imagination becomes so intense and full that we are amazed by what we experience. In my astral projection journal, I often describe the texture of an astral object as being *extremely real*. What I mean by this is that the texture, as touched by my imagination, feels so intense that it easily supersedes anything my physical tactile senses can provide me.

This seems to be true not only for touch, but also for the rest of the senses. I remember eating astral banana bread a few months ago. Although it may not have filled my physical belly (it is the ultimate weight-loss diet), its perfect flavor, moisture, and texture were better than could have been experienced in any physical restaurant.

Still, taste input is not mandatory in the astral. If you do not care much for banana bread, your imagination does not have to supply you with the taste of it. Additionally, there is no rule that says banana bread has to taste like banana bread in the astral, since your astral surroundings are highly subjective (or personalized, if you will). I always say: "The taste of banana bread is in the tongue of the beholder."

Likewise, there is no need to have visual input in the astral, unless you desire a visual experience. Nevertheless, using sensory input that mimics physical senses will make you feel more comfortable traveling through the astral, and this is why the subconscious employs them.

Extraordinary Astral Senses

There are many senses not yet awakened in the physical, senses of knowing and intuition that allow us to sense across time, space, and other dimensions. They can be developed in the physical, but it is easier and faster to access them in the astral. They might provide more input than the common senses. Use them in the astral once you feel comfortable suspending your usual senses.

Exercise: Extrasensory Perception

1. Project into the astral.
2. Find that visual void again, as you did in the previous exercise.
3. Relax your mind.
4. Focus on the center of your astral being (or astral chest).
5. Silence any thoughts.
6. Silence any internal dialogues:
   a. Command: "Rationality: Off!"
   b. Command: "Internal dialogue: Off!"
7. Await input from alternate senses in silence.
8. When you return to the physical, what you have perceived will probably be difficult to describe in a human language, just like dreams may be indescribable. You do not have to describe or analyze it in any way, simply remember the feeling of the information you received.

In truth, senses such as sight, hearing, and touch are of little value in the astral. What matters in an out-of-body state is not how well you perceive an object. What matters is how crisp your mind is, its level of presence and lucidity. When requesting clarity, you should not do it for your eyes, but for your mind.

Physical Attraction

Monday, March 19, 2001
Morning OBE

I have to stay up all night to write a report, so I only get three hours of sleep, from 5:00 to 8:00 A.M. After waking up, I go to the university and deliver the report. When I return, I lie down, turn my attention to my third eye, and wait to get into the body asleep/mind awake state. This is my first morning session. It takes about 40 minutes. I am beginning to slumber. When I wake up from one of several brief dreams, I feel that my body is asleep.

I do a few rounds of the dropping technique (sinking rapidly as I breathe out). Vibrations start. I think, "Hey, this is easy!" I do a few more rounds and suddenly it feels like I am actually floating downward. I float down and out. I can see. My room does not look as it does in physical life, but all the things I feel are important are there.

I am standing with my back to my body. I can briefly see the silver cord. (In retrospect, I think my imagination fabricated a cord that appeared to be attached to my awareness because I intentionally searched for the silver cord. I wanted to see it, so my imagination obliged.) I am being attracted back to my body. I will myself to my desk. I try to hold onto my desk, but my hands do not work. I decide to escape the suction by leaving the room. I will myself to the door, which is in the wrong place. It is closer to my desk than it is in the physical world.

When I float through the door, I lose my vision. I have probably entered a void. I float blindly down what I think is the corridor. My girlfriend, who is next to me in bed, makes a tiny movement and the attraction to my body increases. I wish to go to the university and so begin floating in that direction, but the attraction to my body is too strong. I wake up in my body and open my left eye. My body is paralyzed and my left ankle burns like fire. I attempt a second OBE, but my body is not in the right mode. I estimate that the entire experience lasted about 25 seconds.

One of the things you will notice during your first astral projections is the force with which your physical body pulls you back. The physical body is not *pulling* you, per se, but *calling* you. Your subconscious mind is not used to you being conscious and absent from the physical body at the same time. By old habit, it believes that when you are conscious, the proper place to be is in your body. Consequently, the subconscious instructs your body to call you back. You pick up on the body's signal and immediately shift your awareness to the physical body, where you "wake up." This may feel like the physical body is sucking you back across physical space, but it is actually only a shift in awareness.

Mind Split

Since we are multidimensional beings capable of existing in multiple dimensions and places simultaneously, a part of your awareness may decide to stay in the astral when the rest is called back to the body. It may feel like you are in several places at once, and you are aware of all those places; or it may feel like your awareness is flipping very quickly between those places. As a third alternative, the part of your awareness still in the astral may stay there unnoticed by you, but later call upon your physically based awareness, at which time you are once again "sucked" out into the astral to merge with the already projected part of your being. Astral projector Robert Bruce calls this phenomenon *mind split.*[19]

Wednesday, October 24, 2001
Short Projection

As I fell asleep last night, I visualized myself coming home from school like I did seven years ago. Now I have just awakened and am lying in bed waiting to go back to sleep. I relax. I sense a slight movement in my astral body. Then I get it, I am ready to leave the body. I relax and steer my consciousness out through the top of my head. I float downward and end up somewhere in the astral. I know exactly what I have planned to do: learn to increase and decrease my energy frequency and to create with thoughts.

I can tell that the projection is unstable. I know I can be shot back into my body at any time. I think that I have to ground myself by lowering my frequency. I think, I am lowering my frequency. This was a mistake. I am shot back into my body, either because the frequency is too low or because of the racket my girlfriend makes. Only about five seconds have passed since I exited the body.

What is interesting is that I was in a state that I did not recognize as pre-OBE. I was not paralyzed. I did not have any vibrations or tingling. The only difference from a waking physical state was that my mind was out of sync with my body. There was a light floating feeling around my head. I thought it was just nausea from a hangover (even though I did not party last night). A bubble of energy surrounded my head. What exactly triggers an OBE? Evidently, it is not the body asleep/mind awake state. I think I can obtain that state again without too much work.

Half a minute later, I am suddenly in my mind's eye walking down the middle of a street. My consciousness is projected to that street, but I am not out of my body. I am totally engaged with this part of my consciousness. The other part that is still lying in bed, inside my body, is gone for the moment. Could it be that this part of my consciousness stayed out while the part that I was focusing on during the OBE was pulled back into the body?

The street looks like a street on Earth, but there is such beauty that I think it must be somewhere on a slightly higher plane. There are big, beautiful buildings. On the physical plane, they would have been ugly. There are ordinary trees, but here they look fantastic. Everything has a strong color. I continue to walk down the street. There is not a person in sight. I enter a harbor area where the projection ends.

Reasons for Calling You Back

Being prematurely called back to the physical body can be very frustrating when you want to remain in the astral. It repeatedly happened to me until I started questioning why it happened. Here are a few good reasons for your physical body to call you back:

- Your subconscious mind is confused by the experience of being in a nonphysical environment and decides to go back to familiar ground, your physical body.

- Someone enters your physical room. Even if that person makes no sound, your subconscious picks up on his presence and alerts your awareness.

- Someone or something touches your physical body. Flies and mosquitoes can drive you crazy, even in your absence.

- Your physical ears pick up a disturbing noise.

- Your physical body wakes up naturally like it does after normal sleep. As far as the physical body is concerned, an astral projection *is* nothing but a period of normal sleep. This wake-up will be the ultimate limiting factor to your astral travels after all other disturbances have been dealt with.

- You have a conscious or subconscious thought relating to your physical body. Your astral projection is directed by your thoughts, so anything that passes through your thoughts will happen. The mind is always in charge of the body. The body always follows mental instructions. If you have even the briefest thought about the body, the body will comply by alerting your awareness to its existence. Once the concept of your body enters your awareness in this manner, there is little you can do to prevent the body from increasing its pull.

- You attempt to analyze your projection experience. When you analyze, you inescapably compare the current situation to beliefs formed by old experiences. The bulk of your beliefs deal with the physical world (unless you have vast astral experience), so analyzing naturally leads to subconscious thoughts about your physical body, which increases its pull.

- You project into an area in which you do not yet know how to sustain your awareness. For example, several religious teachings speak of multiple planes of existence, one on "top" (for lack of better word) of the other, or arranged like layers of an onion. Theosophy suggests seven planes of existence, Buddhism 32 planes, Hinduism a throng of realms known as "lokas," and Islam seven heavens. According to the teachings, the planes range from the physical plane to the god-realm, where everything is one: inseparable and separable at the same time. The astral plane is defined to be somewhere in between. Bear in mind that this system of planes is only a model and therefore may or may not illustrate the truth (if there is such a thing). Now, if we were to project from one plane of existence to another, it would be reasonable to assume that the difficulty in sustaining our awareness is proportional to the difference between the nature of the physical plane (since we automatically use the experience gathered in the physical when traveling in other planes) and the nature of the plane into which we are projecting.

• An astral guide decides it is time for you to return to your physical body. He may do this if he deems that you are getting into a situation you are not trained to handle. Astral guides may also deliberately set up small astral lessons to further your knowledge of the astral in preparation for future astral challenges. The lessons are mostly given in the form of distractions or practical obstacles preventing you from getting around in your astral world. The guide may send you back when he deems you have learned enough. Note that it is completely irrelevant whether you successfully conquered the obstacle. The important point is the amount of experience you gained from the obstacle.

False Awakenings

Often, following a pull from the physical body, when it appears you have awakened in your physical body, you are still projected into the astral. More specifically, you are in an astral replica of your bedroom, or a replica of a bedroom from an earlier period of your life, whichever comes most naturally to your subconscious mind. This is a *false awakening*. It is very difficult to tell whether you are in your physical room or in an astral replica. You must use intuition to figure it out. This is even more difficult than knowing that you are dreaming when you are dreaming. I suppose you could always try to create new furniture by thought in the room. If you succeed in creating that furniture, you know you are still in the astral. However, that feat of creation may also be possible in the physical. All it takes is an unlimited mind.

Saturday, March 17, 2001
Four False Awakenings

I wake up beside my girlfriend. I am dizzy and can't see clearly. When I move my arms, it is as if my astral arms are making the same movements, only half a second later. I think, "Wow, I can see my astral body!" I am in my parents' house. I walk downstairs to look in the hall mirror. I make some fast moves with my arms. The astral arms are still outside my physical arms. Cool!

Then I see another face in the mirror. It is a woman in her late twenties with a sweet round face and red hair. She is grabbing for me, as if I have something she just must have. Her arms go right through me. I know she does not have a physical body. I stare at her and try to get her attention. She does not realize I can see her. I grab her hands. She is surprised that I can see and touch her. She introduces herself as some sort of human relations employee at the high school I used to attend. That is strange, because I do not recall any such position. Anyway, she seems like a sweet person.

We walk out into the garden. It is night. She says goodbye and crawls under what appears to be a fallen garden tent. There is another smaller tent in the garden. This one is made of sackcloth. It, too, has fallen and a pair of legs wearing army boots sticks out. I figure that my brother must have had one of his wild parties.

Then I wake up. I think, "What a shame that the astral arms thing was only a dream." I am surprised, because the dream I just woke up from seemed very real. I try the same arm movements in another mirror (I am not in my parents' house anymore, I am at home). Nothing happens. There is something I have to do, but I can't remember what it is. I try to get out of bed, but my girlfriend holds me. She drives her finger into my back in a playful way. It hurts! I bark at her to stop.

Then I wake up. I think, "Enough with the false awakenings!"

Then I wake up. My girlfriend is already awake. She tries to get out of bed. I hold her and drive my finger into her in a playful way. It hurts, so she barks at me to stop. I explain to her that I just had three amazing false awakenings. Suddenly, my mouth is paralyzed and I can only make grunting noises. I sound like a monster. I playfully attack my girlfriend.

Then I awake for real (?) to the physical world.

Prolonging the Projection

Picture yourself in the astral, doing your favorite astral activity. Suddenly, you feel the physical body sucking you back. What do you do? There are techniques you can apply to stay projected, such as relaxing, centering, and remaining focused. However, it is difficult to stay calm enough to do these things when you are being pulled across dimensions; instead I suggest a technique using active force. For some reason, some movements help break off the pull. The *roll* is particularly effective in this. The roll is similar to the exit technique described earlier in this book. In both cases, the roll is applied to break off any attachments to the physical body.

Exercise: Prolonging Roll

1. Project into the astral.
2. Float around for a few seconds to acquaint yourself with your state of mind.
3. Roll as fast as you can. That is, spin around as if you were doing pirouettes.
4. After about ten revolutions, you should clearly sense any attachments to your physical body breaking off. Your awareness becomes more independent from your body.
5. The attachments sneak back on you, so you should get into the habit of rolling every five minutes or so.

Unfortunately, the period between the time the attachments appear and the time you are pulled back into your body is often so brief that, by the time you feel them, it is too late to apply the roll. The pull from the body rapidly increases until you shift your awareness into it against your will. It may take only a few seconds for the body to make the pull irresistible. Obviously, a better technique would be one that prevents those attachments from appearing in the first place. Astral meditation is a good preventive technique.

Meditation generally calms unruly thoughts so we can concentrate on one set of thoughts. However, meditation is always difficult in the physical because physical senses distract us. How many times have you tried to meditate only to be irritated by something like an aching back? Additionally, we have to put effort into quieting our belief system as it continuously tries to convince us that we have more important things to do than doing nothing (which meditation is). When we exit our bodies, we leave the physical senses behind. There are no aching backs in the astral. We also leave most of our belief systems behind. You might say that the astral provides an undistracted channel to our minds, which allows us to optimize our meditation practice. If you think meditation is effective in the physical, try it in the astral.

Do the exercise below first on "dry land" (in waking physical reality) a few times, so you will remember it when you astral project. When you know it by heart, apply the technique every time you go into the astral.

Exercise: Prolonging Meditation

1. The moment you exit your body, float down to the floor or into a void.
2. Cross your astral legs (if you decide to have astral legs) in lotus position.
3. Put your palms together (if you decide to have hands) in front of your chest.
4. Close your astral eyes (if you decide to have eyes).
5. Take a deep (astral) breath.
6. Relax your mind.
7. Quiet all thoughts and internal dialogues.
8. Move the center of thought to your astral chest. Focus on your chest.
9. Stay in this relaxed state of mind for one minute.
10. Go do whatever you set out to do in the astral.
11. Repeat the meditation every time you feel your mind becoming unsynchronized or off balance in any way in the astral.

Meditating in the astral not only prolongs the projection, but also takes you to a more joyous and peaceful astral environment. In the astral, the state of your mind affects your environment. Meditation is the best way I have found to bring about a blissful state of mind and, therefore, is the best way to positively affect any astral environment.

Mind Creation

Now that we have acquired a good degree of self-control—that is, we can astral project without getting sidetracked by our addictions—we can enjoy an incredible freedom of creativity. Have you ever wanted to create music without the hassle of using musical instruments? In the astral, you can. Imagine the time and effort it takes to build a physical castle. In the astral, you can do it in mere seconds. But let us start small.

Decorating the Astral Environment

By now, you should be familiar with how your conscious and subconscious minds create your astral environment, at least theoretically. To recap, this is what happens when you pop out of your body:

1. Your awareness enters a blank astral "space" (the concept of space does not apply in the astral), unless you have an appointment with an already existing astral or physical world.

2. The space is yours to do with whatever you want. The space will

morph to fit even your smallest intentions. If you have (as have most of us) spent too much time in the physical, you will expect to see physical objects. Your expectations quickly turn into intentions. If you expect to see your physical room, the astral space will morph into how you expect your room to look.

3. However, if you expect nothing—and you can do this simply by understanding that the astral is not the physical and does not have to behave even remotely similar to it—your astral space will remain blank. This is the degree of control over our minds we seek. Achieving the astral void may take some practice; so do not worry if you have not come across it yet. In time, you will. Either way, the exercises in this chapter can be done in a void or inside an astral world full of objects.

4. When your astral space is blank, you will have no input from your usual senses, not even vision. From this empty space, you may create an astral world that has visual input, if you so desire. You may just as well create a world without visual input. Visual input is in no way indigenous to the astral, nor is it necessary. Visual input only exists in the astral because we intend it to be so.

Exercise: Creating an Astral Sofa

1. Exit your body and project into the astral.
2. Meditate on your chest as you did in the previous exercise.
3. Select an area in front of you.
4. Think: "I think there is a sofa here. Yes, there is a sofa here. It is white."
5. A sofa should appear before you.
6. Float over to the sofa.
7. Touch the sofa. Feel its texture with your astral fingers.
8. Lie on the sofa. Put your feet up. Enjoy your creation for a minute.
9. Relax your mind.
10. Sense how this sofa came into being, without analyzing.
11. Repeat the exercise, but instead of creating a sofa, you might want to try something different. How about a hot tub?

Testing the Limits

As you probably noticed, the sofa gave you the visual and tactile input you are used to in the physical, perhaps even more intensely so. I am frequently amazed that textures in the astral feel more physically tangible than actual physical textures. Perhaps the reason for this is that the physical is just another astral world, but one with slightly numbed sensory input.

Monday, October 28, 2001
Raising Astral Vibrations

I turn my eyes upward and affirm "I am OBEing" as I fall asleep. The alarm wakes me up after six hours. I spend one hour awake, then I go back to bed. I turn my eyes upward again and repeat the affirmation as I fall asleep. I have two dreams. When I wake up, my body is paralyzed.

I relax my mind and sit my astral body up. I sit on the side of the bed with my legs dangling over. I can't see it, but I hear a radio playing. In waking physical reality, there is no radio. I focus on my heart chakra to tune in on my communication faculties. I need to find out how things work in the astral, so I practice creating a couch with thought. It turns into a black leather couch. I lie on the couch and rest for a while. It feels real enough.

I walk through the room. The feet feel real against the floor. I somehow know my girlfriend is in the kitchen. I walk through the bookshelf and the wall, a funny feeling. I walk down the stairs, through the corridor and into the kitchen. My girlfriend is lying on the sofa. In waking physical reality, she is nowhere near the kitchen. I throw myself in the air and float over to her. I kiss her and she smiles. I am not sure if she can see me. She seems a bit surprised as to where the kiss came from. I blow softly at her neck to convince her that she is not imagining it. Then I am suddenly back in my physical body.

I relax and sit my astral body up. I am blind again, but the vision soon returns. I think of going back to my girlfriend, but suddenly I am standing in my parents' kitchen. My girlfriend is sitting at the table, eating a cucumber and bell pepper sandwich. A familiar spirit or dream character is there, but I do not know who it is and I do not reflect much upon it. I think it would be fun to annoy my girlfriend, now that she can't see me. I throw a piece of cucumber on the floor. When she leans down to pick it up, I grab it and throw it to the other guy. We toss it to each other a few times. Then I am bored.

I want to find out what is in the higher dimensions, so I move away a bit. I repeatedly command, "My frequency is increasing." Suddenly, something grabs me, as if someone pulls my t-shirt from behind. I am a little afraid, but I get over it. Whatever is grabbing me starts running around me in circles, still holding the back of my t-shirt. I rotate with it. I am drilling myself upwards. The scenery is changing. I stop rotating. Everything around me is blindingly bright. There are white and turquoise lights, arranged in vertical layers. I can't make out anything except bright lights. I think, "This kind of change in frequency usually pulls me back to my body," which immediately puts me back in my body.

I relax again and roll out. I want to approach the denser planes, so I command, "My frequency is slowing a little." Not much happens. My girlfriend walks into the room and says she wants to have sex. I say, "Sure," but we hardly get started before I am pulled back into my body. She is not in the physical room.

You may also use other senses to interact with the astral, senses we normally do not use in the physical. We have, as of yet, no names for them. Often we just say: "I *sense* this and that, but I can't explain it." We might call it the sixth sense or intuition, but that would be generalizing. These senses will become useful in later exploration, but for now we will just use the same old senses so we can get acquainted with the astral and understand how it differs from the physical.

Exercise: Walking on Water

1. Exit your body and project into the astral.
2. Meditate on your chest for one minute.
3. Select an area in front of you.
4. Imagine there is a large body of water, for example, a lake. Expect it to be there.
5. Describe every detail of the lake to yourself.
6. The lake should appear before you. If not, increase the detail as you imagine the lake again.
7. Walk on the surface of the water.
8. When you tire of walking, you might want to submerge into the water.
9. If your creation is consistent, you will find that you can breathe under

> water (which of course comes as no surprise to you, since you know anything is possible in the astral).
> 10. If you have not supplied any details for the environment beneath the surface of the lake, you may find yourself in a void or in a totally different world when you do intersect the surface of the lake.

Now, be very careful about whom you tell about this experience. People can be very paranoid, fearful, and defensive and you might end up being crucified. (Well, it has been known to happen, anyway.) If the theory of the physical being an astral world is correct, then Jesus could very well have walked on water. If gravity is just another belief-induced rule to govern our reality, then there is no reason why anybody should not be able to remove that belief and walk on water in the physical.

Astral Persistence

The next thing we should do is to create an *astral home world*. Just as mountain climbers establish a base camp before they explore the mountain, so will we establish a familiar space before we venture further into the astral. Here we will be safe, protected, and at peace. It will also be a place where other astral entities, preferably those interested in our astral progress, can reach us and perhaps give us a few hints on how the astral world works.

Exercise: Creating an Astral Home

1. In the physical, relax your mind.
2. Think of a place that radiates tranquillity. I prefer green meadows and flower gardens, but you can choose any place imaginable.
3. Visualize walking through that area. Touch and smell objects. Pay extra attention to how the vibes of the place feel. They should be uplifting. In other words, walking through the place should make you happy.
4. After returning from your visualization, write down a few notes about what you have felt and seen so that you can refresh your memory tonight.

5. When it is bedtime, visualize walking through that same place again. As you do so, affirm: "Tonight I will AP to this place." Continue the visualization and affirmation as you fall asleep. This is the astral projection technique described earlier in this book.

6. If you wake up in the night, visualize walking through that place again and repeat the affirmation as you drift off to sleep again.

7. When you find yourself in the astral, whether you gained consciousness during sleep or first woke up and then rolled out, imagine yourself being in the place you previously visualized.

8. Start describing the place to yourself. Begin with the large objects near you. They should appear when you intend them to.

9. Next, look closer at your immediate surroundings, discovering more and more details about your space.

10. Walk or float through your space. Expect to see things you previously visualized, and they will be created.

11. When you are happy with your home, surround it with a bubble of white light. The bubble will attract only positive beings. Reinforce the bubble with a shield of your own design (I use metal, but a futuristic plasma shield or anything else should work just as well) to keep out unwanted entities.

12. Define the rules of your newly created world by making a final request by thought: "This is my astral home world. It is persistent and so will remain in existence whether I am here or absent. I will return here at the beginning of every astral projection."

13. Enjoy your new home.

From now on, every time you astral project, remember your astral home, so that you visit it frequently. The more often you visit this place, the more detail you give it by power of creation. Be careful, though, not to get so accustomed to it that you view it as your only true place of existence. Then it will become more like a prison than a home. Because physical existence feels so intense and we spend so much time in it, many of us (not astral projectors, of course) think of it as the only place of existence, which turns it into a sort of prison. It would be unfortunate if we got caught in the same self-invented cell in the astral.

Physical Manifestation

Now that you have exercised the power of creation that is your birthright, we will venture on one last enterprise. Assuming that the physical is an astral world, it should be fairly easy to create objects by thought in the physical. The only thing preventing us is the belief that the feat is impossible. If we can circumvent the belief system somehow, we will meet more success. One way to do this could be to create an object in the astral and then bring it back into the physical. The exercise below has been successfully executed on several occasions, although not by me.

Exercise: Astral-Physical Manifestation

1. When you exit your body and enter the astral, imagine that you have a red rose in your hand.
2. Expect the rose to be in your hand.
3. Look down at the rose and inspect it thoroughly.
4. Touch the smooth petals.
5. Smell the rose.
6. Affirm: "I intend this rose to be physical."
7. Wake up to the physical and find the rose in your physical hand.

Requests

In the exercise called "Clarity Now!" you commanded your subconscious to provide your conscious mind with visual input. The subconscious gladly takes orders from the conscious mind in this manner, as long as the order does not conflict with any beliefs held by the subconscious. For example, the command "Ice Cream Now!" will probably work in the astral, but "Take Flight Now!" only works if the subconscious has removed its belief in gravity or established a new belief that the astral does not succumb to gravity.

You can think up any sort of command you would like to use in the astral. Here are a few examples:

"Clarity Now!"	Initiates visual perception of an already existing astral world, or enforces the creation of a new astral world.
"Stabilize!"	Stabilizes your state of mind so that you can stay longer in your current reality.
"Physical Body Now!"	Takes you back to your physical body, or, if the body is too deeply asleep, creates an astral world in which you will have a false awakening.
"Go to X Now!"	Takes you to the astral world or the person called X,

or creates a replica of X for you, depending on the level of control you have over your mind.

"Go to Astral Home Now!" Takes you to the astral home world you created in the previous chapter, or creates it anew (which is basically the same thing).

"Show me the most important aspect of X!" Shows you, with any means available, the most important aspect of person or place X, unless that person or place is unwilling to reveal that information.

The last request is quite interesting. Let us try it.

Exercise: Show-Me Request

1. Write down a question that you have been turning over in your mind for a while with no results.
2. Project into an astral void.
3. Meditate on the center of your chest for 15 seconds to stabilize the projection.
4. Command: "Show me the most important aspect of the Sphinx of Giza!"
5. Do not move away too quickly; wait for the response to arrive. The response may take any form. It may come in the form of objects or people appearing or simply in the form of a knowing.
6. When you have the answer, continue the inquiry by commanding: "Show me the most important aspect of me!"
7. When you get the response, ask the question you wrote down in step 1.

Note that the answers you received were fetched from a subconscious place and may therefore be colored or misinterpreted by your subconscious. The answers may not reflect the exact truth but, still, they should be more accurate than the answers the conscious mind can come up with. For example, if the subconscious received information about the nature of life, the subconscious might represent that information with a closet. Suddenly, a closet appears before you in the astral. To the conscious mind, the closet is just a closet, but to the subconscious mind, the closet is a representation of the nature of life, although much information was lost in the translation from truth to closet.

Note also that as the answers were not constructed by the conscious mind, the conscious mind may not be able to grasp them. If you receive an answer you do not understand, do not attempt to understand it by further consciously analyzing it. This will only force a misinterpretation, because the analytical mind feels that a misinterpretation is still better than confusion. Other parts of you, unbeknownst to your conscious mind, understand exactly what is meant by the answer. They operate outside the bounds of reason and logic.

Replenishing Energy

Monday, February 5, 2001
Fatigue

My energy reserves have been exhausted for a while now. This has resulted in bad moods. However, I am getting better. I think that my "First Contact" drained my nonphysical energy. I will have to build my energy centers from the ground up to make them stronger.

Today, I did my first energy exercises for some time. I noticed that my left side is more sensitive than my right. For example, if I tickle my left palm or sole, I will feel it for about half a minute. If I tickle my right palm or sole, the sensation disappears after only a few seconds. This is probably because the left side of my nonphysical energy is more active than my right side. I will have to do many exercises to activate my right side.

The day following an astral projection, you will probably feel physically tired. The second day, you might feel mentally exhausted, leading to boredom, hopelessness, and perhaps even depression. This is caused by a lack of mental energy. Projecting into the astral takes a lot of energy, and this is where you spent it. But do not worry, you will automatically replenish your energy and in a few days you will be energetically restored.

To avoid mental exhaustion, I recommend that you do not astral project too often. Once a week is excellent for beginners. In time, we adapt to the astral and learn not to waste so much energy while we are there. You might say we are optimizing our astral energy usage. This done, we can project about twice a week. Under no circumstances would I recommend projecting more often than three times a week. The strain on the mental energy reserves would be too high. In any case, there are exercises we can do in order to accelerate the replenishing of energy.

Exercise: Personal Impeccability

The fastest way to stock up on energy is by making decisions for yourself and following through on them. When there are no what-ifs and no maybes, energy will go straight into your reservoir. For example, you may decide to go on a diet in which you will only eat three times a day with no in-between snacks. Or, if you are a smoker, you might decide to quit. If you stand by that decision in spite of your sweet tooth or nicotine cravings, energy will automatically flow into you.

1. Make a decision you think will improve your daily life.
2. Stand by that decision, no matter how difficult it gets. Do not postpone.

Exercise: The Effect of Beauty

1. Intentionally seek to see the uniqueness and beauty of ordinary things in your physical environment. People, plants, animals, objects, even freeways are incredibly beautiful, but often we forget to appreciate their beauty.
2. Tie a string around one of your fingers to remind you to focus on the beauty of each thing that comes your way. The beauty will put you in a state of awe, which is beneficial for replenishing energy.

Exercise: Aiming Higher

1. In each person you meet, see the silver-blue luminous bubble that is her beautiful higher self, instead of seeing the ego and its doings. Every person has a positive higher self.

2. Connect with other people's higher selves. In doing so, you connect with your own higher self, which is a groovy feeling.

3. Your higher self will then automatically attract energy from the universe and replenish your reserves.

Exercise: Energetic Meditation

1. Close your eyes.

2. Relax your mind and go into a calm state.

3. Ground your mind by shooting all upsetting emotions into the ground below you.

4. Think of your spine as a flexible organic tube, through which energy flows between your head and the rest of your body.

5. Make that tube expand, as if to let more energy flow through it.

6. Imagine the tube leading all the way up to the top of your head. Open that end of the tube.

7. Imagine some of the energy in the tube flowing out of the top of the tube and mixing with the rest of the energy in the universe.

8. Start absorbing energy from the universe in through the top of the tube.

9. After a few minutes, close the top of the tube.

Exercise: Restoring Meditation

1. Close your eyes.

2. Visualize how your body and mind would look and feel if they were in perfect shape. Pay special attention to the emotions a perfect body and mind would give you.

3. Put that image in the center of your chest.

4. Open the spine tube, as you did in the previous exercise.

5. Let energy from the universe flow in through the top of the tube, down your spine, and let it wash over the image in your chest, making the image become reality.

6. After a few minutes, close the top of the tube.

The Nature of Reality

Find the truth about life, the universe, and everything.

They say that dreams are only real as long as they last. Couldn't you say the same thing about life?

—*Waking Life* (movie)[20]

Welcome to Circle 4, where we delve into the mysteries of our existence. By now, you have surely experienced how simple thoughts affect your perception of the astral. The next step is to attempt to grasp the enormity of these abilities. Do they represent our natural capabilities? Are they part of who we are as nonphysical beings? Can we use them in a waking physical state of mind? How do they affect our view of reality?

The Meaning of Life

Why are we here? Where did we come from? Are we just irrelevant specks in an incomprehensibly large universe or is there some purpose to our lives? These questions will find answers in time. We have asked them for a hundred thousand years, but now I think we are closer to finding out the answers than we ever were. The psychic skills of our species are awakening, and with those skills we can explore more of our nature and the world around us.

Most likely, the meaning of life can't be put into words, at least not with our current vocabulary. For now, the meaning will have to become a feeling inside each one of us, a subjective impression that we can lean back on when times get tough.

Why Incarnate?

Some Eastern traditions speak of automatic reincarnation: When you die, you instantly pop into another human body. (Hinduism includes the possibility of incarnating into an animal body.) This automatic birth process seems contradictory to our nature, and our lives appear far too well prepared to occupy just any body.

It is more likely that we have free will on a soul level, just as we have free will on Earth. Therefore, we choose whether we want to incarnate. We can stay between lives indefinitely if we so choose. We also choose where, when, how, and why to live. Then we spend most of our lives wondering what that "why" was.

Considering how harsh life can be, it takes a brave soul to incarnate. We, the incarnate, are the brave ones. It could also be that we are fools. I can imagine that it is difficult to foresee just how physical life will feel when we are not engulfed in it. It may look easy in the planning stage, but when we are stuck in it with no recollection of our soul lives, it is very hard to cope. We are all probably very cocky about our abilities on a soul level, but when we are stripped from them at birth, life presents an entirely different challenge.

But that is also the reason we came to be: to experience ourselves without the aid of our soul abilities. We want to interact as human beings because they have a lot to teach us about ourselves. As an analogy: If you take a course in survival in the wilderness, you can read all you want and still not know anything about how to function in the wild. You must get out there, eat your last bologna sandwich, get lost, and then try to survive.

The Privilege of the Living

By incarnating, we are willing to go through all the pain that life has to offer: grief, disease, homesickness. Not only that, once we have been through it, we choose to come back time after time, subjecting ourselves to the same suffering again. Either we just do not get the message or we are looking for something so rewarding that the suffering is insignificant in comparison. What could the physical hold that is so valuable? Could it be the thrill of simply being here? Could it be that we look our whole lives for the adventures in projecting or ascending to a spiritual plane, to open the way to the soul, but when we get there, we realize that it is nothing—that physical life was the excitement, the intriguing part, and the adventure? Are we, as incarnates, in the most exciting place ever constructed, but we do not have the brains to take advantage of the opportunity, to live life to its fullest?

Monday, August 12, 2002
Past-Life Mother and Bliss!

It is 2 P.M. I am half awake. I dream I am in a car. My mother (from a past life?) is in the car, too. I feel love for her. She gets out and leaves. Then there is a flashback. I see that as she leaves, she playfully shoots water at me with a garden hose, which is next to the car. I am behind the car. I raise my hand and catch the water. As the water hits me, I have an amazing feeling: Life is so beautiful! Life is bliss. Living is a chance to be in bliss all the time. In each second of life, we have the choice to be in bliss. Bliss is only a simple decision away. We decide how we want to feel. We can decide to remove the concepts of fear and anger. The theme from Forrest Gump *is playing in the background.*

Someone has recently died in the dream (could my past-life mother, leaving the car, represent dying?), but I know death is nothing. My sense of respect and loyalty tells me to mourn, but I choose to be in bliss. In waking reality, Jazz's tail is thumping against the floor as she sleeps. I wonder if she can feel the bliss, too. I open my eyes to see if there is a spirit in the room but can't see anything out of the ordinary.

There is so much pleasure in Earth life, but only seldom do we allow ourselves to feel it. I love the smells, the energy of trees, the feeling of air against my skin, the breath in my lungs, the smell of my skin, and the throbbing of blood as it rushes through my veins. I also love the uncertainty: to not know what will happen next. Life is a blank story-book we fill with adventures as we go along. These are things we can't experience anywhere else, and yet they are the simplest things in life. They are so simple that we do not notice them. And still, they are the treasures for which we came, the reasons for our incarnation.

The School of Life

In addition to the wonderful sensations on this plane, we come here to evolve. The limitations of the physical provide a good learning ground. While we are in this "school," we have no idea what lies beyond graduation. Perhaps there is another school, and one after that, and so on into infinity. Or perhaps we are released into real life upon graduation. In the movie *Defending Your Life*,[21] Earth is described as a school in which the goal for the students is to lose their fears so they can become citizens of the universe. Perhaps that is not too far from the truth.

We are our own teachers, and the thoughts we conjure up are our teaching tools. We also have assistants residing outside the physical, continuously engaged in helping us prepare the lessons.

Wednesday, October 30, 2002
Discovering Faith

A few days ago, Barb and I had a few drinks. I got a floating sensation. It was a thrill. My body went numb. Barb had to feed me, because I could not control my arms enough to hold anything. I felt like I was ready to astral project, but when I attempted to exit my body by rolling out, the physical body rolled with me.

Tonight we are drinking once more. Barb sees the big black scarab from another world run across the floor again. She points out her observation to me and I say, "Cool!" Things are happening in my head. Suddenly, there is a knock on the door. Barb opens it and in steps Susanne and her dog Little Paw. She goes on and on about how Eric left a supposedly rude note by the dishwasher or something. Barb runs around in the kitchen, trying to keep busy and not look at Susanne. She does not want Susanne to know we have been drinking. She drops things and wiggles now and then. It looks like she is directing all her energy to trying to walk straight, or it could just be that I interpret it that way. It looks funny and I giggle to myself. Little Paw jumps up on the bed and licks my face.

I don't want to talk because the world is getting slurred and I can imagine my voice will sound retarded and give me away. Susanne turns around and sees me sitting in bed. "Oh, hi Mag!" I wave (a mistake, as I must look drunk as hell) at her and say, "Hi." It feels like someone else said that, someone who was in a different reality. I am slipping away. I can't concentrate on waking reality. I want to escape into an alternate reality and explore it, but Susanne just goes on and on about how rude Eric is, which is a lie, of course, because we know Eric is a good man. Why won't she leave? It feels like I am on the verge of astral projecting, but her negativity keeps pulling me back to waking reality.

Then it hits me. This altered state allows me to see with incredible clarity: Susanne is addicted to pity! Her subconscious is deliberately looking for things in other people's actions to feel hurt about. Therefore, she interprets most events as attacks on her person. She also sets up harmful situations in which she can feel emotionally and physically hurt, so she can attract pity from her fellow beings. She wants love, and, subconsciously, she thinks she can get it through the pity from others. This is the underlying cause of her faltering physical health. Right now, she is complaining about

Eric in order to get pity from Barb. It does not work though, because in Barb's intoxicated state, there is no such thing as pity. I have an urge to tell Susanne about my insight, but at the last moment, I manage to conceive that in an ordinary state of mind, such as Susanne's, this would be considered rude.

I am holding the cat in my arms. The next thing I know, the cat is running on the floor. How did it get there? What is going on? I try to step back in my memory, but I have no recollection of what happened during the last seconds. I can't focus on waking reality anymore. I get short glimpses of it, that is all. I take off my glasses and pretend to inspect them. I keep my eyes fixed on them. I can't look at a living thing, because it changes all the time. It does things and I repeatedly forget what it did during the last second I looked at it. Looking at an unchanging object helps me retain my sense of reality. Susanne sees me staring at the glasses and I can feel she takes it as hint that I am not interested in having her in the apartment. "Come here, Little Paw!" She walks out. At last, she leaves us to enjoy our altered state of consciousness.

The next thing I know, I "wake up" and Barb is talking to me. I have a vague memory of telling Barb that I had almost astral projected when Susanne was there, but it feels like our conversation has taken place in a dream from which I have just awakened. Barb says, "Really, you almost projected?" Jesus, what is going on? How did she know that? I thought I dreamt that? I do not know what to tell her.

Now I do not know what we talked about, because the memory of the dream is fading. I just stare at her, dumbfounded. I am getting a short glimpse of waking physical reality. It lasts ten milliseconds. Then I spend the following 40 milliseconds in a dream world. Then I get another glimpse of waking reality, and so it continues. I can't control it. I am trying to figure out whether waking reality is the dream and the dream is real or if it is some other way. It feels like I am having a lucid dream, but the dream is taking place in waking reality.

I am living only in the moment. Each moment I create anew all my intentions and plans. From one moment to the next, I can't remember what I did or what I planned to do. My mind is falling asleep and waking up 20 times per second. I am rushing between dream realities and waking reality. I hate it. I hate waking up in the morning, and now I am waking up 20 times every second! Each time I am confused and can hardly remember what I dreamt about. I unintentionally blame different noises for waking me up. I am getting irritated.

Barb and I talk. She talks to make sure I am all right and perhaps keep me focused in waking reality. I think she talks so much because the alcohol makes her talkative. Suddenly, I wake up and she asks, "Are you getting angry?" I can't remember what we talked about that might have led her to thinking I am angry. I search any memory from a dream, knowing that what I find could actually have happened in waking reality.

Then I start to suspect that I had an overdose of alcohol or an allergic reaction, although I have never heard of the latter. Jesus, I have to do something. I think it will help if I get up and walk around for a while; this would get my blood moving and my brain would get fresh oxygen. Can I control my body enough to stand up? I can't feel my body. I get up.

I am moving purely by will. By wanting to walk, I walk. I think that my subconscious is controlling the body, and I am instructing it via my will. Or maybe I am just floating outside my body? A few steps later, I wake up to see Barb standing in my way. She asks me why I am walking around. Hell if I know. I can't remember anything. The last thing I remember, I was sitting in the bed, but that too feels like it happened in a dream.

I continue skipping back and forth into a dream world. Sometimes I have nightmares. When I wake up from them, which I do 20 times per second, I am panicked and my heart is racing. My ego takes charge. I am fear-struck. Am I going to have a heart attack? Did the alcohol kill my brain? Am I going to turn into a drooling vegetable? Am I dying? I have to get help.

I want to beg Barb to take me to a hospital where they can give me a shot of adrenaline or something that will restore me to waking physical reality. I so miss the clarity of thought in a sober mind. I hate being in the dream world. I love the smell, taste, and feel of waking reality. I love breathing the air, but in the dream world, there is no way to experience those things. But most of all, I hate being in two realities at the same time.

I panic. I try to ask Barb to take me to a hospital but can't formulate the words, and from one moment to the next, I can't remember what it is I want to say. Then I remember—only to forget as I fall into another dream. I reach out with the intention of touching Barb. If this is a dream, then I can alter it. I try to do that, but it does not work. I must still be in waking reality.

Dreams are popping in and out between my glimpses of being awake, and they are confusing me. I put my hands over my face, desperately trying to create a beacon in waking reality that will hold my focus there. Barb is getting freaked out. She fears for my health. I do, too. Am I going insane? Is the brain damaged and now I am destined to spend the rest of my life flipping between waking reality and dreaming reality, not being able to tell them apart and not remembering what happened just a few seconds before?

Barb leads me back to bed. I go along; after all, I can't remember why I got up in the first place. I work very hard during many wake-sleep cycles to formulate a cry for help. I ask her, "What do you do when you've had too much?" She says, "You had better eat something. Want me to get you a sandwich and milk?" "Yes. And a banana." How do I remember that we just bought bananas? The bananas feel like a spectacular memory, sticking out from the blur in which I float. She returns with a cheese sandwich. I try to hold it in my hand, but I have no feeling in my palm. The sandwich slides out of my hand and the cat eats from it. I want to say, "Jesus, I can't even hold a sandwich." But I only get as far as "Jesus." Then I forget what I was going to say. Each time I wake up, I can see the sandwich has slid farther in my hand.

I can't feel my stomach, but I suspect that I am very close to puking. I should be, shouldn't I? I get up and will myself to the bathroom. I sit on the toilet, trying to hold my perception of waking reality together. I want to get back to waking reality. I stick my head into the shower, drenching it with cold water for several minutes. After a while, my body is freezing, so I have to give it up. My sensory perception is so numbed that I can't feel the cold, but I know from how the skin reacts (goose bumps) that it can't take much more. My state has improved only slightly.

I get back into bed and try to get warm. In spite of several layers of blankets, I can't raise my body temperature. Now I have done it. I have accelerated the dying process by cooling my body. I am getting increasingly convinced that I am dying. This is probably going to get worse. I will be flipping between waking reality and the dream realm until I can't tell which is which. At some point, I will be completely in the dream world, leaving my body behind to rot. Is this how death is, a confusing haze? It sure is not how I envisioned it.

This is not fair! I have so many things yet to complete. I am writing a book. Now I will never see it finished. I have been cheated out of the rest of my life. Nobody ever told me such a small amount of ethanol could kill you. I had no warning. It is not fair. This makes me angry.

Then something peculiar happens. The next time I wake up from a micro-slumber, Barb's face is very close to mine. It has a layer of shimmering tranquillity. Her eyes calmly look into mine. A moment ago, she was freaking out, but now she is completely serene. What brought about this change? She does not feel like Barb anymore. Is it Barb or is some wise spirit borrowing her body to relay a message to me? Or is Barb perhaps inspired by such a spirit? Or perhaps Barb is such a wise spirit, but only lets its true nature surface when it is needed? Who am I looking at?

When she speaks, that does not matter anymore: "You are very close to your soul right now. Go with it and I will watch over your body while you are gone." That is exactly what I need to hear. A wave of relief washes over my being. But how did Barb know to say that? The next moment, the layer of tranquillity disappears from her face, as if the spirit who addressed me left her body. Was Barb aware of what she told me? She seems to be, but she also seems surprised to have said it.

Reassured of my safety, I finally stop trying to hold onto waking reality. I slip into another conscious state. It is dark. Wait a moment; there is something out here. I can sense it. It is huge! It is getting closer. I can't find a name for it. The closest I can come to describing it is as the universe. It is a gigantic swirl of black and dark red. Oh, wow! It is alive.

It wants me to know that whether we are in physical bodies or without them (i.e., dead), the universe takes care of us. In all possible outcomes of all our actions, the universe is there to take care of us. We are always safe. Suddenly, worries of the future wash away. It does not matter whether I am dying or not. I understand that either way, I am and will always be completely safe. Jesus, this is so unlike me! Where did this serenity come from? It is an improvement.

The universe sends thoughts to me. In order to feel this care, all we have to do is face the direction the universe is going in and we will flow with its movement. There are no obstacles in life when you are facing the direction of the universe. I think I have just found faith, something I never had in life. There was never any reason to believe there was something that took care of me, but here it is, swirling about to my upper right. I think I can drop my chronic worry about my problems in life now. A life without worry, what bliss.

What is more, I feel this incredible love between all beings in the universe. There is a universal love that will never diminish or go away. We all love each other, even though we may not know it. I also get a feeling that our physical bodies are not ours. We are just borrowing them.

There is another presence here. The universe fades away as I turn my attention to the new presence. It is a small, red, metallic creature sitting just by my right ear, telling me things. I know he is my ego. I do not reflect on his purpose. It feels like he has always been sitting there next to me, telling me things. Has he been there all my life and only now do I notice him? I know without a doubt that he is telling me lies. I tell him "no" in my mind, over and over.

I wave my hands before him as a sign of rejection. I deny the lies he is telling me. I reject his advice. I am rebelling against this creature for the first time in my life. I know he only wants to control me. He invents ugly lies to trick me into believing I need to fol-

low his advice. Funny now, in retrospect, how the creature fits the description of the Devil. I do not believe in the existence of a Devil, though.

At the same time, I notice lots of little people running around. They are dressed in the colors of the woods, green and brown. Is their skin green, too? What the hell—gnomes? They seem awfully busy, running here and there. I know what they are doing without asking. They are working intensely to arrange the experience I am having. They control every event by some invisible machinery.

And sitting on a platform overlooking the working gnomes are my spirit guides. There are three or four of them. I sense they have invested great effort in preparing the experience for me and now they relax and observe the gnomes carrying it out. They are the masterminds behind this whole experience. I am impressed by the time and effort I sense it took to put this experience together. I sense that the guides have spent over six months planning the experience in detail.

I now see the reason for the experience. The guides saw an opportunity to run me through a large number of lessons when my brain state was altered by alcohol. The goal of the lessons was to shed parts of the ego and strengthen my faith. The best way to do this was to make me confront the thought of death, but also to show me the truth about the universe. The lessons could not have been learned in an ordinary state of mind. The rational mind had to be put aside.

As if on a signal, all the gnomes stop working. The gnomes and spirit guides applaud. They applaud themselves for a job well done, and they applaud me for making the best of their efforts by learning what they intended me to learn. This marks the end of a project they have been working on for a long time.

When I was young, I was taught that angels are watching over each one of us. I thought the angels were there to help me if I got into too much trouble. Now it turns out that the job of the angels is the opposite: It is to get me *into* trouble! Even so, it is all according to my will. I wanted to experience what I have just described. I wanted to confront my fear of death so I could live more fully. I also wanted to know what was out there, beyond the limits of the physical. I had never verbally uttered these wishes, but they were there, in my consciousness. And so my guides obliged.

In the same way, the experiences we desire are set up in life. The subconscious is a sponge, full of desires from our past. Each thought we have, enforced with emotion, ends up in the subconscious in the form of a desire. If we, for example, fear snakes, then that fear, being a strong emotion, will establish a desire to overcome the fear of snakes in our subconscious. The desire will in turn arrange for an experience in which we have a chance to experience the fear so that we may understand and dissolve it. It may take years to manifest the experience. The time depends on our reluctance to have it. We can set up those experiences ourselves, or we can ask others, fellow humans and discarnate guides, to help us.

The strong emotion, of course, does not have to be a negative emotion. We can create equally well with happiness and bliss. If we decide to experience bliss, then that strong emotion will create a subconscious desire to experience more bliss.

Our Nature

Dusting Off the Soul

There are a multitude of papers presenting the out-of-body and near-death phenomena in academic ways, such as with witness testimony, EEG charts, and everything else representing scientific investigation. The papers are written by medical and psychological professionals simply because they have stumbled upon something that, in spite of thorough education and experience, they can't explain. Often, the author has no personal experience with these phenomena but is intrigued by the accounts of patients and coworkers.

Unfortunately, without personal experience, they inescapably give a distorted picture of the phenomena, which misleads the masses. For example, the average person thinks of the out-of-body experience as a brief trip in the physical realm, but outside of the body. He has no idea of the abundance of beautiful worlds to be found outside the physical and the immensity behind the worlds. Uninformed papers only reinforce this picture. They do little to explain the actual nature of the out-of-body experience.

Such authors, using all the latest technology, can't explain what the phenomena are or what causes them. They can't, because the phenomena do not fit into their worldview. Their understanding of the world tells them to look to the physical for explanations. Commonly, they expect the biological brain to provide them with answers. The brain is supposedly the most complex object in the known physical universe, so if there is anything that can't be explained (telepathy, precognition, OBE, NDE), they can explain it away as some yet unknown brain function. But the brain remains silent. No answers come. We have all these cool color printouts of brain activity, but none of them says: "Hey, I am what you have been looking for all these years! I am the one whose complicated effects you have attributed to a soul. Hah, hah, can you imagine that?—A soul!"

What is missing in these accounts? Why can't we explain OBE and NDE from our current scientific standpoint? Well, isn't it obvious? Out-of-body and near-death experiences happen because we, contrary to contemporary scientific beliefs, *are not physical beings*. We are not minds created by biological circuitry. We are minds creating the biological circuitry and all other physical objects. Our lives did not begin when papa sperm met mama egg; they have been going on since long before Earth was even thought up. This fact is ignored by science, which is why scientists can't explain the OBE phenomenon. Out of the fear of being upset, science does not delve into the mind to explore it. The unfortunate fate of science is to investigate everything except the only important thing: who we are.

From their personal experience with leaving the body and entering the astral, most astral projectors conclude that they are mostly nonphysical beings. The rest of humanity, or at least Western society, still believes they are physical all the way, perhaps with a twist of weird psychic abilities (contributed by the brain, of course). To them, it is easy to conceive that the physical is our natural state. After all, we spend most of our time there.

To those who have not yet had the opportunity to astral project or try out other impressive human abilities, the OBE phenomenon appears amazing, far out, even abnormal. They push it away as if it were a disease threatening their very existence (rightly so; it will indeed upset their lives). But if they change their physical point of view to one from which they can see also their nonphysical nature, OBE becomes completely natural.

We are only physical because we have chosen to project to the physical for a while. When we have had enough of that, we turn our attention elsewhere. Contrary to conventional beliefs, it would be strange if we could not leave our physical bodies whenever we wanted in order to get back to that larger existence with which we are so familiar. Humans can leave their physical bodies, so what is the big deal? We should be more surprised if we could not, if we were stuck in the physical, in these cramped bodies.

Waking Up to Our True Nature

If this is all true, if we are nonphysical beings having a dream of the physical, why can't we wake up to the "real" world? We are living the dream for a reason: to grow in ways we can't in the real world. We are having this awesome dream and, deep inside it, we do not want to wake up. We will wake up when we are ready, count on that, but not before. No night lasts forever.

The challenge is to figure out how to get ready. How do we take full advantage of this dream and learn as much as we can from it? How do we treat our minds so that they will be ready to wake up? We experience life to the fullest. We smell the flowers and look at the sky until we are satiated with the experience of life. What we do *not* do is run around, stressed out every second of the day, always planning for tomorrow, constantly building our personal empires. When we have seen the sky without the limits of beliefs and expectations, we know there is nothing more for us to see in the physical, and we choose to wake up.

The moment we wake up, we shake off the limitations of our physical lives. We realize that we are vast beings. We see that we are so huge that our galaxy, the Milky Way, is but a tiny speck in comparison. Ironically, it is that small, insignificant, self-created piece of our attention that we have considered reality for so long, lifetime after lifetime, on so many different planets. We realize that the time we spent in the astral was an extension of the dream, but on the brink of waking up to the real life. How could we have been so blind? How could we have avoided seeing what we are? It seems incredible how we created the dream and stepped into it. And how it engulfed us and made us forget the real life.

Then it hits us: The reason we could not figure out what we were, is that we are *everything*. We are even whatever we think we are. We are everywhere and everything. We think of a thing and then we become it, just like we became our physical bodies. During our trip to the physical, we *were* the worlds around and inside the physical. This is a mind-blowing realization.

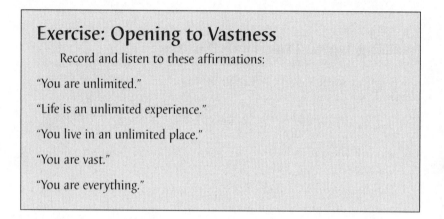

Exercise: Opening to Vastness

Record and listen to these affirmations:

"You are unlimited."

"Life is an unlimited experience."

"You live in an unlimited place."

"You are vast."

"You are everything."

The Worlds Beyond

So, you thought life is all there is and, when it is over, you do not have to worry about anything anymore? Well, tough luck! It looks like we are all going to continue to exist for a very long time, possibly forever. But where and how? Surely we can't stay in physical life all the time?

The Physical Is a Dream

I have written at great length about our physical reality and the beliefs that govern it. You have seen for yourself how the beliefs affect the mind and how the mind in turn governs the astral. Consider again the idea that the physical is an astral world, completely at the mercy of your creative powers. Therefore, what you created in the astral, you can create in the physical.

Just as in the astral, the physical relies so much on our mind to sustain its existence that it can't be anything else than our own creation. Physical reality seems to be a practical joke we have played on ourselves, but it is not a distasteful joke.

Tuesday, February 11, 2003
Waking Up

I wake up in the hypnopompic state. Ramtha²² must have made a big impression on me, because the realization, "The physical is a dream," seems natural to me as I open my eyes. I look around the room. My perception is exactly like it is in my lucid dreams: distinct and vibrating. I know I am looking at physical reality, but still I understand that it is just another dream. Physical reality is as flexible and unimportant (or important, whichever way you prefer to look at it) as a dream. A floating and tingling sensation surrounds my being. The walls seem to be vibrating like static on a TV screen, but more smoothly.

At my command, the room bends like a sheet of paper into an arc before my eyes. The room looks like it has been stuffed into a cylinder. I find nothing unusual about this. After all, since physical reality is a dream, anything is possible. I go back to sleep. Or am I just waking up from a lifelong dream?

If the physical world is a dream world, what is a dream world? Since we can create any object in a dream just as we can in an astral world, it is reasonable to assume that a dream world is an astral world. This means that the physical is indeed an astral world. The question now is: Do we want to wake up from this dream and, if so, how do we do it? In the journal entry above, I saw through the illusion of physical solidity. I was able to do this because I had the belief (shaped by Ramtha) to support it, and my reason was still too deeply asleep to tell me it was impossible.

As we know, an astral world is governed by the mind and that mind is highly affected by our beliefs. Beliefs are in turn adjusted by thoughts. Affirmations are just thoughts specifically designed to adjust beliefs. So, in order to see through the illusion of the physical, we have to turn the majority of our thoughts in the direction of what lies beyond the physical, preferably as if we already know the physical is an illusion. Furthermore, we have to get to know reason, so that we can halt it. We do not want reason interfering with our intuitive understanding of the physical. Reason is not easily halted though, because it fears relinquishing control, so instead we could use a natural sleep state to accomplish this.

The Nature of the Astral

All we have is a bunch of astral worlds, among them, the physical universe(s) and the dream worlds. However different they appear, they are all connected, and we, their creators, are that connection. Have you ever had a precognitive dream that came true? If you have, you probably embrace the fact that dreams are real. Your precognition happened in another world—that is all.

An angel or agent of special divine intervention did not come down and drop the information into your dream. The future did not fold back into your dreaming mind, nor did your dreaming mind extend into the future. You simply created the event in a world you were visiting while dreaming, and then you created the same event in the world you were visiting while you were physically awake. You are the creator of any astral world you happen to be in, including the physical.

It may be difficult to accept this, especially since we sometimes have precognitive dreams of coming tragedies. Such tragedies are often cocreated, meaning that a group of people planned the event. For a tragedy to occur in your life, you also must create it. As we plan such events on a soul level, they are not tragedies but experiences we can learn from, or experiences leading to future learning experiences.

We have spoken of astral replicas, astral worlds that resemble the physical world, and, hopefully, you have floated through them. Are they any less real than the physical? No, they are the same as the physical world, made from the same stuff—thought—and conjured up by the same being—you. The so-called original of the replicas is just another replica of whatever lives in your mind, whatever you desire to think of.

The astral can hold an infinite number of worlds, because it is not limited by space or time. We choose to create physical, astral, and dream worlds therein. In so doing, we decide their preferences: whether they should have space, time, gravity, matter, and so on. We think up these worlds, because the creative process thrills us, just like decorating a room or a dollhouse or building a snow fortress thrills us. Then, of course, when we spend too much time inside our creations, we forget that we made them, and we desperately try to figure out what they are and how to get out. The astral is indeed a wondrous place, the perfect playground for the ones brave enough to incarnate into one of its worlds, and the perfect educational facility for the same.

If you are the creator, where do you put the creation? Hardly in an external world, since that would be outside of you. You put your creation within you, in what we term perception. Your perception is a self-invented picture of the world, but it is also your entire world. There is no external world. If you project into the astral and create an astral world, you are putting the new world in your perception. The astral is your mind and the worlds you create live in the perception of that mind. The physical also only lives in the perception of your mind. There is no external physical world.

When people come together in the same space, as we are together in this universe, we are sharing not the space, but our individual perceptions. Your perception is picked up by people around you and used to reinvent what you see into their own perception. A shared world appears similar in all inhabitants' minds because of mind transference. Our universe is just a virtual concept described by the perception of all its inhabitants. The perception in turn is continuously modified by their imagination.

The reason why we do not know whether the physical universe is infinite or ends somewhere is that nobody has yet decided to make it one way or another. All the laws of physics were invented in the minds of our ancestors. Because of reincarnation, we are our ancestors, of course. Everything happened now until one of us decided to invent time. We were formless until someone invented matter. We were floating around in an undefined haze until someone decided to invent gravity.

Everything around you is your perception. There is nothing underlying it. You are creating your perception, and people who see the same are creating the same perception, influenced by your perception. This is apparent in dreams and astral projections, where you can change your environment. If a second person were to project into your dream world, he would create the same dream world within his perception. Additionally, he will tweak some objects and add others in order to fit the dream to his personality.

In other words, when manipulating a dream world, as you may have tried in a lucid dream, you are not changing the surrounding dream world, because there is none, but you are changing your perception. The same applies to the physical. There is no space, mass, or time. All that exists is your perception. You take nothingness and turn it into a made-up world of space, mass, and time.

If there is no external world, then what is real? What can we rely upon not to be figments of our imagination? The only constant object is our mind. The mind is the only "real" thing. The physical brain, the body, the whole universe, and all the astral worlds are merely inventions of that mind.

The Pure Mind

If the astral worlds are just inventions of our minds, we should be able to cease inventing long enough to investigate the only real thing: the mind—us. Earlier in this book, I referred to this as the meta-world, the deeper astral, or the pure astral. The pure astral is the mind with an empty perception. If you leave your body and end up in a dark void, your perception is blank. This can be scary in the beginning, since we are used to perceiving something at all times.

From the astral void, we are able to fully disable the perception mechanism. It is easy to manipulate the perception mechanism when we

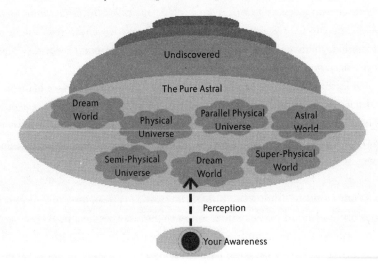

Figure 8. The mind is clouded by self-created astral worlds.

do not have a world to clutter up our perception. We can then sense the mind as it is without its inventions. This can be a powerful experience. It is a feeling of knowing and presence. When first I reached it, it was like sensing something real for the first time. It was the only steady component of existence. For the first time, I found something I was not perceiving and creating simultaneously (see figure 8).

We can also reach the pure mind in the physical. All we have to do is stop the activity of the part of us that constantly creates our current astral world (i.e., the physical), namely, our internal dialogue. This is what Don Juan refers to when he speaks about stopping the world.[23] The only way to stop the world is by stopping our thoughts, because this world is nothing but our thoughts.

Saturday, October 12, 2002
Illusory Layer of the Astral

I wake up in the hypnopompic state. Barb turns on the second computer. As its CPU cooler fan winds up, my mind somehow listens to it and winds up with it. I am buzzing slightly. My awareness is floating an inch over my body. It is a luxurious feeling. I do not recognize the state of mind as anything I have felt before, but I suspect it is good for astral projection. I consider attempting to roll out of my body, but something tells me to do nothing but observe.

I sense a layer of existence. It is the world I have called the astral during all my travels. It is an illusion. It feels like lumps of gray fog covering what is real. I move my center of thought to my chest. I do my best to cease thinking, but it is not easy. Small thoughts keep popping up.

The lumps of fog clear away to the sides and I can sense the surface of the pure astral. It is smooth, dense, and gray. I think of extending my senses into it, but in doing so, I invoke thoughts, which bring back the fog of illusion. Learning not to think is going to take a lot of practice. My body calls me back as it wakes up. The floating sensation ceases.

What could be hiding behind the smooth, gray surface of the mind? Is it simply a feeling of existing, or is there another set of worlds contained within the perception of a super-mind? Are they untouchable by our creative powers, or at least untouchable by thought, as we know thought? There are plenty of unknowns to explore in this area. The good thing is, we do not have to spend half a day preparing astral projection in order to do it. All we have to do is cease thinking for a minute.

Exercise: Stop the World

1. Tonight, as you go to bed, relax your mind.
2. Close your eyes.
3. Move your attention to your head. Do not move it to the chest. The chest produces thoughts in the form of images. The head produces "verbal" thoughts. Verbal thoughts are easier to stop than images, at least for me.
4. Command: *Rationality: Off!*
5. Command: *Internal dialogue: Off!*
6. Cross your eyes and look up slightly. This is a diversion for the mind.
7. Stop the thinking process. Simply decide not to use it. Do not try to quiet the thoughts; instead stop your whole thinking machinery altogether. Thoughts do not pop into your head by some inexplicable magic—*you* create them. You have created every thought you have ever had. And if you can create them, you can refuse to create them for a minute.
8. Sit in a thoughtless void for several seconds. If the thinking process resumes, stop it again.
9. Do not look for anything. Just enjoy the peace.
10. At some point, you will fall asleep.
11. If you wake up in the night, continue stopping the thought process.
12. In the morning when you wake up, before doing anything (do not even try to figure out where you are), stop it again for several minutes. There are always fewer thoughts just after waking up, so this should have some exciting results.

In the exercise above, did you manage to stop your thoughts so that you could break through the physical world and sense what is beyond it? If you did not, I have an even better idea. Everything happens faster when we are outside this particular physical world. For that reason, it might be easier and more effective to cease the thinking process while projecting into another astral world, as in the next exercise.

Exercise: Stop the Other World

1. Project into the astral.
2. Relax your mind.
3. Sit down and meditate upon the center of your chest for half a minute, to stabilize the projection.
4. Command: *Rationality: Off!*
5. Command: *Internal dialogue: Off!*
6. Cross your eyes.
7. Stop the thinking process. Simply decide not to use it. Do not try to shush the thoughts; instead stop your whole thinking machinery altogether.
8. Sit in a thoughtless void for several seconds. If the thinking process resumes, stop it again.
9. Do not look for anything. Just enjoy the peace.

Ascension

The buzz in New Age circles for the last 30 years has been ascension. In short, one by one or all at once, Earth and her inhabitants will raise their energy frequencies from the third dimension (the physical) to the fourth (or fifth, depending on whether you count time as a dimension). I have not explored this sufficiently in nonphysical realms, so I will refrain from speculating on it too much here. In any case, it seems to me that the destination is a little closer to our unlimited potential. The event will unlock much of our minds and give us our power back, if we are ready for it.

Tuesday, October 15, 2002
Seeing the Other World

I am convinced now that the humans are ascending from the third dimension to the fifth dimension. Don Juan from Carlos Castaneda's books seems to spend his life halfway there, even if he calls it by other names. I am doing what he told Carlos Castaneda to do: crossing my eyes in order to stop the world and leaving it to the subconscious to figure things out instead of consciously analyzing.

After just two days, I can see things out of the ordinary. I serve Barb ice cream and the cat is desperately trying to get to Barb's bowl. He is unusually unruly tonight, it seems. As I walk around the TV set to my side of the bed, I see the cat running toward me on the bed. I see him in full detail for two seconds. Suddenly, he disappears. I assume he has jumped off the bed or behind the TV. Then I see him sitting at the side of the bed, calmly watching Barb as she eats her ice cream. I ask Barb if he has moved within the last minute and she says no. What I saw was the cat, but not in this world.

I go to sleep. The cat wakes me up. He is sitting next to my head in bed. I am in the hypnopompic state. I can feel the cat showing me around in the fourth dimension, the destination of our ascension, and telling me what it is like to live there. I fall asleep and the cat wakes me up many times. Each time, I find myself being shown around by the cat in the fifth dimension. I suspect the cat is a power animal that is capable of traveling between dimensions. He is here to show Barb and me a few things that are in store for humankind.

The next day, Barb sees a black scarab running across the floor. Then it disappears. A few days later, I see the cat jumping at something on the wall. He is playing. I wonder what he is jumping at, because the wall is smooth and white. The next time I look over at him, I see a black speck on the wall. I can't believe my eyes. In that moment of disbelief, the speck disappears.

The destination of ascension could, of course, be just another astral world, like the physical but with fewer limitations. Perhaps we are already underway creating this next world through our thoughts, just by wondering what it will be like. By the ways of the astral, just the expectation of ascending to another world will actually create that other world and move us there. Most likely, we are copying some characteristics of the old world into it, because that is how we think a world should look. Hopefully, we will avoid copying too many of the physical limitations.

The destination could also be the pure astral, where the "real" world is. This would mean the end of physical beauty. No more blue skies viewed through limited eyes. This brings us to the next question: Why would we want to ascend? After all, unless we waste life by being too busy, life is quite nice. So why leave it? We need to check our motives here. If we want to leave because life is too hard, then we have missed the point of being alive, which is to enjoy life in its simplicity, knowing that life, both hard and easy, is whatever we make of it.

We created the physical world for a reason: to experience the beauty of our creation from a first-person perspective. Is that reason no longer valid? Have we experienced all the beauty we came to experience? Have we outgrown our current reality? If so, then ascension should be the next step. There is no point in staying here when there is so much beauty to discover elsewhere.

Ramtha ascended because he wanted to be free like the wind. Ramtha discovered that he was more than a physical being. With that, he was no longer engulfed in the physical and so the physical held little interest for him. I can imagine that physical life is quite boring when you know you can do so much more. Why live on a tiny planet when you created the whole galaxy? Ramtha left by raising the energy frequency of his body.

Are we there yet? Do we have the same understanding of ourselves that Ramtha had? Do we accept the idea that we are vast nonphysical beings? With the exception of a handful of enlightened ones, not by a long shot. But slowly we will get there. Person by person, we will wake up to our larger selves. The wake-up call has been spreading across humanity for decades. As part of the wake-up call, astral projection gives us personal proof that we are much larger than we thought we were.

The Nature of Reality

Nothing but Opinions

Because physical reality is a highly subjective environment (we create it within ourselves), we find it difficult to communicate our perceptions to each other. In fact, no one can tell another what the world is like, for the world differs from one individual to another. All we have are our own creations, none like those of others. In spite of this, more than a few attempt to force their worldview upon others. Preachers have been doing it for millennia, politicians have been doing it for decades, and I have been doing it throughout this book.

Religion, intellect, science, literature, expertise, authority, the job market, gravity—all of these are merely *opinions*. They rise and fall by the ideas of people. The good thing about opinions is that we do not have to embrace them unless we want to. We have the choice to reject them. And we should reject many of them. We should be very picky when it comes to opinions, for the moment we accept them, they turn into beliefs, which in turn govern our reality.

Nothing is nailed down, absolutely nothing. There are no constant qualities of nature, no absolute laws, no forever facts. There is no path of scientific or spiritual discovery leading up to the final revelation of nature. There is only the never-ending path that we create as we go along. No truth remains a truth indefinitely and no higher truth exists that is not constructed by us. We live in a fluid world that changes at our own whim.

Reality changes at your command. You can change anything you want. As quickly as you think a thought, your reality changes. By using this understanding, you can make reality progress in whatever direction you want. Life is yours to do with what you desire.

Exercise: Manifestation

1. Close your eyes.
2. Picture in your mind something that you want (money, a nice car or home, psychic abilities, understanding, skills, happiness, etc.).
3. Write down that thing on a piece of paper.
4. Visualize what it would be like to have it. Be as precise and detailed as possible. Most importantly, visualize the emotions evoked by having it.
5. Make a note on your calendar. In one year's time, look at the note. You may just find that you have that thing you desired.

Reality Is What You Make of It

Tuesday, June 24, 2003
Sleep Paralysis

At about 10 A.M., I am reading Whitley Strieber's Confirmation[24] when I start drifting back to sleep. Before I fully fall asleep, I have a thought that startles me back to a waking state. I can't remember the contents of the thought. However, I notice that my chest and arms are rendered immobile by sleep paralysis. I think "Hey, I bet I can Reiki myself really well now. There will be no tension in the arms to obstruct the energy flow because of the paralysis, and there will be no doubting thoughts because of my dazed mind."

After a few minutes of Reiki, I fall back to sleep. I dream I am in a stadium. I am 12 years old. A group of kids, me included, are playing some sport. There are aliens here, but we can't see them. Our minds perceive their presence as gray rats. The fear of what the rats could be (aliens) makes me hysterical, as it does the other kids. In the locker room, we try to get rid of the rats, but they are hiding. I am getting more hysterical, almost panicking. I decide I must wake up. I seek the waking state of consciousness the way an eel swims to the ocean surface.

I come to in my bed. The sleep paralysis is now in full bloom. Suddenly, the door opens and someone walks into the room. It must be Barb. At least, I think it is Barb. She must be home early from work. I have to check that it really is Barb, to make sure one of those aliens did not follow me here from the dream. I try to turn my head but am prevented by the sleep paralysis. I hear footsteps, like wet plastic soles rubbing against linoleum. The person, whoever it is, walks up to the left side of the bed and stops. It seems the person is standing next to the bed, staring at me, but my head is turned the other way, so I can't see it.

The uncertainty gets to me. I have to know who is there! With extreme effort, I break free from the sleep paralysis and forcefully turn my head to the left. There is nobody there. The bed is perfectly normal, as is the wall, and there is not a person in sight. This is too weird. I decide to get out of bed and flee the room, preferably screaming in terror. I try to roll out of the bed on my right side but am shot back to a lying position as if attached to a rubber band. Something is holding me to the bed. I try repeatedly to escape to no avail.

I realize now that I am in a dazed kind of state, one of those states that are especially beneficial for astral projection. I get a weird idea: If I can't see the person with my physical eyes, maybe I can see her with my astral eyes. I roll again, but this time with the intention of rolling out of my body. Same results: I am shot back into the bed. Is there no escape from this person? Then I realize, as I did a few minutes ago, that I must wake up again. I struggle to arouse my awareness in the direction of the physical. After some time, I successfully wake up in the bed.

As my mind leaves the sleep state, the invisible person puts a thought in my head: "Reality is what you make it, not what you perceive to be true." I think that is a great point of view. It holds a doer's attitude. I have to remember that. But the person is not content with that: "Put it in your book!" The thought echoes through my mind. Put it in my book? Then, finally, I realize the importance of the thought. It is the conclusion of the whole book. That simple statement describes the nature of reality.

Reality is what you make it says that life in general and the environment that surrounds you are of your own creation. This is true for all dimensions. On a physical level, if you move the pen on your desk from one place to another, you have changed your reality. On a higher level, you are not moving pens, but life situations and even the look and feel of life. All situations we get ourselves into are of our own making. This can be difficult to accept, as we sometimes find ourselves in harmful or traumatic situations. But on a higher level, we may appreciate those situations as the great tools for growth they are.

Of course, we do not *have* to create such situations. The entity creating them is still you, although it may be inaccessible from your waking physical frame of mind. But no matter what frame of mind you are in, if you do not want a situation, you will not have it. I think the best lesson here is the understanding that you can do anything if you put your mind to it and get your emotions involved.

We also choose how we want to interact with what we have created. We do not necessarily have to use our arms, legs, eyes, ears, etc. They are just something we have created for ourselves. We might want to use our mind to directly interact with our creation, or perhaps invent a new tool for interaction.

Not what you perceive to be true means that whether we perceive something to be true or false has no bearing on how real it is. Everything is part of reality, because you put it there. You can't create something, claim it is false, and deny its part in reality. Nothing unreal exists. The core of the statement is that reality is not an external agent that can either be true or false. Instead, reality is an internal part of you, because it springs from your own mind.

I know from experience that messages like this never come alone. They are always accompanied by practical examples. Good teachers know that a theory will not be accepted or appreciated unless exemplified by personal experience (we first count oranges and apples instead of numbers in school because we have personal experience with oranges and apples). Skilled guides, likewise, offer us the practical examples first, and then the message is presented as a conclusion so that we students can experience the examples uncolored by the conclusion. This also allows students an opportunity to draw the intended conclusion from the examples by themselves, which is a much better method for learning. Usually, I don't draw the intended conclusions. The majority of dreams and astral experiences leave me puzzled as to what their meaning might be. But the meaning is there, awaiting delivery.

In order to see what practical examples have been provided, I backtrack through what happened during sleep. First, I woke up, or at least I thought I woke up, to find that I could not move. That event has an intense feeling of example to it: I *created* the event of paralysis. This rings a bell. The concept of self-created paralysis reminds me of something I read in Whitley Strieber's *Breakthrough: The Next Step*. What a synchronicity that I read another of Strieber's books before I fell asleep. Or perhaps Strieber is one of those authors who have it all.

In short, what happens in this particular part of *Breakthrough* is that Strieber is invited by the Visitors (his name for the gray aliens) to accompany them during a classical alien abduction, for lack of better word. The Visitors and Strieber cruise down to his friend Dora's house, which is about seven states from where Strieber is picked up. The trip takes mere minutes. Whether they travel in physical or nonphysical form remains unclear, but what is clear is that Strieber is in an altered state of mind. His job, apparently, is to keep Dora in her bed while Dora's daughter's "spine was being stiffened, as if it was being adjusted to provide her with a strength and determination she would need all her life."[25]

What happens in Dora's bedroom resembles the practical example that was provided to me. Dora wakes up as her daughter, who is in another bedroom, screams in horror from the Visitor presence. Strieber says: "Then a scream came—a horrible shriek. It went through me like a burning arrow. Dora's eyes flew open, she lurched up, staring right at me, but her eyes were strange and dark and I knew immediately that they were seeing only into the world of nightmare. She struggled, but something prevented her from rising. She would lunge forward, then stop as if she was slamming into a glass wall. *It looked like she was doing this to herself, in an odd way holding herself back* [emphasis mine]. But I also felt somehow responsible. Very responsible. I was holding her down somehow."[26]

Was Strieber holding her down or was Dora holding herself down? Perhaps the suggestion to be held down was provided by Strieber, but the ultimate decision to be held down was Dora's? Why would one make a decision to be held down? One would surely not make it in a waking physical state of mind, but perhaps it would seem like the correct thing to do in a more informed state of mind. Strieber even mentions that Dora's eyes were "seeing only into the world of nightmare," which could mean that she was tuned into a nonphysical state that allowed her to see the benefit of not interfering with the Visitors' work.

I have a feeling Dora's daughter was given a wonderful gift by the Visitors and, in an informed state of mind, Dora knew better than to take that gift away from her daughter. That would be a good argument for creating a paralysis that would restrict her physical body to the bed. Likewise, I created a sleep paralysis to ensure I would pay attention to the message relayed to me in the previous journal excerpt. Of course, after the return to a waking physical state of mind, Dora would assume, as would anyone of us, that the paralysis was forced upon her by an external agent.

If the statement *Reality is what you make it* is correct, a conclusion must be that we subconsciously access the informed state in order to continuously create our realities. But if we create our realities subconsciously, we can probably turn this creation into a conscious action, or at least have some conscious say in the subconscious process. However, before we do, we need to achieve an informed state of mind, or we would not know which is the optimal reality to create. But how does one access such an informed state of mind? The subconscious accesses it all the time, so why should we not be able to do that consciously? One way to do it could be to stop the world, as in the exercises described earlier. Astral projection might provide a good opportunity to reach that state of mind by conscious intent, but I do not doubt there are other ways. All we have to do is to be willing to work on ourselves and, most importantly, to work through our minds.

Even if we can't yet control a subconscious process such as the creation of our realities, we can influence it. The subconscious is not a clearly separated part of us. It has many connections to the conscious mind by which we can consciously affect it. For example, before the dream, I read about Visitors, or *aliens,* if you will. This was a conscious action. The subconscious was influenced in a way that made it create a dream containing aliens. This is just one of many ways we can influence the subconscious in its creation of reality, for the dream became my reality, if only for an hour.

The subconscious may also be influenced through hypnosis, visualization, affirmation, and daydreaming. There might be other, more direct, approaches to influence it. Perhaps we can even develop technical tools to access our subconscious. The Visitors in Strieber's books seem to possess that kind of technology. They accessed Dora's subconscious, so why can't we access ours?

Exercise: Reality Is—Affirmations

1. Record the affirmation: "Reality is what you make of it."
2. Listen to the affirmation in the background for six days.

Before I created the paralysis for myself, I created the event in which I woke up, although it was not to a waking physical state of mind. Waking up became my reality. What reason would there be for me to wake up other than that I created it? Waking up does not just happen; it is created. Not by the physical body or a force of nature, but by *me*. And when you wake up in the morning, that waking up is *your* doing. Whether you wake up in your physical bedroom or in an astral replica of the same is irrelevant. The two bedrooms are both your creation, and that creation becomes your reality.

Then there was the event of audible footsteps. That was spooky, but educational. There is no reason there would be footsteps in my bedroom, other than that I put them there. Even if there had been a person accompanying the footsteps, that person would be of my creation. The person may originate from its own consciousness, but that does not matter. Whether he is a conscious person or a figment of my imagination, in order for him to exist in my reality, I have to create him inside my own mind.

With the simple statement, *Reality is what you make it,* comes freedom of choice: If I choose to have something in my world, I create it. If I choose not to have it, I refrain from creating it. We all have this freedom. Reality can be whatever we want it to be. All that is required is that we know what kind of reality we wish to create. In that freedom, we have the power to change our worlds. It is up to us what we want to do with this power. This could be the end to suffering, something that has been our companion for far too many millennia. We only have suffering because we choose to create it. Now it is time to choose to fill our realities instead with beautiful things, breathtaking colors, and radiant feelings. Let us here and now decide to have only the best in our lives. Let us turn the warmth of our thoughts into the brightness of our world. Let us commit to the laughter and friendship of the future.

Further Exploration

The goal of this book was to provide you with the tools (astral projection techniques) needed to explore other dimensions. This book was never intended to present packaged discoveries ready for digestion, although it was necessary at times to present some of my own experiences in order to widen your notion of possibilities. I would be a fool to attempt to convert anyone to my belief system. Instead, I choose to provide the tools for exploration and encourage you to form your own view of the world.

In the late nineteenth century, many scientists were depressed because of the "fact" that the current scientific community had already discovered all there was to discover. Now, more than one century and a few thousand discoveries later, we chuckle at how naïve we were back then. But still we hold the same belief: We think we have a good grip on how most things work. We do not. We are just afraid of how small we would feel if we were to admit how little we really know.

Creation is packed with unknowns. A discovery is not just the revelation of a habit of our nature, but also the revelation of a hundred other questions awaiting answers. We should never assume that there is nothing left to discover. When we have discovered the meaning of life, we will have yet to discover the meaning of the meaning of life. Our journey of exploration is never-ending.

Horizons to Explore

I would like to give a few last hints on what to explore. These are questions I have been asking myself for a long time but have not had the time to explore myself. If you find these questions intriguing, then embark upon your own expedition to find your own answers.

- Explore your being outside physical life.
- Explore the pure astral by ceasing all thoughts.
- Visit astral worlds created by other beings.
- Visit friends currently not incarnated.
- Visit other nonphysical civilizations.
- Visit physical beings on distant planets.
- Visit yourself in a previous lifetime.
- Investigate the reincarnation process.

Exploration Procedure

It always helps if the exploration process is somewhat structured. The following set of steps is a good framework from which you can form your personalized exploration process.

Exercise: Exploration

1. Write down a question you want answered. Your nonphysical friends will oblige you by preparing an astral experience for you. With their help, you will set up astral energies, objects, and people to interact with.
2. The evening before your next astral projection, read the note, so that you will remember your mission.
3. When you astral project, enjoy the experience.

4. When you return to the body, ponder how the astral experience relates to your question.

5. Also, ponder how you and your nonphysical friends set up the experience. In my case, they usually provide a series of lessons. Each lesson comprises a series of practical examples. At the end of each lesson, I tie together the examples by drawing a conclusion or having an insight. Once a conclusion has been made, the next lesson begins. Taken together, the lessons provide the answer to my question.

Remember, astral projection is only a tool. It is not the goal. You can use this tool in your quest for what is important to you. And only you can decide what that is.

Astral Troubleshooter

This chart is provided as a quick reference for overcoming obstacles commonly encountered by astral projectors before the exit, during the exit, and in the astral realm. For each obstacle, several possible solutions are suggested. For example, if you are losing the out-of-body state, to regain it you may roll, meditate, or move your center of thought.

Problem	Solution
Body aches	Stretch muscles.
	Bend elbows by putting hands on hips.
	Relieve pressure against mattress by elevating feet with a pillow.
	Try a different body position.
Noise	Use earplugs.
Bed shaking	Use the motion to intensify your visualization. Visualize being in a shaking location, e.g., on a ship or a volcano, or inside a giant milkshake.

Itch	Observe the start, middle, and end of the itch. As you observe the end, the itch will go away.
	Scratch. It takes more effort to ignore than to scratch and get back into the same state.
Can't relax	Visualize floating downward.
	Focus on your breathing.
	Take long exhales.
	Let your mind wander.
Mind in turmoil	Postpone the astral projection session and welcome the turmoil. Experience it. Heal it once and for all.
	Decide to deal with all problems tomorrow. They can wait until you wake up in the morning.
Can't fall asleep	Let your mind wander. Forget the body.
Can't maintain visualization	Increase your motivation by increasing the desire to AP.
	Visualize something fun or intriguing. Go explore.
Sex drive takes over	Remove drive before session by masturbating.
	Realize that the whole universe loves you, as the motivation for the sex drive often is a need for love.
OBE vision is absent or blurred	Create an object with your mind and place it before you.
	Meditate on your third eye during OBE.
	Command *Clarity Now!*
Losing OBE state	Roll.
	Sit down and meditate on third eye or center of chest during OBE.
	Move center of thought to chest, as the head often destabilizes the state.
Can't move where you want	Expect to be there.
	Bring to mind the feeling the place evokes.

Endnotes

1. Deepak Chopra, *Body, Mind, and Soul: The Mystery and the Magic,* video (Alexandria, Va.: PBS Home Video, 1995).
2. Steven Lee Weinberg, *Ramtha* (Eastsound, Wash.: Sovereignty, 1986.)
3. Henry K. Beecher, "The Powerful Placebo," *Journal of the American Medical Association* 159: 1602, 1955.
4. J. Hall, C. Kim, B. McElroy, and A. Shimoni, "Wave-Packet Reduction as a Medium of Communication," *Foundations of Physics* 7: 759–767, 1977.
5. Hugh Everett, "Relative State Formulation of Quantum Mechanics," *Reviews of Modern Physics* 29: 454–462 (Everett's Princeton Ph.D. thesis, 1957).
6. R. Omnès, *Understanding Quantum Mechanics* (Princeton, N.J.: Princeton University Press, 1999). Chapter 13 describes consistent histories.
7. William Gammill, *The Gathering: Meetings in Higher Space* (Charlottesville, Va.: Hampton Roads, 2001), p. 72.
8. Robert Perala, with Tony Stubbs, *The Divine Blueprint* (Campbell, Calif.: United Light Publishing, 1998), p. 73.
9. Bruce Moen, *Voyages into the Unknown* (Charlottesville, Va.: Hampton Roads, 1997), p. 155.
10. Weinberg, *Ramtha,* p. 16.
11. Robert Peterson, *Out-of-Body Experiences: How to Have Them and What to Expect* (Charlottesville, Va.: Hampton Roads, 1997), p. 216.
12. Louis de Broglie, *Researches on the Quantum Theory* (Paris, France: Faculty of Sciences at Paris University, 1924).
13. Jane Roberts, *Seth: Dreams and Projection of Consciousness* (Manhasset, N.Y.: New Awareness Network, 1998), p. 335.

14. Carlos Castaneda, *The Wheel of Time* (New York: Washington Square Press, 2001), from front cover.
15. Roberts, *Seth,* p. 333.
16. Ken Keys, *How to Enjoy Your Life in Spite of It All* (St. Mary, Ky.: Living Love Publications, 1980), p. 5.
17. Roberts, *Seth,* p. 327.
18. William Buhlman, *Adventures beyond the Body: How to Experience Out-of-Body Travel* (New York: HarperSanFrancisco, 1996), p. 172.
19. Robert Bruce, *Astral Dynamics: A New Approach to Out-of-Body Experiences* (Charlottesville, Va.: Hampton Roads, 1999), p. 44.
20. *Waking Life,* movie (Beverly Hills, Calif.: Fox Home Entertainment, 2001).
21. *Defending Your Life,* movie (Burbank, Calif.: Warner Studios, 1991).
22. Weinberg, *Ramtha,* p. 19.
23. Carlos Castaneda, *Tales of Power* (New York: Simon & Schuster, 1974), p. 22.
24. Whitley Strieber, *Confirmation: The Hard Evidence of Aliens among Us?* (New York: St. Martin's Press, 1998).
25. Whitley Strieber, *Breakthrough: The Next Step* (New York: Harper Paperbacks, 1995), p. 47.
26. Ibid., p. 45.

Additional Resources

The reference material previously listed is well worth a read. On top of that, I guarantee that the following material is riveting for anyone interested in either astral projection or the nature of reality.

Castaneda, Carlos. 1993. *The Art of Dreaming*. New York: HarperCollins.

Monroe, Robert. 1994. *Ultimate Journey*. New York: Doubleday.

Redfield, James. 1993. *The Celestine Prophecy: An Adventure*. New York: Warner Books.

Strieber, Whitley. 1987. *Communion: A True Story*. New York: Avon Books.

——. 1988. *Transformation: The Breakthrough*. New York: Avon Books.

Talbot, Michael. 1991. *The Holographic Universe*. New York: HarperCollins.

I also highly recommended the following films.

Communion. 1989. Los Angeles: New Line Home Entertainment.

Lucky People Center International. 1997. Stockholm, Sweden: Lucky People Center.

Out on a Limb. 1986. Troy, Mich.: Anchor Bay Entertainment.

What Dreams May Come. 1998. Beverly Hills, Calif.: Polygram Films.

About the Author

John Magnus is a technical writer, software engineer, interdimensional traveler, and musician. Since his birth in Halmstad, Sweden, in 1977, John had lived a quiet and dull life until one day he discovered the discipline of astral projection. This event aroused a fierce desire to understand the out-of-body phenomenon and, in conjunction, to understand physical reality.

Toward this goal, John has undertaken countless investigative expeditions into the astral. His findings are presented in this book. Because of the commonly hard-to-digest nature of the unknown, the book is designed to gently guide readers toward their own astral discoveries, rather than merely to disclose his own opinions.

In order to spread the knowledge of astral projection, John gives workshops on related subjects. To make reservations or to request more information, please visit John Magnus's website at *www.johnmagnus.com.*

John's physical body currently resides in Boise, Idaho, with his wife Barbara (a crystal practitioner), Jazz the Dalmatian, and several cats.

HAMPTON ROADS
PUBLISHING COMPANY, INC.

Astral Dynamics
A NEW Approach to Out-of-Body Experience
Robert Bruce

This encyclopedic out-of-body masterpiece gives you everything you need to understand the practice and go out exploring on your own. *Astral Dynamics* includes a practical "how-to" guide, troubleshooting advice, and a fascinating theoretical perspective on astral travel.

Paperback • 560 pages • ISBN 1-57174-143-7 • $18.95

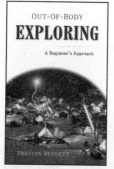

Out-of-Body Exploring
A Beginner's Approach
Preston Dennett

Novice, intermediate, or expert—anyone interested in the spiritual art of astral travel will benefit from Dennett's 20 years of out-of-body traveling. Including his initial forays into expanded consciousness, he shares the many techniques he experimented with, and discusses the people and sights he encountered. Plus, he offers tips on how to go reliably out of body and maintain this enhanced awareness.

Paperback • 200 pages • ISBN 1-57174-409-6 • $13.95

Cosmic Journeys
My Out-of-Body Explorations with Robert A. Monroe
Rosalind A. McKnight • Foreword by Laurie Monroe

Paperback • 296 pages • ISBN 1-57174-123-2 • $13.95

Eternal Life and How to Enjoy It
A First-Hand Account
Gordon Phinn

Paperback • 224 pages • ISBN 1-57174-408-8 • $13.95

Afterlife Knowledge Guidebook
A Manual for the Art of Retrieval and Afterlife Exploration
Bruce Moen

Paperback • 328 pages • ISBN 1-57174-450-9 • $16.95

Exploring the Afterlife Series (vols. 1–4)
by Bruce Moen

Voyages into the Unknown
Paperback • 256 pages
ISBN 1-57174-068-6 • $12.95

Voyage Beyond Doubt
Paperback • 296 pages
ISBN 1-57174-101-1 • $13.95

Voyages into the Afterlife
Paperback • 320 pages
ISBN 1-57174-139-9 • $13.95

Voyage to Curiosity's Father
Paperback • 320 pages
ISBN 1-57174-203-4 • $13.95

Hampton Roads Publishing Company

... for the evolving human spirit

HAMPTON ROADS PUBLISHING COMPANY publishes books on a variety of subjects, including metaphysics, spirituality, health, visionary fiction, and other related topics.

For a copy of our latest trade catalog, call toll-free, 800-766-8009, or send your name and address to:

HAMPTON ROADS PUBLISHING COMPANY, INC.
1125 STONEY RIDGE ROAD • CHARLOTTESVILLE, VA 22902
e-mail: hrpc@hrpub.com • www.hrpub.com